FOS·BOS 13 2017
Abitur-Prüfungsaufgaben mit Lösungen

Englisch

Bayern

2009–2016

© 2016 Stark Verlagsgesellschaft mbH & Co. KG
18. ergänzte Auflage
www.stark-verlag.de

Das Werk und alle seine Bestandteile sind urheberrechtlich geschützt. Jede vollständige oder teilweise Vervielfältigung, Verbreitung und Veröffentlichung bedarf der ausdrücklichen Genehmigung des Verlages.

Inhalt

Vorwort
Stichwortverzeichnis

Hinweise und Tipps

Vorbereitung auf die Abiturprüfung I
Aufbau der Prüfung I
Zeitmanagement II
Multiple Choice II
Multiple Matching III
Mediation Englisch–Deutsch III
Mediation Deutsch–Englisch IV
Argumentative Writing IV
Mündliche Gruppenprüfung VI
Useful Phrases VI

Englische Kurzgrammatik

Besonderheiten einiger Wortarten .... G 1
1 Adjektive und Adverbien – *Adjectives and Adverbs* .... G 1
2 Artikel – *Article* .... G 5
3 Pronomen – *Pronouns* .... G 6
4 Präpositionen – *Prepositions* .... G 8
5 Modale Hilfsverben – *Modal Auxiliaries* .... G 9

Infinitiv, Gerundium oder Partizip? – Die infiniten Verbformen .... G 10
6 Infinitiv – *Infinitive* .... G 10
7 Gerundium (*-ing*-Form) – *Gerund* .... G 11
8 Infinitiv oder Gerundium? – *Infinitive or Gerund?* .... G 13
9 Partizipien – *Participles* .... G 14

Bildung und Gebrauch der finiten Verbformen .... G 17
10 Zeiten – *Tenses* .... G 17
11 Passiv – *Passive Voice* .... G 24

Der Satz im Englischen .... G 25
12 Wortstellung – *Word Order* .... G 25
13 Konditionalsätze – *Conditional Sentences* .... G 25
14 Relativsätze – *Relative Clauses* .... G 27
15 Indirekte Rede – *Reported Speech* .... G 29

Anhang .... G 31
16 Liste wichtiger unregelmäßiger Verben – *List of Irregular Verbs* .... G 31

Übungsaufgaben zum mündlichen Teil

Beispiele für Themen der mündlichen Prüfung 1
Beispieldiskussion zum Thema „Global warming" 2

Abiturprüfungen

Abiturprüfung 2009
Aufgabenteil: *Reading* 2009-1
Aufgabenteil: *Writing* 2009-9
Lösungsvorschläge 2009-12

Abiturprüfung 2010
Aufgabenteil: *Reading* 2010-1
Aufgabenteil: *Writing* 2010-10
Lösungsvorschläge 2010-12

Abiturprüfung 2011
Aufgabenteil: *Reading* 2011-1
Aufgabenteil: *Writing* 2011-9
Lösungsvorschläge 2011-11

Abiturprüfung 2012
Aufgabenteil: *Reading* 2012-1
Aufgabenteil: *Writing* 2012-10
Lösungsvorschläge 2012-12

Abiturprüfung 2013
Aufgabenteil: *Reading* 2013-1
Aufgabenteil: *Writing* 2013-10
Lösungsvorschläge 2013-12

Abiturprüfung 2014
Aufgabenteil: *Reading* 2014-1
Aufgabenteil: *Writing* 2014-11
Lösungsvorschläge 2014-13

Abiturprüfung 2015
Aufgabenteil: *Reading* 2015-1
Aufgabenteil: *Writing* 2015-9
Lösungsvorschläge 2015-11

Abiturprüfung 2016
Aufgabenteil: *Reading* 2016-1
Aufgabenteil: *Writing* 2016-10
Lösungsvorschläge 2016-12

Jeweils im Herbst erscheinen die neuen Ausgaben
der Abiturprüfungsaufgaben mit Lösungen.

Autoren:

Kurzgrammatik: Redaktion
Hinweise, Übungsaufgaben, Lösungen zu den Prüfungsaufgaben: Peter Warlimont

Vorwort

Liebe Schülerinnen und Schüler,

dieses Buch hilft Ihnen dabei, sich ideal auf die **Abiturprüfung** zum Erwerb der fachgebundenen oder allgemeinen Hochschulreife an den Beruflichen Oberschulen in Bayern **im Fach Englisch** vorzubereiten.

Mithilfe der **Original-Prüfungsaufgaben** der letzten Jahrgänge können Sie genau sehen, was Sie in der Prüfung erwartet. Zu allen Aufgaben finden Sie **ausführliche Lösungen und Musteraufsätze**. Sie können Ihre eigenen Lösungen damit überprüfen und korrigieren. **Viele Tipps bei den Lösungen** geben Ihnen Hinweise darauf, wie Sie am besten mit der Aufgabenstellung umgehen, und erklären Ihnen genau, wie Sie zur richtigen Lösung kommen.

Zu den einzelnen Prüfungsteilen *Reading* und *Writing* finden Sie in diesem Buch **ausführliche Hinweise zur Bearbeitung** sowie Beispiele und *useful phrases* für das *composition writing*. Sie können noch einmal nachlesen, wie die Prüfung abläuft, welche Aufgabentypen Sie erwarten, was Sie in die Prüfung mitnehmen dürfen und was in der mündlichen Prüfung von Ihnen erwartet wird. **Tipps zur Prüfungsvorbereitung** helfen Ihnen, die Zeit vor der Abiturprüfung sinnvoll zu nutzen und sich so eine sichere Ausgangsbasis zu verschaffen. **Beispielthemen der mündlichen Prüfung** und ein **Transkript einer Beispieldiskussion** zeigen Ihnen, wie die mündliche Prüfung ablaufen kann.

Sollten nach Erscheinen dieses Bandes noch **wichtige Änderungen** in der Prüfung 2017 vom bayerischen Kultusministerium bekannt gegeben werden, finden Sie aktuelle Informationen dazu im Internet unter:
www.stark-verlag.de/pruefung-aktuell

Ich wünsche Ihnen Freude bei der Arbeit mit diesem Buch und *„good luck"* in der Abiturprüfung!

Stichwortverzeichnis

adolescence 2014-5
America's economic crisis 2010-7
anorexia 2009-4
baby boomers 2011-6
bilingual teaching 1
border control 2014-8
changing the world 2014-12
child labour 2011-10
Chopin, Kate 2011-1
(American) citizenship 2012-4
demography 2011-6
dialects 2013-11
disaster fatigue 2011-10
eating disorder 2009-4
economy 2012-7, 2013-4
English-Scottish relations 2009-7
English: world language 2010-10
environment 2, 2009-11, 2010-11
European Union 2013-4
fashion industry 2016-1
food production/consumption 2013-11
frugality 2010-7
Gandhi, Mahatma 2012-11
globalisation 4, 2012-7
global warming 2, 2009-11, 2010-11
"Globish" 2010-10
good looks 2012-11
Hawks, Tony 2012-1
holiday 2016-10
immigration 2011-4, 9, 2013-4, 2014-8, 2016-4
internet addiction 2009-9
internet and democracy 2013-10
Ireland 2012-1, 2015-1
Joseph 2013-1

Keret, Etgar 2013-1
lying 2010-5
masculinities studies 2016-7
McCourt, Frank 2010-1
megacities 2014-12
Mexican border 2014-8
Middle East conflict 2013-1
Nobel Peace Prize 2010-11
nuclear power 2012-10
Obama, Barack 2010-11
pandemics 2015-6
political commitment 2009-11
procrastination 2015-4
refugee crisis 2016-4
saving money 2010-7
Sayers, Dorothy 2014-1
Scotland 2009-7; 2015-9
Sedaris, David 2009-1
selfish lifestyles 2015-10
social inequality 2014-11
social freezing 2015-10
speech defects 2009-1
Smyth, Bernadette 2015-1
teaching 2010-1
teenager 2014-5
terrorism 2013-1
The Devil Wears Prada 2016-1
The Inspiration 2014-1
The Story of an Hour 2011-1
taxes 2016-11
Tuvalu 2010-11
urbanisation 2014-12
vegetarianism/veganism 2016-11
Weisberger, Lauren 2016-1

Hinweise und Tipps

Vorbereitung auf die Abiturprüfung

- Arbeiten Sie im Laufe des Schuljahres kontinuierlich mit und beteiligen Sie sich aktiv am Unterricht. Fangen Sie frühzeitig an, sich vorzubereiten!
- Lernen Sie Wortschatz und machen Sie Ihre Hausaufgaben gewissenhaft.
- Beschäftigen Sie sich auch in Ihrer Freizeit mit Englisch. Lesen Sie englische Bücher oder sehen Sie Filme und Serien in der Originalsprache. Hören oder sehen Sie Nachrichten oder Sendungen in Englisch, z. B. Podcasts oder Videoclips, die auf den Websites englischer Zeitungen, Radio- und TV-Sender angeboten werden. Sie erweitern so Ihren Wortschatz und werden feststellen, wie viel leichter Sie Englisch verstehen.
- Suchen Sie den Kontakt zu *native speakers* und sprechen Sie oft Englisch. In vielen Städten gibt es deutsch-amerikanische Institute oder Zentren, die Stammtische und regelmäßige Treffen abhalten. Je mehr Sie aktiv sprechen, desto sicherer werden Sie und desto gelassener können Sie in die mündliche Prüfung gehen.
- Haben Sie keine Angst vor Fehlern, Sie lernen daraus.
- Der Bereich *Composition* lässt sich leichter bewältigen, wenn Sie sich auf hilfreichen Wortschatz stützen, die sogenannten *useful phrases*.
- Beziehen Sie Ihre(n) Lehrer(in) in Ihre Übungsaktivitäten ein. Lassen Sie Hausaufgaben und freiwillige Übungen korrigieren. Lehrer freut es in der Regel, wenn ihre Schüler sich engagieren, und Sie werden davon profitieren, denn Sie erhalten Rückmeldungen über Ihre Schwächen und Ihre Stärken.

Aufbau der Prüfung

- Die Abiturprüfung besteht aus einem schriftlichen und einem mündlichen Teil.
- Der schriftliche Prüfungsteil umfasst die Bereiche *reading* und *writing*.
  - Die üblichen Aufgabenformen im Bereich *reading* sind *multiple choice*, Mediation Englisch–Deutsch und *multiple matching*. Sie müssen aber auch damit rechnen, dass ein *gapped summary* oder *short answer questions* vorkommen. Sie haben für die *reading*-Aufgaben 90 Minuten Zeit und können maximal 24 Punkte erreichen.
  - Der *writing*-Teil besteht aus einer Mediationsaufgabe Deutsch–Englisch und einer *argumentative writing*-Aufgabe mit der Wahlmöglichkeit zwischen zwei *composition*-Themen. Für den *writing*-Teil haben Sie 75 Minuten zur Verfügung. Sie können insgesamt 36 Punkte erreichen.

- In der mündlichen Prüfung werden 4 bis 6 Schüler in einer Gruppe geprüft und diskutieren mit verteilten Rollen über ein vom Prüfer festgelegtes Thema. Die mündliche Prüfung dauert ca. 20–30 Minuten. Sie können maximal 30 Punkte erhalten.

Zeitmanagement

- Ein durchdachtes Zeitmanagement ist für die Bewältigung der Prüfung von enormer Bedeutung.
- Für die *reading*-Aufgaben müssen Sie bis zu drei Texte lesen, die meist mehr als eine DIN-A-4-Seite umfassen. Außerdem müssen Sie rund 20 Teilfragen beantworten.
- Für die *writing*-Aufgaben müssen Sie einen Text von ca. 150 Wörtern und einen Text von mindestens 220 Wörtern verfassen.
- Wenn Sie sich bewusst machen, was von Ihnen verlangt wird, werden Sie feststellen, dass während der Prüfung keine Zeit zum Trödeln oder Träumen bleibt. Bereiten Sie sich daher im Vorfeld gezielt auf die Prüfung vor:
  - Notieren Sie beim Bearbeiten der Übungsaufgaben, wie lange Sie für die einzelnen Aufgaben brauchen und welche Aufgabenstellung Sie besonders schnell lösen können oder welche Ihnen Schwierigkeiten bereitet.
  - Machen Sie sich anhand Ihrer Erfahrungen mit den Übungsaufgaben vor der Prüfung einen Zeitplan.
  - Legen Sie darin fest, wie viel Zeit Sie pro Aufgabenstellung veranschlagen.
  - Halten Sie sich während der Prüfung unbedingt an diesen Plan!
  - Hören Sie mit der Bearbeitung einer Aufgabenstellung auf, wenn die veranschlagte Zeit vorüber ist. Sonst verbeißen Sie sich in Schwierigkeiten, die Sie nur Zeit kosten.
  - Beginnen Sie mit der Aufgabenstellung, die die meisten Punkte gibt.

Multiple Choice

- Lesen Sie den ganzen Text ruhig und konzentriert.
- Schlagen Sie zunächst keine unbekannten Wörter nach – tun Sie das erst, wenn Sie merken, dass ein unbekanntes Wort für die Bearbeitung einer Aufgabe wichtig ist.
- Bei den meisten *multiple choice*-Aufgaben müssen Sie die relevante Passage für die jeweilige Aufgabe im Text selbst finden, manche Aufgaben verweisen aber mit einer Zeilenangabe direkt auf die entsprechende Textstelle.
- Die Aufgaben sind meist in der Reihenfolge der dazugehörigen Textstellen geordnet.
- Lesen Sie konzentriert alle angebotenen Antwortmöglichkeiten – auch dann, wenn Ihnen eine davon gleich ins Auge springt.

- Die Aufgabenstellung lautet immer: "*Mark the most suitable option*". Manchmal gibt es zwei oder mehr plausible Antworten, die sehr ähnlich klingen. Machen Sie sich die exakte Bedeutung jeder Antwort klar und vergleichen Sie jede Option noch einmal genau mit der Fragestellung. Wählen Sie dann diejenige Antwort aus, die am treffendsten ist.
- Lesen Sie bei diesem Aufgabentyp wirklich genau und Wort für Wort, denn schon ein geringer Bedeutungsunterschied kann eine Antwort ausschließen.

Multiple Matching

- Lesen Sie den Text ruhig und konzentriert durch.
- Schlagen Sie zunächst keine unbekannten Wörter nach – tun Sie das erst, wenn Sie merken, dass ein unbekanntes Wort für die Bearbeitung einer Aufgabe wichtig ist!
- Machen Sie sich den Inhalt des Textes klar und gehen Sie in Gedanken die Handlungsabfolge des Textes durch. Achten Sie auf markante Ereignisse im Text oder auf wörtliche Rede. So können Sie einzelne Sätze für bestimmte Lücken leichter finden und unpassende schneller aussortieren.
- Die Umgebung der Textlücken verrät manchmal etwas über den passenden Satz, den Sie zuordnen sollen. Wörter aus dem Satz finden sich unter Umständen in der näheren oder weiteren Umgebung.
- Prüfen Sie, ob der gewählte Antwortsatz im Kontext Sinn ergibt und sich logisch zwischen den vorausgehenden und nachfolgenden Satz im Text einfügt.

Mediation Englisch–Deutsch

- Bei diesem Typ von Mediationsaufgabe müssen Sie Fragen zu einem englischen Text auf Deutsch beantworten. Dabei sollen Sie Informationen sinngemäß ins Deutsche übertragen.
- Lesen Sie die relevanten Textpassagen ruhig und konzentriert.
- Schlagen Sie zunächst keine unbekannten Wörter nach – tun Sie das erst, wenn Sie merken, dass ein unbekanntes Wort für die Bearbeitung der Aufgabenstellung wichtig ist.
- Versuchen Sie, die relevanten Inhalte präzise zu erfassen und mit Ihren eigenen Worten zu formulieren.
- Oft wiederholen die Formulierungen der Aufgaben Formulierungen aus dem Text. Das kann Ihnen helfen, die relevante Textstelle schneller zu finden.
- Die Bewertung orientiert sich vor allem an der inhaltlichen Richtigkeit und Vollständigkeit. Sie müssen aber auch auf angemessenes Deutsch achten.

Mediation Deutsch–Englisch

- Bei dieser Aufgabe müssen Sie markierte Passagen eines deutschen Textes ins Englische übertragen. Dabei steht die korrekte sinngemäße Übertragung im Vordergrund, nicht eine Übersetzung. Eine Abrundung durch Einleitung und Schluss ist nicht verlangt. Eigene Überlegungen oder persönliche Meinung dürfen Sie nicht einbringen.
- Sie erhalten für Ihren englischen Text oft einen vorformulierten Anfang, an den Sie anknüpfen sollen.
- Konzentrieren Sie sich auf die markierten Textstellen – das spart Zeit und Energie und eliminiert Fehlerquellen.
- Bilden Sie aus den übertragenen Textstellen einen zusammenhängenden Text und reihen Sie nicht nur die Fakten lose aneinander.
- Die Bewertung erfolgt nach den Kriterien: Inhaltliche Richtigkeit und Vollständigkeit – Sprachliche Qualität (Grammatik, Wortschatz, Idiomatik).

Argumentative Writing

- In der Aufgabenstellung *Argumentative Writing* sollen Sie zeigen, dass Sie in der Lage sind, einen zusammenhängenden argumentativen Text auf Englisch zu einem vorgegebenen Thema zu verfassen. Sie sollen Ansichten begründen und nachvollziehbar und zusammenhängend präsentieren.
- In der Prüfung haben Sie die Wahl zwischen zwei *Composition*-Themen.
- Die Bewertung Ihrer Arbeit erfolgt nach folgenden Kriterien:
Inhalt: Themabezug, Qualität der Argumente, Aufbau, Geschlossenheit der Darstellung ...
Sprachliche Richtigkeit: Grammatik, Rechtschreibung ...
Ausdrucksvermögen: angemessener Wortschatz, Satzstrukturen, Herstellen von Zusammenhängen ...

Themenwahl

- Lesen Sie konzentriert jede angebotene Themenstellung.
- Analysieren Sie die einzelnen Themen und machen Sie sich klar, was jeweils von Ihnen verlangt wird.
- Versuchen Sie zu überschlagen, wie viel Sie zu dem jeweiligen Thema wissen und welche Stichpunkte Ihnen dazu auf Anhieb einfallen.
- Legen Sie sich nicht voreilig fest, sondern treffen Sie eine bewusste Entscheidung.

Aufbau und Schreiben

- Der Aufbau ist klassisch: Einleitung – Hauptteil – Schluss. Denken Sie daran: Sie verschenken wertvolle Punkte, wenn Sie sich nicht an diese Form halten.

– Der geforderte Umfang lässt normalerweise eine detaillierte Auseinandersetzung mit dem Thema nicht zu. Darum geht es auch bei diesem Aufgabentyp nicht. Vielmehr sollen Sie zeigen, dass Sie ein Thema in seinen relevanten Aspekten erkennen und bearbeiten können.

Sprache
– Schreiben Sie einfach und verständlich. Lange, verschachtelte Sätze sind typisch für das Deutsche und im Englischen eher unnatürlich. Machen Sie lieber aus einem längeren Satz zwei kürzere.
– Verwenden Sie Ausdrücke aus der Liste der *useful phrases* und bringen Sie Fachbegriffe zu dem jeweiligen Thema ein, wenn Ihnen solche bekannt sind.

Checkliste
Erstellen Sie während Ihrer Vorbereitungszeit eine Liste Ihrer häufigsten Fehler (Rechtschreibung und Grammatik) und überprüfen Sie Ihren Text nach dem Schreiben auf diese Fehler. So könnte Ihre Liste z. B. aussehen:
– Satzstellung S-V-O
– Plural oder Singular?
– 3. Person Singular-s
– unregelmäßige Verben
– *who* für Personen, *which* für Dinge
– *this* oder *these*, *that* oder *those*
– Adverbien erkannt?
– kein *will/would* im *if*-Satz

Tipps zur *composition*
– Achten Sie darauf, dass Sie das Thema richtig und vollständig erfasst haben. („*Discuss …*" bedeutet, dass Sie sich mit Pro und Contra auseinandersetzen müssen.)
– Sammeln Sie relevante Ideen – Vor- und Nachteile, Argumente, Beispiele, Belege, Fachausdrücke – auf einem Konzeptpapier, bevor Sie zu schreiben beginnen!
– Führen Sie den Leser mit einem einleitenden Gedanken an die Thematik heran. Versuchen Sie, Ihren Leser neugierig zu machen.
– Machen Sie Ihren Standpunkt deutlich. Beispielsweise können Sie erst eine kurze Einschätzung der Problematik geben und daran anschließend die pro- und dann die contra-Argumente anführen. Alternativ können Sie auch auf jedes Pro sofort ein Contra folgen lassen.
– Achten Sie darauf, dass Ihr Text inhaltlich und sprachlich schlüssig, verständlich und überzeugend ist. Gliedern Sie den Text in Absätze entsprechend der einzelnen Sinnabschnitte und verbinden Sie diese sinnvoll. Arbeiten Sie Spezialwortschatz und passende *useful phrases* ein.
– Runden Sie Ihren Text mit einer Schlussbemerkung (z. B. Resümee) ab.
– Schreiben Sie sachlich.

Mündliche Gruppenprüfung

- In der mündlichen Prüfung werden 4 bis 6 Schüler in einer Gruppe geprüft. In der Vorbereitungszeit (15 Min.) erhält jeder Schüler der Gruppe ein Arbeitsblatt mit Arbeitsanweisungen. Die Arbeitsanweisungen beziehen sich auf die individuelle Aufgabe jedes Schülers und auf die Aufgabe der Gruppe.
- Es gibt Aufgaben, bei denen Sie mit verteilten Rollen verschiedene festgelegte Positionen einnehmen und verteidigen sollen, und Aufgaben, bei denen Sie ohne festgelegte Rolle in der Gruppe diskutieren sollen.
- Zu Beginn der Prüfung stellt jeder Teilnehmer sich/seine Rolle und seine Position vor. Dazu haben Sie etwa 1 Minute Zeit.
- Im weiteren Prüfungsverlauf sollen Sie mit Ihren Mitschülern nach den Vorgaben der Aufgabenstellung/Ihrer jeweiligen Rolle über das gegebene Thema diskutieren. Dabei sollen Sie Ihr Ziel durch gute Argumente und eine überlegte Redestrategie erreichen.
- Beteiligen Sie sich am Gespräch und versuchen Sie, in die Diskussion einzugreifen. Gehen Sie auch auf die Argumente Ihrer Mitprüflinge ein, sodass ein echtes Gespräch zustande kommt.

Useful Phrases

starting off / getting into the stuff			
In view of …	– Angesichts	As we know from …	– Wie wir aus … wissen
When it comes to …	– Wenn es um … geht	For many years …	– Seit vielen Jahren
According to …	– laut, nach Angaben von	Many years ago …	– Vor vielen Jahren

listing / grouping / linking			
first(ly) / second(ly) / …	– erstens / zweitens / …	however	– jedoch, aber
		in other words	– mit anderen Worten
finally	– schließlich	yet	– allerdings, jedoch
in addition (to that)	– zusätzlich, außerdem	consequently	– folglich
additionally	– zusätzlich, außerdem	as a result	– folglich
moreover	– außerdem, darüber hinaus	for this reason	– daher, aus diesem Grund
furthermore	– weiterhin, außerdem	That's why	– daher, deshalb
what is more …	– dazu kommt …	therefore	– deshalb
provided that	– vorausgesetzt, dass …	on the one hand / on the other hand	– einerseits / andererseits

conclusion

Considering all this …	– Betrachtet man all dies …	To cut a long story short …	– Um es kurz zu sagen …
Taking all this into account …	– Wenn man all dies berücksichtigt …	To sum it up...	– Zusammengefasst …
		On the whole …	– Insgesamt …

discussing a topic

as far as … is concerned	– was … betrifft	actually	– eigentlich, im Grunde
unlike	– im Gegensatz zu	to take into account	– berücksichtigen
in contrast to	– im Gegensatz zu	to take into consideration	– in Betracht ziehen
contrary to	im Gegensatz zu		
in spite of / despite	– trotz	to think sth. over	– etw. überdenken
obviously	– offensichtlich	to make a difference	– unterscheiden
apparently / seemingly	– anscheinend	to examine	– untersuchen
		to doubt	– bezweifeln
on the one hand / on the other hand	– einerseits / andererseits	doubt	– Zweifel
		to question	– in Frage stellen
whereas	– während, wohingegen	to suggest / to propose	– vorschlagen
instead of	– anstatt	suggestion / proposal	– Vorschlag
nevertheless	– nichtsdestoweniger, dennoch, trotzdem	to prove	– beweisen
		proof	– Beweis
however	– jedoch, aber	to disprove	– widerlegen
although	– obwohl	to contradict	– widersprechen
in particular	– insbesondere	contradiction	– Widerspruch
above all	– vor allem	to conclude	– schlussfolgern
This does not go for …	– Das gilt nicht für …	conclusion	– Schlussfolgerung
		to consider	– bedenken, überlegen
to a certain extent / degree	– bis zu einem gewissen Grad	opinions are divided as to …	– die Meinungen bzgl. … gehen auseinander
in the short / long run	– auf kurze / lange Sicht		
The same goes for …	– Dasselbe gilt für …		

problem and solution

A problem can be:

serious	– ernst
complicated	– kompliziert
difficult	– schwierig
easy	– einfach
pressing	– drängend
delicate	– delikat
insurmountable	– unüberwindlich
a major problem	– ein größeres Problem
a minor problem	– ein kleineres Problem

What you can do with a problem:

to discuss	– diskutieren
to outline	– umreißen
to face	– konfrontiert sein mit, sich gegenübersehen
to deal with	– sich befassen mit
to tackle	– anpacken, angehen
to get to the heart of	– zum Kern vorstoßen
to avoid	– vermeiden
to ignore	– ignorieren
to cope with	– fertig werden mit
to cause	– verursachen
to raise	– aufwerfen
to settle	– beilegen
to solve	– lösen

A solution can be:

complicated	– kompliziert
difficult	– schwierig
easy	– einfach
quick	– schnell
satisfactory	– befriedigend
unsatisfactory	– unbefriedigend
convincing	– überzeugend
ideal	– ideal
neat	– sauber
practicable	– praktikabel
useful	– nützlich
helpful	– hilfreich
possible	– möglich
lasting	– dauerhaft

What you can do with a solution:

to work out	– ausarbeiten
to go over again	– überarbeiten
to reject	– zurückweisen
to suggest / to propose	– vorschlagen

dispute	– Disput, Streit
controversy	– Kontroverse
controversial	– strittig
debatable	– umstritten, fraglich
compromise	– Kompromiss

Kurzgrammatik

Besonderheiten einiger Wortarten

1 Adjektive und Adverbien – *Adjectives and Adverbs*
Bildung und Verwendung von Adverbien – *Formation and Use of Adverbs*

Bildung
Adjektiv + *-ly*   glad → glad<u>ly</u>

Ausnahmen:
- *-y* am Wortende wird zu *-i*   ea<u>sy</u> → ca<u>si</u>ly
  funn<u>y</u> → funn<u>i</u>ly
- auf einen Konsonanten folgendes   sim<u>ple</u> → sim<u>ply</u>
  -le wird zu *-ly*   probab<u>le</u> → probab<u>ly</u>
- *-ic* am Wortende wird zu *-ically*   fantas<u>tic</u> → fantas<u>tically</u>
  Ausnahme: pub<u>lic</u> → pub<u>licly</u>

Beachte:
- Unregelmäßig gebildet wird: good → well
- Endet das Adjektiv auf *-ly*, so kann kein Adverb gebildet werden; man verwendet deshalb: in a + Adjektiv + *manner/way*   friendly → in a friendly manner
- In einigen Fällen haben Adjektiv und Adverb dieselbe Form, z. B.:   daily, early, fast, hard, long, low, weekly, yearly
- Manche Adjektive bilden zwei Adverbformen, die sich in der Bedeutung unterscheiden, z. B.:

Adj./Adv.	Adv. auf *-ly*
hard	hardly
schwierig, hart	kaum
late	lately
spät	neulich, kürzlich
near	nearly
nahe	beinahe

The task is <u>hard</u>.   (adjective)
Die Aufgabe ist schwierig.
She works <u>hard</u>.   (adverb)
Sie arbeitet hart.
She <u>hardly</u> works.   (adverb)
Sie arbeitet kaum.

Verwendung
Adverbien bestimmen
- Verben,

- Adjektive,

- andere Adverbien oder

- einen ganzen Satz näher.

She <u>easily</u> <u>found</u> her brother in the crowd.
Sie fand ihren Bruder leicht in der Menge.
This band is <u>extremely</u> <u>famous</u>.
Diese Band ist sehr berühmt.
He walks <u>extremely</u> <u>quickly</u>.
Er geht äußerst schnell.
<u>Fortunately</u>, <u>nobody was hurt</u>.
Glücklicherweise wurde niemand verletzt.

Beachte:
Nach bestimmten Verben steht nicht das Adverb, sondern das Adjektiv:
- Verben, die einen **Zustand** ausdrücken, z. B.:

to be	sein
to become	werden
to get	werden
to seem	scheinen
to stay	bleiben

- Verben der **Sinneswahrnehmung**, z. B.:

to feel	sich anfühlen
to look	aussehen
to smell	riechen
to sound	sich anhören
to taste	schmecken

Everything <u>seems</u> <u>quiet</u>.
Alles scheint ruhig zu sein.

This dress <u>looks</u> <u>fantastic</u>!
Dieses Kleid sieht toll aus!

Steigerung des Adjektivs – *Comparison of Adjectives*

Bildung
Man unterscheidet:
- Grundform/Positiv *(positive)*
- Komparativ *(comparative)*
- Superlativ *(superlative)*

Peter is y<u>oung</u>.
Jane is y<u>ounger</u>.
Paul is <u>the youngest</u>.

Steigerung auf -er, -est
- einsilbige Adjektive

old, old<u>er</u>, old<u>est</u>
alt, älter, am ältesten

- zweisilbige Adjektive, die auf -er, -le, -ow oder -y enden

clever, clever<u>er</u>, clever<u>est</u>
klug, klüger, am klügsten

simple, simpl<u>er</u>, simpl<u>est</u>
einfach, einfacher, am einfachsten

narrow, narrow<u>er</u>, narrow<u>est</u>
eng, enger, am engsten

funny, funn<u>ier</u>, funn<u>iest</u>
lustig, lustiger, am lustigsten

Beachte:
- stummes -e am Wortende entfällt
- nach einem Konsonanten wird -y am Wortende zu -i-
- nach kurzem Vokal wird ein Konsonant am Wortende verdoppelt

simpl<u>e</u>, simpl<u>er</u>, simpl<u>est</u>

funn<u>y</u>, funn<u>ier</u>, funn<u>iest</u>

fi<u>t</u>, fi<u>tt</u>er, fi<u>tt</u>est

Steigerung mit *more ..., most ...*
- zweisilbige Adjektive, die nicht auf -er, -le, -ow oder -y enden
- Adjektive mit drei und mehr Silben

useful, <u>more</u> useful, <u>most</u> useful
nützlich, nützlicher, am nützlichsten

difficult, <u>more</u> difficult, <u>most</u> difficult
schwierig, schwieriger, am schwierigsten

Unregelmäßige Steigerung
Die unregelmäßig gesteigerten Adjektive muss man auswendig lernen. Einige sind hier angegeben:

good, better, best
gut, besser, am besten

bad, worse, worst
schlecht, schlechter, am schlechtesten

many, more, most
viele, mehr, am meisten

much, more, most
viel, mehr, am meisten

little, less, least
wenig, weniger, am wenigsten

Steigerungsformen im Satz – *Sentences with Comparisons*

Es gibt folgende Möglichkeiten, Steigerungen im Satz zu verwenden:

- **Positiv:** Zwei oder mehr Personen oder Sachen sind **gleich oder ungleich:** *(not) as* + Grundform des Adjektivs + *as*

    Anne is <u>as</u> t<u>all</u> <u>as</u> John (and Steve).
    Anne ist genauso groß wie John (und Steve).
    John is <u>not as</u> t<u>all</u> <u>as</u> Steve.
    John ist nicht so groß wie Steve.

- **Komparativ:** Zwei oder mehr Personen/Sachen sind **verschieden** (größer/besser …): Komparativform des Adjektivs + *than*

    Steve is tall<u>er</u> <u>than</u> Anne.
    Steve ist größer als Anne.

- **Superlativ:** Eine Person oder Sache wird besonders hervorgehoben (der/die/das größte/beste …): *the* + Superlativform des Adjektivs

    Steve is <u>the</u> tall<u>est</u> boy in class.
    Steve ist der größte Junge in der Klasse.

Steigerung des Adverbs – *Comparison of Adverbs*

Adverbien können wie Adjektive auch gesteigert werden.

- Adverbien auf *-ly* werden mit *more, most* bzw. mit *less, least* gesteigert.

    She talks <u>more</u> quick<u>ly</u> than John.
    Sie spricht schneller als John.

- Adverbien, die dieselbe Form wie das Adjektiv haben, werden mit *-er, -est* gesteigert.

    fast – fast<u>er</u> – fast<u>est</u>
    early – earl<u>ier</u> – earl<u>iest</u>

- Manche Adverbien haben unregelmäßige Steigerungsformen, z. B.:

    well – better – best
    badly – worse – worst
    little – less – least
    much – more – most

Die Stellung von Adverbien im Satz

Adverbien können verschiedene Positionen im Satz einnehmen:

- Am **Anfang des Satzes**, vor dem Subjekt *(front position)*

    <u>Tomorrow</u> he will be in London.
    Morgen [betont] wird er in London sein.
    <u>Unfortunately</u>, I can't come to the party.
    Leider kann ich nicht zur Party kommen.

- **Im Satz** *(mid position)*
  vor dem Vollverb,

  nach *to be,*

  nach dem ersten Hilfsverb.

- Am **Ende des Satzes** *(end position)*

  Gibt es mehrere Adverbien am Satzende, so gilt die **Reihenfolge**: Art und Weise – Ort – Zeit *(manner – place – time)*

She <u>often</u> goes to school by bike.
Sie fährt oft mit dem Rad in die Schule.
She is <u>already</u> at home.
Sie ist schon zu Hause.
You can <u>even</u> go swimming there.
Man kann dort sogar schwimmen gehen.
He will be in London <u>tomorrow</u>.
Er wird morgen in London sein.

The snow melts <u>slowly</u> <u>in the mountains</u> <u>at springtime</u>.
Im Frühling schmilzt der Schnee langsam in den Bergen.

2 Artikel – *Article*

Der **bestimmte Artikel** steht, wenn man von einer **ganz bestimmten Person oder Sache** spricht.

Beachte: Der bestimmte Artikel steht unter anderem **immer** in folgenden Fällen:
- **abstrakte Begriffe**, die näher erläutert sind

- **Gebäudebezeichnungen**, wenn man vom Gebäude und nicht von der Institution spricht
- **Eigennamen im Plural** (Familiennamen, Gebirge, Inselgruppen, einige Länder etc.)
- Namen von **Flüssen** und **Meeren**

<u>The</u> cat is sleeping on the sofa.
Die Katze schläft auf dem Sofa. [nicht irgendeine Katze, sondern eine bestimmte]

<u>The</u> agriculture practised in the USA is very successful.
Die Landwirtschaft, wie sie in den USA praktiziert wird, ist sehr erfolgreich.

<u>The</u> university should be renovated soon.
Die Universität sollte bald renoviert werden.

<u>the</u> Johnsons, <u>the</u> Rockies, <u>the</u> Hebrides, <u>the</u> Netherlands, <u>the</u> USA

<u>the</u> Mississippi, <u>the</u> North Sea, <u>the</u> Pacific Ocean

Der **unbestimmte Artikel** steht, wenn man von einer **nicht näher bestimmten Person oder Sache** spricht.

<u>A</u> man is walking down the road.
Ein Mann läuft gerade die Straße entlang. [irgendein Mann]

G 5

Beachte:
In einigen Fällen steht **stets** der unbestimmte Artikel:
- **Berufsbezeichnungen** und **Nationalitäten**
- Zugehörigkeit zu einer **Religion** oder **Partei**

She is a̱ engineer. *Sie ist Ingenieurin.*
He is a̱ Scot(sman). *Er ist Schotte.*
She is a̱ Catholic. *Sie ist katholisch.*
He is a̱ Tory. *Er ist Mitglied der Tories.*

In diesen Fällen steht **kein Artikel**:
- **nicht zählbare** Nomen wie z. B. **Stoffbezeichnungen**
- **abstrakte Nomen** ohne nähere Bestimmung
- **Kollektivbegriffe**, z. B. *man, youth, society*
- **Institutionen**, z. B. *school, church, university, prison*
- **Mahlzeiten**, z. B. *breakfast, lunch*
- *by* + **Verkehrsmittel**
- **Personennamen** (auch mit Titel), **Verwandtschaftsbezeichnungen**, die wie Namen verwendet werden
- Bezeichnungen für **Straßen, Plätze, Brücken, Parkanlagen**
- Namen von **Ländern, Kontinenten, Städten, Seen, Inseln, Bergen**

Gold is very valuable.
Gold ist sehr wertvoll.

Buddhism is widespread in Asia.
Der Buddhismus ist in Asien weit verbreitet.

Man is responsible for global warming.
Der Mensch ist für die Klimaerwärmung verantwortlich.

We went to school together.
Wir gingen zusammen zur Schule.

Dinner is at 8 p.m.
Das Abendessen ist um 20 Uhr.

I went to school by bike.
Ich fuhr mit dem Fahrrad zur Schule.

Tom, Mr Scott, Queen Elizabeth, Dr Hill, Dad, Uncle Harry

Fifth Avenue, Trafalgar Square, Westminster Bridge, Hyde Park

France, Asia, San Francisco, Loch Ness, Corsica, Ben Nevis

3 Pronomen – *Pronouns*

Possessivpronomen – *Possessive Pronouns*

Possessivpronomen *(possessive pronouns)* verwendet man, um zu sagen, **wem etwas gehört**.
Steht ein Possessivpronomen allein, so wird eine andere Form verwendet als in Verbindung mit einem Substantiv:

mit Substantiv	ohne Substantiv		
my	*mine*	This is my bike.	– This is mine.
your	*yours*	This is your bike.	– This is yours.
his/her/its	*his/hers/–*	This is her bike.	– This is hers.
our	*ours*	This is our bike.	– This is ours.
your	*yours*	This is your bike.	– This is yours.
their	*theirs*	This is their bike.	– This is theirs.

Reflexivpronomen – *Reflexive Pronouns*

Reflexivpronomen *(reflexive pronouns)* **beziehen sich auf das Subjekt** des Satzes **zurück**. Es handelt sich also um dieselbe Person:

myself	I will buy myself a new car.
yourself	You will buy yourself a new car.
himself / herself / itself	He will buy himself a new car.
ourselves	We will buy ourselves a new car.
yourselves	You will buy yourselves a new car.
themselves	They will buy themselves a new car.

Beachte:
- Einige Verben stehen ohne Reflexivpronomen, obwohl im Deutschen mit „mich, dich, sich etc." übersetzt wird.
- Einige Verben können sowohl mit einem Objekt als auch mit einem Reflexivpronomen verwendet werden. Dabei ändert sich die Bedeutung, z. B. bei *to control, to enjoy, to help, to occupy.*

I apologize …
Ich entschuldige mich …
He is hiding.
Er versteckt sich.

He is enjoying the party.
Er genießt die Party.
She is enjoying herself.
Sie amüsiert sich.
He is helping the child.
Er hilft dem Kind.
Help yourself!
Bedienen Sie sich!

Reziprokes Pronomen – *Reciprocal Pronoun* ("each other / one another")

each other / one another ist unveränderlich. Es bezieht sich auf **zwei oder mehr Personen** und wird mit „sich (gegenseitig) / einander" übersetzt.

Beachte:
Einige Verben stehen ohne *each other*, obwohl im Deutschen mit „sich" übersetzt wird.

They looked at each other and laughed.
Sie schauten sich (gegenseitig) an und lachten.
oder:
Sie schauten einander an und lachten.

to meet	*sich treffen*
to kiss	*sich küssen*
to fall in love	*sich verlieben*

4 Präpositionen – *Prepositions*

Präpositionen *(prepositions)* drücken **räumliche, zeitliche oder andere Arten von Beziehungen** aus.

Die wichtigsten Präpositionen mit Beispielen für ihre Verwendung:

- *at*
  Ortsangabe: *at home*

  Zeitangabe: *at 3 p.m.*

- *by*
  Angabe des Mittels: *by bike*

  Angabe der Ursache: *by mistake*

  Zeitangabe: *by tomorrow*

- *for*
  Zeitdauer: *for hours*

- *from*
  Ortsangabe: *from Dublin*

  Zeitangabe: *from nine to five*

- *in*
  Ortsangabe: *in England*

The ball is under the table.
He came home after six o'clock.

I'm at home now. *Ich bin jetzt zu Hause.*
He arrived at 3 p.m. *Er kam um 15 Uhr an.*

She went to work by bike.
Sie fuhr mit dem Rad zur Arbeit.

He did it by mistake.
Er hat es aus Versehen getan.

You will get the letter by tomorrow.
Du bekommst den Brief bis morgen.

We waited for the bus for hours.
Wir warteten stundenlang auf den Bus.

Ian is from Dublin.
Ian kommt aus Dublin.

We work from nine to five.
Wir arbeiten von neun bis fünf Uhr.

In England, they drive on the left.
In England herrscht Linksverkehr.

Zeitangabe: *in the morning*

- *of*
  Ortsangabe: *north of the city*

- *on*
  Ortsangabe: *on the left,*
  on the floor
  Zeitangabe: *on Monday*

- *to*
  Richtungsangabe: *to the left*

  Angabe des Ziels: *to London*

They woke up in the morning.
Sie wachten am Morgen auf.

The village lies north of the city.
Das Dorf liegt nördlich der Stadt.

On the left you see the London Eye.
Links sehen Sie das London Eye.

On Monday she will buy the tickets.
(Am) Montag kauft sie die Karten.

Please turn to the left.
Bitte wenden Sie sich nach links.

He goes to London every year.
Er fährt jedes Jahr nach London.

5 Modale Hilfsverben – *Modal Auxiliaries*

Zu den **modalen Hilfsverben** *(modal auxiliaries)* zählen z. B. *can, may* und *must.*

Bildung

- Die modalen Hilfsverben haben für alle Personen **nur eine Form**: kein *-s* in der 3. Person Singular.

- Auf ein modales Hilfsverb folgt der **Infinitiv ohne** *to*.

- **Frage und Verneinung** werden nicht mit *do/did* umschrieben.

I, you, he/she/it,
we, you, they } must

You must listen to my new CD.
Du musst dir meine neue CD anhören.

Can you help me, please?
Kannst du mir bitte helfen?

Die modalen Hilfsverben können nicht alle Zeiten bilden. Deshalb benötigt man **Ersatzformen** (können auch im Präsens verwendet werden).

- *can* (können)
  Ersatzformen:
  (to) be able to (Fähigkeit),
  (to) be allowed to (Erlaubnis)

  Beachte: Im *simple past* und *conditional I* ist auch *could* möglich.

I can sing. / I was able to sing.
Ich kann singen. / Ich konnte singen.

You can't go to the party. /
I wasn't allowed to go to the party.
Du darfst nicht auf die Party gehen. /
Ich durfte nicht auf die Party gehen.

When I was three, I could already ski.
Mit drei konnte ich schon Ski fahren.

- *may* (dürfen) – sehr höflich
  Ersatzform: *(to) be allowed to*

  You may go home early. /
  You were allowed to go home early.
  Du darfst früh nach Hause gehen. /
  Du durftest früh nach Hause gehen.

- *must* (müssen)
  Ersatzform: *(to) have to*

  He must be home by ten o'clock. /
  He had to be home by ten o'clock.
  Er muss um zehn Uhr zu Hause sein. /
  Er musste um zehn Uhr zu Hause sein.

Beachte:
must not/mustn't = „nicht dürfen"

You must not eat all the cake.
Du darfst nicht den ganzen Kuchen essen.

„nicht müssen, nicht brauchen" =
not have to, needn't

You don't have to / needn't eat all the cake.
Du musst nicht den ganzen Kuchen essen. /
Du brauchst nicht ... zu essen.

Infinitiv, Gerundium oder Partizip? – Die infiniten Verbformen

6 Infinitiv – *Infinitive*

Der **Infinitiv** (Grundform des Verbs) mit *to* steht z. B. nach
- bestimmten **Verben**, z. B.:

to decide	(sich) entscheiden, beschließen
to expect	erwarten
to hope	hoffen
to manage	schaffen
to plan	planen
to promise	versprechen
to want	wollen

  He decided to wait.
  Er beschloss zu warten.

- bestimmten **Substantiven und Pronomen** *(something, anything)*, z. B.:

attempt	Versuch
idea	Idee
plan	Plan
wish	Wunsch

  We haven't got anything to eat at home.
  Wir haben nichts zu essen zu Hause.
  It was her plan to visit him in May.
  Sie hatte vor, ihn im Mai zu besuchen.

- bestimmten **Adjektiven** (auch in Verbindung mit *too/enough*) und deren Steigerungsformen, z. B.:

certain	sicher
difficult/hard	schwer, schwierig
easy	leicht

  It was difficult to follow her.
  Es war schwer, ihr zu folgen.

- **Fragewörtern**, wie z. B. *what, where, which, who, when, how* und nach *whether*. Diese Konstruktion ersetzt eine indirekte Frage mit modalem Hilfsverb.

We knew <u>where</u> <u>to find</u> her. /
We knew <u>where</u> <u>we</u> <u>would find</u> her.
Wir wussten, wo wir sie finden würden.

Die Konstruktion **Objekt + Infinitiv** wird im Deutschen oft mit einem „dass"-Satz übersetzt.
Sie steht z. B. **nach**
- bestimmten **Verben**, z. B.:
to allow	erlauben
to get	veranlassen
to help	helfen
to persuade	überreden

  She <u>allowed</u> him <u>to go</u> to the cinema.
  Sie erlaubte ihm, dass er ins Kino geht. / ... ins Kino zu gehen.

- **Verb + Präposition**, z. B.:
to count on	rechnen mit
to rely on	sich verlassen auf
to wait for	warten auf

  She <u>relies on</u> him <u>to arrive</u> in time.
  Sie verlässt sich darauf, dass er rechtzeitig ankommt.

- **Adjektiv + Präposition**, z. B.:
easy for	leicht
necessary for	notwendig
nice of	nett
silly of	dumm

  It is <u>necessary</u> <u>for you</u> <u>to learn</u> maths.
  Es ist notwendig, dass du Mathe lernst.

- **Substantiv + Präposition**, z. B.:
opportunity for	Gelegenheit
idea for	Idee
time for	Zeit
mistake for	Fehler

  Work experience is a good <u>opportunity</u> <u>for you</u> <u>to find out</u> which job suits you.
  Ein Praktikum ist eine gute Gelegenheit, herauszufinden, welcher Beruf zu dir passt.

- einem **Adjektiv**, das durch *too* oder *enough* näher bestimmt wird.

  The box is <u>too</u> <u>heavy</u> <u>for me</u> <u>to carry</u>.
  Die Kiste ist mir zu schwer zum Tragen.

  The weather is <u>good</u> <u>enough</u> <u>for us</u> <u>to go</u> for a walk. *Das Wetter ist gut genug, dass wir spazieren gehen können.*

7 Gerundium (*-ing*-Form) – *Gerund*

Bildung
Infinitiv + *-ing*   read → read<u>ing</u>

Beachte:
- stummes -*e* entfällt
- nach kurzem betontem Vokal: Schlusskonsonant verdoppelt
- -*ie* wird zu -*y*

wri<u>te</u> → writ<u>ing</u>
sto<u>p</u> → sto<u>pp</u>ing
l<u>ie</u> → l<u>y</u>ing

Verwendung
Die -*ing*-Form steht nach bestimmten Ausdrücken und kann verschiedene Funktionen im Satz einnehmen, z. B.:
- als **Subjekt** des Satzes
- nach bestimmten **Verben** (als **Objekt** des Satzes), z. B.:

to avoid	vermeiden
to enjoy	genießen, gern tun
to keep (on)	weitermachen
to miss	vermissen
to risk	riskieren
to suggest	vorschlagen

<u>Skiing</u> is fun. *Skifahren macht Spaß.*

He <u>enjoys</u> <u>reading</u> comics.
Er liest gerne Comics.

You <u>risk</u> <u>losing</u> a friend.
Du riskierst, einen Freund zu verlieren.

- nach **Verb + Präposition**, z. B.:

to agree with	zustimmen
to believe in	glauben an
to dream of	träumen von
to look forward to	sich freuen auf
to talk about	sprechen über

She <u>dreams</u> <u>of</u> <u>meeting</u> a star.
Sie träumt davon, einen Star zu treffen.

- nach **Adjektiv + Präposition**, z. B.:

afraid of	sich fürchten vor
famous for	berühmt für
good/bad at	gut/schlecht in
interested in	interessiert an

He is <u>afraid</u> <u>of</u> <u>losing</u> his job.
Er hat Angst, seine Arbeit zu verlieren.

- nach **Substantiv + Präposition**, z. B.:

chance of	Chance, Aussicht
danger of	Gefahr
reason for	Grund
way of	Art und Weise

Do you have a <u>chance</u> <u>of</u> <u>getting</u> the job?
Hast du Aussicht, die Stelle zu bekommen?

- nach **Präpositionen** und **Konjunktionen der Zeit**, z. B.:

after	nachdem
before	bevor
by	indem, dadurch, dass
in spite of	trotz
instead of	statt

Before leaving the room he said goodbye.
Bevor er den Raum verließ, verabschiedete er sich.

8 Infinitiv oder Gerundium? – *Infinitive or Gerund?*

Einige Verben können sowohl **mit dem Infinitiv** als auch **mit der -ing-Form** stehen, **ohne** dass sich die **Bedeutung ändert**, z. B.
to love, to hate, to prefer, to start, to begin, to continue.

I hate getting up early.
I hate to get up early.
Ich hasse es, früh aufzustehen.

Bei manchen Verben **ändert sich** jedoch die **Bedeutung**, je nachdem, ob sie mit Infinitiv oder mit der -ing-Form verwendet werden, z. B. *to remember, to forget, to stop.*

- to remember + Infinitiv:
  „daran denken, etwas zu tun"

  I must remember to post the invitations.
  Ich muss daran denken, die Einladungen einzuwerfen.

  to remember + ing-Form:
  „sich erinnern, etwas getan zu haben"

  I remember posting the invitations.
  Ich erinnere mich daran, die Einladungen eingeworfen zu haben.

- to forget + Infinitiv:
  „vergessen, etwas zu tun"

  Don't forget to water the plants.
  Vergiss nicht, die Pflanzen zu gießen.

  to forget + ing-Form:
  „vergessen, etwas getan zu haben"

  I'll never forget meeting the President.
  Ich werde nie vergessen, wie ich den Präsidenten traf.

- to stop + Infinitiv:
  „stehen bleiben, um etwas zu tun"

  I stopped to read the road sign.
  Ich hielt an, um das Verkehrsschild zu lesen.

  to stop + ing-Form:
  „aufhören, etwas zu tun"

  He stopped laughing.
  Er hörte auf zu lachen.

9 Partizipien – *Participles*

Partizip Präsens – *Present Participle*

Bildung
Infinitiv + *ing*
Sonderformen: siehe *gerund*
(S. G 11 f.)

talk → talking

Verwendung
Das *present participle* verwendet man:
- zur Bildung der Verlaufsform *present progressive*,
- zur Bildung der Verlaufsform *past progressive*,
- zur Bildung der Verlaufsform *present perfect progressive*,
- zur Bildung der Verlaufsform *future progressive*,
- wie ein Adjektiv, wenn es vor einem Substantiv steht.

Peter is reading.
Peter liest (gerade).
Peter was reading when I saw him.
Peter las (gerade), als ich ihn sah.
I have been living in Sydney for 5 years.
Ich lebe seit 5 Jahren in Sydney.
This time tomorrow I will be working.
Morgen um diese Zeit werde ich arbeiten.
The village hasn't got running water.
Das Dorf hat kein fließendes Wasser.

Partizip Perfekt – *Past Participle*

Bildung
Infinitiv + *-ed*

Beachte:
- stummes *-e* entfällt
- nach kurzem betontem Vokal wird der Schlusskonsonant verdoppelt
- *-y* wird zu *-ie*
- unregelmäßige Verben (S. G 31 f.)

talk → talked
live → lived
stop → stopped

cry → cried
be → been

Verwendung
Das *past participle* verwendet man
- zur Bildung des *present perfect*,

He hasn't talked to Tom yet.
Er hat noch nicht mit Tom gesprochen.

- zur Bildung des *past perfect*,

- zur Bildung des *future perfect*,

- zur Bildung des Passivs,

- wie ein Adjektiv, wenn es vor einem Substantiv steht.

Before they went biking in France, they had bought new bikes.
Bevor sie nach Frankreich zum Radfahren gingen, hatten sie neue Fahrräder gekauft.
The letter will have arrived by then.
Der Brief wird bis dann angekommen sein.
The fish was eaten by the cat.
Der Fisch wurde von der Katze gefressen.
Peter has got a well-paid job.
Peter hat eine gut bezahlte Stelle.

Verkürzung eines Nebensatzes durch ein Partizip

Adverbiale Nebensätze (meist kausale oder temporale Bedeutung) und **Relativsätze** können durch ein Partizip verkürzt werden.

She watches the news, because she wants to stay informed.
Wanting to stay informed, she watches the news.
Sie sieht sich die Nachrichten an, weil sie informiert bleiben möchte.

Aus der Zeitform des Verbs im Nebensatz ergibt sich, welches Partizip für die Satzverkürzung verwendet wird:

- Steht das Verb im Nebensatz im *present* oder *past tense* (*simple* und *progressive form*), verwendet man das *present participle*.

he finishes
he finished } → finishing

- Steht das Verb im Nebensatz im *present perfect* oder *past perfect*, verwendet man *having* + *past participle*.

he has finished
he had finished } → having finished

- Das *past participle* verwendet man auch, um einen Satz im Passiv zu verkürzen.

Sally is a manager in a five-star hotel which is called Pacific View.
Sally is a manager in a five-star hotel called Pacific View.

Beachte:
- Man kann einen Temporal- oder Kausalsatz verkürzen, wenn **Haupt- und Nebensatz dasselbe Subjekt** haben.

When he was walking down the street, he saw Jo.
(When) walking down the street, he saw Jo.
Als er die Straße entlangging, sah er Jo.

- Bei **Kausalsätzen** entfallen die Konjunktionen *as, because* und *since* im verkürzten Nebensatz.
- In einem **Temporalsatz** bleibt die einleitende **Konjunktion** häufig erhalten, um dem Satz eine **eindeutige Bedeutung** zuzuweisen.

As <u>he</u> was hungry, <u>he</u> bought a sandwich.
<u>Being</u> hungry, <u>he</u> bought a sandwich.
Da er hungrig war, kaufte er ein Sandwich.
When <u>he</u> left, <u>he</u> forgot to lock the door.
<u>When leaving</u>, <u>he</u> forgot to lock the door.
Als er ging, vergaß er, die Tür abzuschließen.
Tara got sick <u>eating</u> too much chocolate.
Tara wurde schlecht, als/während/da sie zu viel Schokolade aß.

Die Vorzeitigkeit einer Handlung kann durch *after + present participle* oder durch *having + past participle* ausgedrückt werden.
- Bei **Relativsätzen** entfallen die Relativpronomen *who, which* und *that*.

<u>After</u> <u>finishing</u> / <u>Having finished</u> breakfast, he went to work.
Nachdem er sein Frühstück beendet hatte, ging er zur Arbeit.
I saw a six-year-old boy <u>who</u> <u>played</u> the piano.
I saw a six-year-old boy <u>playing</u> the piano.
Ich sah einen sechsjährigen Jungen, der gerade Klavier spielte. / ... Klavier spielen.

Verbindung von zwei Hauptsätzen durch ein Partizip

Zwei Hauptsätze können durch ein Partizip verbunden werden, wenn sie **dasselbe Subjekt** haben.

Beachte:
- Das Subjekt des zweiten Hauptsatzes und die Konjunktion *and* entfallen.
- Die Verbform des zweiten Hauptsatzes wird durch das Partizip ersetzt.

<u>He</u> did his homework and <u>he</u> listened to the radio.
<u>He</u> did his homework <u>listening</u> to the radio.
Er machte seine Hausaufgaben und hörte Radio.

Unverbundene Partizipialkonstruktionen – *Absolute Participle Constructions*

Unverbundene Partizipialkonstruktionen haben ein **eigenes Subjekt**, das nicht mit dem Subjekt des Hauptsatzes übereinstimmt. Sie werden in **gehobener Sprache** verwendet. Mit einleitendem *with* werden sie auf allen Stilebenen verwendet.

The sun having come out, the ladies went for a walk in the park.
Da die Sonne herausgekommen war, gingen die Damen im Park spazieren.

With the telephone ringing, she jumped out of bed.
Als das Telefon klingelte, sprang sie aus dem Bett.

Bildung und Gebrauch der finiten Verbformen

10 Zeiten – *Tenses*

Simple Present

Bildung
Infinitiv, Ausnahme 3. Person Singular: Infinitiv + -*s*

stand – he/she/it stand**s**

Beachte:
- Bei Verben, die auf -*s*, -*sh*, -*ch*, -*x* und -*z* enden, wird in der 3. Person Singular -*es* angefügt.

kiss – he/she/it kiss**es**
rush – he/she/it rush**es**
teach – he/she/it teach**es**
fix – he/she/it fix**es**

- Bei Verben, die auf Konsonant + -*y* enden, wird -*es* angefügt; -*y* wird zu -*i*-.

carry – he/she/it carr**ies**

Bildung von Fragen im *simple present*
(Fragewort +) *do/does* + Subjekt + Infinitiv

Where does he live? / Does he live in London?
Wo lebt er? / Lebt er in London?

Beachte:
Die Umschreibung mit *do/does* wird nicht verwendet,
- wenn nach dem Subjekt gefragt wird (mit *who, what, which*),

Who likes pizza?
Wer mag Pizza?
Which tree has more leaves?
Welcher Baum hat mehr Blätter?

- wenn die Frage mit *is/are* gebildet wird.

Are you happy?
Bist du glücklich?

Bildung der Verneinung im *simple present*
don't/doesn't + Infinitiv

He <u>doesn't like</u> football.
Er mag Fußball nicht.

Verwendung
Das *simple present* wird verwendet:
- bei Tätigkeiten, die man **gewohnheitsmäßig** oder häufig ausführt Signalwörter: z. B. *always, often, never, every day, every morning, every afternoon*

Every morning John <u>buys</u> a newspaper.
Jeden Morgen kauft John eine Zeitung.

- bei **allgemeingültigen** Aussagen

London <u>is</u> a big city.
London ist eine große Stadt.

- bei **Zustandsverben**: Sie drücken Eigenschaften / Zustände von Personen und Dingen aus und stehen normalerweise nur in der *simple form*, z. B. *to hate, to know, to like*.

I like science-fiction films.
Ich mag Science-Fiction-Filme.

Present Progressive / Present Continuous

Bildung
am/is/are + *present participle*

read → <u>am/is/are</u> <u>reading</u>

Bildung von Fragen im *present progressive*
(Fragewort +) *am/is/are* + Subjekt + *present participle*

Is Peter reading? / What is he reading?
Liest Peter gerade? / Was liest er?

Bildung der Verneinung im *present progressive*
am not/isn't/aren't + *present participle*

Peter <u>isn't</u> reading.
Peter liest gerade nicht.

Verwendung
Mit dem *present progressive* drückt man aus, dass etwas **gerade passiert** und **noch nicht abgeschlossen** ist. Es wird daher auch als **Verlaufsform** der Gegenwart bezeichnet.

Signalwörter: *at the moment, now*

At the moment, Peter <u>is drinking</u> a cup of tea.
Im Augenblick trinkt Peter eine Tasse Tee.
[Er hat damit angefangen und noch nicht aufgehört.]

Simple Past

Bildung
Regelmäßige Verben: Infinitiv + *-ed*   walk → walk<u>ed</u>

Beachte:
- stummes *-e* entfällt   hop<u>e</u> → hop<u>ed</u>
- Bei Verben, die auf Konsonant + *-y* enden, wird *-y* zu *-i-*.   car<u>ry</u> → carr<u>ied</u>
- Nach kurzem betontem Vokal wird der Schlusskonsonant verdoppelt.   sto<u>p</u> → sto<u>pped</u>

Unregelmäßige Verben: siehe Liste S. G 31 f.
be → was
have → had

Bildung von Fragen im *simple past*
(Fragewort +) *did* + Subjekt + Infinitiv

(<u>Why</u>) <u>Did</u> he <u>look</u> out of the window?
(Warum) Sah er aus dem Fenster?

Beachte:
Die Umschreibung mit *did* wird nicht verwendet,
- wenn nach dem Subjekt gefragt wird (mit *who, what, which*),

<u>Who</u> <u>paid</u> the bill?
Wer zahlte die Rechnung?

<u>What</u> happ<u>ened</u> to your friend?
Was ist mit deinem Freund passiert?

- wenn die Frage mit *was/were* gebildet wird.

<u>Were</u> you happy?
Warst du glücklich?

Bildung der Verneinung im *simple past*
didn't + Infinitiv

He <u>didn't</u> <u>call</u> me.
Er rief mich nicht an.

Verwendung
Das *simple past* beschreibt Handlungen und Ereignisse, die **in der Vergangenheit passierten** und **bereits abgeschlossen** sind.

Signalwörter: z. B. *yesterday, last week/year, two years ago, in 2008*

Last week, he <u>helped</u> me with my homework.
Letzte Woche half er mir bei meinen Hausaufgaben. [Die Handlung fand in der letzten Woche statt, ist also abgeschlossen.]

Past Progressive / Past Continuous

Bildung
was/were + present participle

watch → was/were watching

Verwendung
Die **Verlaufsform** *past progressive* verwendet man, wenn **zu einem bestimmten Zeitpunkt** in der Vergangenheit eine **Handlung ablief**, bzw. wenn eine **Handlung** von einer anderen **unterbrochen** wurde.

Yesterday at 9 o'clock I was still sleeping.
Gestern um 9 Uhr schlief ich noch.

I was reading a book when Peter came into the room.
Ich las (gerade) ein Buch, als Peter ins Zimmer kam.

Present Perfect (Simple)

Bildung
have/has + past participle

write → has/have written

Verwendung
Das *present perfect* verwendet man,
- wenn ein Vorgang **in der Vergangenheit begonnen** hat und **noch andauert**,
- wenn das Ergebnis einer vergangenen Handlung **Auswirkungen auf die Gegenwart** hat.

Signalwörter: z. B. *already, ever, just, how long, not ... yet, since, for*

Beachte:
- *have/has* können zu *'ve/'s* verkürzt werden.
- Das *present perfect* wird oft mit *since* und *for* verwendet („seit").
  - *since* gibt einen **Zeitpunkt** an:
  - *for* gibt einen **Zeitraum** an:

He has lived in London since 2008.
Er lebt seit 2008 in London.
[Er lebt jetzt immer noch in London.]

I have just cleaned my car.
Ich habe gerade mein Auto geputzt.
[Man sieht evtl. das saubere Auto.]

Have you ever been to Dublin?
Warst du schon jemals in Dublin?

He's given me his umbrella.
Er hat mir seinen Regenschirm gegeben.

Ron has lived in Sydney since 2007.
Ron lebt seit 2007 in Sydney.

Sally has lived in Berlin for five years.
Sally lebt seit fünf Jahren in Berlin.

Present Perfect Progressive / Present Perfect Continuous

Bildung
have/has + been + present participle

write → has/have been writing

Verwendung
Die **Verlaufsform** *present perfect progressive* verwendet man, um die **Dauer einer Handlung** zu **betonen**, die in der Vergangenheit begonnen hat und noch andauert.

She has been sleeping for ten hours.
Sie schläft seit zehn Stunden.

Past Perfect (Simple)

Bildung
had + past participle

write → had written

Verwendung
Die Vorvergangenheit *past perfect* verwendet man, wenn ein Vorgang in der Vergangenheit **vor einem anderen Vorgang in der Vergangenheit abgeschlossen** wurde.

He had bought a ticket before he took the train to Manchester.
Er hatte eine Fahrkarte gekauft, bevor er den Zug nach Manchester nahm. [Beim Einsteigen war der Kauf abgeschlossen.]

Past Perfect Progressive / Past Perfect Continuous

Bildung
had + been + present participle

write → had been writing

Verwendung
Die **Verlaufsform** *past perfect progressive* verwendet man für **Handlungen**, die in der Vergangenheit **bis zu dem Zeitpunkt andauerten**, zu dem eine neue Handlung einsetzte.

She had been sleeping for ten hours when the doorbell rang.
Sie hatte seit zehn Stunden geschlafen, als es an der Tür klingelte. [Das Schlafen dauerte bis zu dem Zeitpunkt an, als es an der Tür klingelte.]

Will-future

Bildung
will + Infinitiv

buy → will buy

Bildung von Fragen im *will-future*
(Fragewort +) *will* + Subjekt + Infinitiv

What will you buy?
Was wirst du kaufen?

Bildung der Verneinung im *will-future*
won't + Infinitiv

Why won't you come to our party?
Warum kommst du nicht zu unserer Party?

Verwendung
Das *will-future* verwendet man, wenn ein Vorgang **in der Zukunft stattfinden** wird:
- bei Vorhersagen oder Vermutungen,
- bei spontanen Entscheidungen.

Signalwörter: z. B. *tomorrow, next week, next Monday, next year, in three years, soon*

The weather will be fine tomorrow.
Das Wetter wird morgen schön (sein).
[doorbell] "I'll open the door."
"Ich werde die Tür öffnen."

Going-to-future

Bildung
am/is/are + *going to* + Infinitiv

find → am/is/are going to find

Verwendung
Das *going-to-future* verwendet man, wenn man ausdrücken will:
- was man für die Zukunft **plant** oder **zu tun beabsichtigt**.

- dass ein **Ereignis bald eintreten wird**, da bestimmte **Anzeichen** vorhanden sind.

I am going to work in England this summer.
Diesen Sommer werde ich in England arbeiten.

Look at those clouds. It's going to rain soon.
Schau dir diese Wolken an. Es wird bald regnen.

Simple Present und *Present Progressive* zur Wiedergabe der Zukunft

Verwendung
- Mit dem *present progressive* drückt man **Pläne** für die Zukunft aus, für die bereits **Vorkehrungen** getroffen wurden.
- Mit dem *simple present* wird ein zukünftiges Geschehen wiedergegeben, das **von außen festgelegt** wurde, z. B. Fahrpläne, Programme, Kalender.

We <u>are flying</u> to New York tomorrow.
Morgen fliegen wir nach New York.
[Wir haben schon Tickets.]

The train <u>leaves</u> at 8.15 a.m.
Der Zug fährt um 8.15 Uhr.

The play <u>ends</u> at 10 p.m.
Das Theaterstück endet um 22 Uhr.

Future Progressive / Future Continuous

Bildung
will + be + present participle

work → <u>will</u> be <u>working</u>

Verwendung
Die **Verlaufsform** *future progressive* drückt aus, dass ein **Vorgang** in der Zukunft zu einem bestimmten Zeitpunkt **gerade ablaufen wird**.

Signalwörter: *this time next week / tomorrow, tomorrow* + Zeitangabe

This time tomorrow I <u>will</u> be <u>sitting</u> in a plane to London.
Morgen um diese Zeit werde ich gerade im Flugzeug nach London sitzen.

Future Perfect (Future II)

Bildung
will + have + past participle

go → <u>will</u> have <u>gone</u>

Verwendung
Das *future perfect* drückt aus, dass ein **Vorgang** in der Zukunft **abgeschlossen sein wird** (Vorzeitigkeit in der Zukunft).

Signalwörter: *by then, by* + Zeitangabe

By 5 p.m. tomorrow I <u>will</u> have <u>arrived</u> in London.
Morgen Nachmittag um fünf Uhr werde ich bereits in London angekommen sein.

11 Passiv – *Passive Voice*

Bildung
Form von *(to) be* in der entsprechenden Zeitform + *past participle*

The bridge was finished in 1894.
Die Brücke wurde 1894 fertiggestellt.

Zeitformen:
- *simple present*

  Aktiv: Joe buys the milk.
  Passiv: The milk is bought by Joe.

- *simple past*

  Aktiv: Joe bought the milk.
  Passiv: The milk was bought by Joe.

- *present perfect*

  Aktiv: Joe has bought the milk.
  Passiv: The milk has been bought by Joe.

- *past perfect*

  Aktiv: Joe had bought the milk.
  Passiv: The milk had been bought by Joe.

- *will-future*

  Aktiv: Joe will buy the milk.
  Passiv: The milk will be bought by Joe.

- *future perfect (future II)*

  Aktiv: Joe will have bought the milk.
  Passiv: The milk will have been bought by Joe.

- *conditional I*

  Aktiv: Joe would buy the milk.
  Passiv: The milk would be bought by Joe.

- *conditional II*

  Aktiv: Joe would have bought the milk.
  Passiv: The milk would have been bought by Joe.

Aktiv → Passiv
- Das Subjekt des Aktivsatzes wird zum Objekt des Passivsatzes. Es wird mit *by* angeschlossen.
- Das Objekt des Aktivsatzes wird zum Subjekt des Passivsatzes.
- Stehen im Aktiv **zwei Objekte**, lassen sich zwei verschiedene Passivsätze bilden. Ein Objekt wird zum Subjekt des Passivsatzes, das zweite bleibt Objekt.

Beachte:
Das indirekte Objekt muss im Passivsatz mit *to* angeschlossen werden.

Aktiv: Joe   buys   the milk.
       Subjekt   Objekt

Passiv: The milk   is bought   by Joe.
        Subjekt   by-agent

Aktiv: They   gave   her   a ball.
       Subjekt   ind. Obj.   dir. Obj.

Passiv: She   was given   a ball.
        Subjekt   dir. Obj.

oder:

Aktiv: They   gave   her   a ball.
       Subjekt   ind. Obj.   dir. Obj.

Passiv: A ball   was given   to her.
        Subjekt   ind. Obj.

Passiv → Aktiv

- Der mit *by* angeschlossene Handelnde *(by-agent)* des Passivsatzes wird zum Subjekt des Aktivsatzes; *by* entfällt.
- Das Subjekt des Passivsatzes wird zum Objekt des Aktivsatzes.
- Fehlt im Passivsatz der *by-agent*, muss im Aktivsatz ein Handelnder als Subjekt ergänzt werden, z. B. *somebody, we, you, they*.

Passiv: The milk is bought by Joe.
        Subjekt   *by-agent*
Aktiv: Joe buys the milk.
      Subjekt   *Objekt*

Passiv: The match was won.
        Subjekt
Aktiv: They won the match.
      (ergänztes)   *Objekt*
      Subjekt

Der Satz im Englischen

12 Wortstellung – *Word Order*

Im Aussagesatz gilt die Wortstellung
Subjekt – Prädikat – Objekt
(subject – verb – object):

- Subjekt: Wer oder was tut etwas?
- Prädikat: Was wird getan?
- Objekt: Worauf / Auf wen bezieht sich die Tätigkeit?

Für die Position von Orts- und Zeitangaben vgl. S. G 4 f.

Cats catch mice.
Katzen fangen Mäuse.

13 Konditionalsätze – *Conditional Sentences*

Ein Konditionalsatz (Bedingungssatz) besteht aus zwei Teilen: einem Nebensatz *(if-clause)* und einem Hauptsatz *(main clause)*. Im *if*-Satz steht die **Bedingung** *(condition)*, unter der die im **Hauptsatz** genannte **Folge** eintritt. Man unterscheidet drei Arten von Konditionalsätzen:

Konditionalsatz Typ I

Bildung
- *if*-Satz (Bedingung): *simple present*
- Hauptsatz (Folge): *will-future*

Der *if*-Satz kann auch nach dem Hauptsatz stehen. In diesem Fall entfällt das Komma:
- Hauptsatz: *will-future*
- *if*-Satz: *simple present*

Im Hauptsatz kann auch
- *can* + Infinitiv,
- *must* + Infinitiv,
- der Imperativ

stehen.

If you read this book,
Wenn du dieses Buch liest,
you will learn a lot about music.
erfährst du eine Menge über Musik.

You will learn a lot about music
Du erfährst eine Menge über Musik,
if you read this book.
wenn du dieses Buch liest.

If you go to London, you can see Bob.
Wenn du nach London fährst, kannst du Bob treffen.
If you go to London, you must visit me.
Wenn du nach London fährst, musst du mich besuchen.
If it rains, take an umbrella.
Wenn es regnet, nimm einen Schirm mit.

Verwendung
Bedingungssätze vom Typ I verwendet man, wenn die **Bedingung erfüllbar** ist. Man gibt an, was unter bestimmten Bedingungen **geschieht** oder **geschehen kann**.

Konditionalsatz Typ II

Bildung
- *if*-Satz (Bedingung): *simple past*
- Hauptsatz (Folge): *conditional I* = *would* + Infinitiv

If I went to London,
Wenn ich nach London fahren würde,
I would visit the Tower.
würde ich mir den Tower ansehen.

Verwendung
Bedingungssätze vom Typ II verwendet man, wenn die **Bedingung nur theoretisch erfüllt** werden kann oder **nicht erfüllbar** ist.

Konditionalsatz Typ III

Bildung
- *if*-Satz (Bedingung):
  past perfect

- Hauptsatz (Folge):
  conditional II = would + have + past participle

If I had gone to London,
Wenn ich nach London gefahren wäre,
I would have visited the Tower of London.
hätte ich mir den Tower of London angesehen.

Verwendung
Bedingungssätze vom Typ III verwendet man, wenn sich die **Bedingung auf die Vergangenheit bezieht** und deshalb **nicht mehr erfüllbar** ist.

14 Relativsätze – *Relative Clauses*

Ein Relativsatz ist ein Nebensatz, der sich **auf eine Person oder Sache** des Hauptsatzes **bezieht** und diese **näher beschreibt**:
- Hauptsatz:
- Relativsatz:

The boy who looks like Jane is her brother.
Der Junge, der Jane ähnlich sieht, ist ihr Bruder.

The boy ... is her brother.
... who looks like Jane ...

Bildung
Haupt- und Nebensatz werden durch das Relativpronomen verbunden.
- *who* (Nominativ oder Akkusativ),

Peter, who lives in London, likes travelling.
Peter, der in London lebt, reist gerne.

whose (Genitiv) und

whom (Akkusativ) beziehen sich auf **Personen**,

- *which* bezieht sich auf **Sachen**,

- *that* kann sich auf **Sachen** und auf **Personen** beziehen und wird nur verwendet, wenn die **Information** im Relativsatz **notwendig** ist, um den ganzen Satz zu verstehen.

Sam, whose mother is an architect, is in my class.
Sam, dessen Mutter Architektin ist, geht in meine Klasse.
Anne, whom/who I like very much, is French.
Anne, die ich sehr mag, ist Französin.
The film "Dark Moon", which we saw yesterday, was far too long.
Der Film „Dark Moon", den wir gestern sahen, war viel zu lang.
The film that we saw last week was much better.
Der Film, den wir letzte Woche sahen, war viel besser.

Verwendung
Mithilfe von Relativpronomen kann man **zwei Sätze miteinander verbinden**.

London is England's biggest city. London has about 7.2 million inhabitants.
London ist Englands größte Stadt.
London hat etwa 7,2 Millionen Einwohner.
London, which is England's biggest city, has about 7.2 million inhabitants.
London, die größte Stadt Englands, hat etwa 7,2 Millionen Einwohner.

Beachte:
Man unterscheidet zwei Arten von Relativsätzen:
- **Notwendige Relativsätze**
 (defining relative clauses) enthalten Informationen, die **für das Verständnis** des Satzes **erforderlich** sind.

 Hier kann das Relativpronomen entfallen, wenn es Objekt ist; man spricht dann auch von *contact clauses*.

The man who is wearing a red shirt is Mike.
Der Mann, der ein rotes Hemd trägt, ist Mike.

The book (that) I bought yesterday is thrilling.
Das Buch, das ich gestern gekauft habe, ist spannend.

- **Nicht notwendige Relativsätze** *(non-defining relative clauses)* enthalten **zusätzliche Informationen** zum Bezugswort, die für das Verständnis des Satzes nicht unbedingt notwendig sind. Dieser Typ von Relativsatz wird **mit Komma** abgetrennt.

Sally, who went to a party yesterday, is very tired.
Sally, die gestern auf einer Party war, ist sehr müde.

15 Indirekte Rede – *Reported Speech*

Die indirekte Rede verwendet man, um **wiederzugeben, was ein anderer gesagt** oder **gefragt hat.**

Bildung
Um die indirekte Rede zu bilden, benötigt man ein **Einleitungsverb.** Häufig verwendete Einleitungsverben sind:

to say, to tell, to add, to mention, to think, to ask, to want to know, to answer

In der indirekten Rede verändern sich die **Pronomen**, in bestimmten Fällen auch die **Zeiten** und die **Orts-** und **Zeitangaben.**

- Wie die Pronomen sich verändern, hängt vom jeweiligen **Kontext** ab.

direkte Rede	indirekte Rede
Bob says to Jenny: "I like y<u>ou</u>."	Jenny tells Liz: "Bob says that he likes <u>me</u>."
Bob sagt zu Jenny: „Ich mag dich."	*Jenny erzählt Liz: „Bob sagt, dass er mich mag."*
Aber:	Jenny tells Liz that Bob likes <u>her</u>.
	Jenny erzählt Liz, dass Bob sie mag.

- **Zeiten:**
Keine Veränderung, wenn das Einleitungsverb
im *simple present* oder
im *present perfect* steht:

direkte Rede	indirekte Rede
Bob <u>says</u>, "I <u>love</u> dancing."	Bob <u>says</u> (that) he <u>loves</u> dancing.
Bob sagt: „Ich tanze sehr gerne."	*Bob sagt, er tanze sehr gerne.*

In folgenden Fällen wird die Zeit der direkten Rede in der indirekten Rede **um eine Zeitstufe zurückversetzt**, wenn das **Einleitungsverb** im *simple past* steht:

simple present	→	*simple past*
simple past	→	*past perfect*
present perfect	→	*past perfect*
will-future	→	*conditional I*

- **Zeitangaben** verändern sich, wenn der Bericht zu einem späteren Zeitpunkt erfolgt, z. B.:
- Welche **Ortsangabe** verwendet wird, hängt davon ab, wo sich der Sprecher im Moment befindet.

Bob said, "I love dancing."
Bob sagte: „Ich tanze sehr gerne."

Bob said (that) he loved dancing.
Bob sagte, er tanze sehr gerne.

Joe: "I like it."
Joe: "I liked it."

Joe said he liked it.
Joe said he had liked it.

Joe: "I've liked it."

Joe said he had liked it.

Joe: "I will like it."

Joe said he would like it.

now	→	then, at that time
today	→	that day, yesterday
yesterday	→	the day before
the day before yesterday	→	two days before
tomorrow	→	the following day
next week	→	the following week
here	→	there

Bildung der indirekten Frage
Häufige Einleitungsverben für die indirekte Frage sind:

- **Fragewörter** bleiben in der indirekten Rede **erhalten**. Die **Umschreibung** mit *do/does/did* **entfällt** in der indirekten Frage.

- Enthält die direkte Frage **kein Fragewort**, wird die indirekte Frage mit *whether* oder *if* eingeleitet:

to ask, to want to know, to wonder

Tom: "When did they arrive?"
Tom: „Wann sind sie angekommen?"

Tom asked when they had arrived.
Tom fragte, wann sie angekommen seien.

Tom: "Are they staying at the hotel?"
Tom: „Übernachten sie im Hotel?"

Tom asked if/ whether they were staying at the hotel.
Tom fragte, ob sie im Hotel übernachten.

Befehle/Aufforderungen in der indirekten Rede
Häufige Einleitungsverben sind:
In der indirekten Rede steht hier **Einleitungsverb + Objekt + *(not) to* + Infinitiv**.

to tell, to order, to ask

Tom: "Leave the room."
Tom: „Verlass den Raum."

Tom told me to leave the room.
Tom forderte mich auf, den Raum zu verlassen.

Anhang

16 Liste wichtiger unregelmäßiger Verben – *List of Irregular Verbs*

Infinitive	Simple Past	Past Participle	*Deutsch*
be	was/were	been	*sein*
begin	began	begun	*beginnen*
blow	blew	blown	*wehen, blasen*
break	broke	broken	*brechen*
bring	brought	brought	*bringen*
build	built	built	*bauen*
buy	bought	bought	*kaufen*
catch	caught	caught	*fangen*
choose	chose	chosen	*wählen*
come	came	come	*kommen*
cut	cut	cut	*schneiden*
do	did	done	*tun*
draw	drew	drawn	*zeichnen*
drink	drank	drunk	*trinken*
drive	drove	driven	*fahren*
eat	ate	eaten	*essen*
fall	fell	fallen	*fallen*
feed	fed	fed	*füttern*
feel	felt	felt	*fühlen*
find	found	found	*finden*
fly	flew	flown	*fliegen*
get	got	got	*bekommen*
give	gave	given	*geben*
go	went	gone	*gehen*
grow	grew	grown	*wachsen*
hang	hung	hung	*hängen*
have	had	had	*haben*
hear	heard	heard	*hören*
hit	hit	hit	*schlagen*
hold	held	held	*halten*
keep	kept	kept	*halten*
know	knew	known	*wissen*

Infinitive	Simple Past	Past Participle	*Deutsch*
lay	laid	laid	*legen*
leave	left	left	*verlassen*
let	let	let	*lassen*
lie	lay	lain	*liegen*
lose	lost	lost	*verlieren*
make	made	made	*machen*
meet	met	met	*treffen*
pay	paid	paid	*bezahlen*
put	put	put	*stellen/setzen*
read	read	read	*lesen*
ring	rang	rung	*läuten/anrufen*
run	ran	run	*rennen*
say	said	said	*sagen*
see	saw	seen	*sehen*
send	sent	sent	*schicken*
show	showed	shown	*zeigen*
sing	sang	sung	*singen*
sit	sat	sat	*sitzen*
sleep	slept	slept	*schlafen*
smell	smelt	smelt	*riechen*
speak	spoke	spoken	*sprechen*
spend	spent	spent	*ausgeben/ verbringen*
stand	stood	stood	*stehen*
steal	stole	stolen	*stehlen*
swim	swam	swum	*schwimmen*
take	took	taken	*nehmen*
teach	taught	taught	*lehren*
tell	told	told	*erzählen*
think	thought	thought	*denken*
throw	threw	thrown	*werfen*
wake	woke	woken	*aufwachen*
wear	wore	worn	*tragen*
win	won	won	*gewinnen*
write	wrote	written	*schreiben*

Berufliche Oberschulen Bayern – Englisch 13. Klasse
Beispiele für Themen der mündlichen Prüfung

Beispiel für eine Aufgabenstellung ohne festgelegte Rollen

Bilingual teaching

Situation:
The PISA studies have revealed that there is a need to raise German standards of achievement in education. According to them, the German school system does not prepare pupils and students adequately for the future.
The headmaster in your school now wants to introduce bilingual classes (e. g. teaching history in English). He has set up a committee of students and teachers to discuss the topic of "bilingual education".
You are a member of the committee.

TASK 1: In the first meeting, your first task will be to present what you think of bilingual education. Is it a step in the right direction?

TASK 2: Then it is the task of the group to decide whether bilingual education should be introduced and which subjects should be affected by it.

Beispiel für eine Aufgabenstellung mit festgelegten Rollen

Smoking in school

Situation:
At your FOS/BOS smoking is allowed where ashtrays have been installed – that is, in the entrance area and the schoolyard.
The headmaster wants to forbid smoking in school in general. Yet, his plan has aroused some protest by students. Thus he has invited some "important" people to discuss the problem of smoking in school.

Roles:
– headmaster: non-smoker, wants to ban smoking
– student: smoker, is against the headmaster's plan
– student: non-smoker, supports the plan
– representative of parents: non-smoker, is against the plan
– caretaker: non-smoker, supports the plan

TASK 1: Take a role and point out the reasons why you are for/against the plan.

TASK 2: Then it is the task of the group to discuss the pros and cons and to try to reach an agreement or to find another solution.

> **Berufliche Oberschulen Bayern – Englisch 13. Klasse**
> **Beispieldiskussion zum Thema „Global warming"**

Situation:
Global warming appears to be one of the big issues – if not the biggest – in the 21st century. In Germany there have been lively discussions recently on how to deal with this challenge. Suggestions for countermeasures range from a speed limit on German highways to banning SUVs[1] and limiting the number of long-distance flights.

You are members of the "German Federal Task Force on Climate Change" and your job is to work out a priority list of suggestions on how to cope with global warming. The list you are going to make up will be of vital importance for the future decisions made by the federal government.

INDIVIDUAL TASK:
Develop short-term und long-term suggestions on how to deal with the issue of global warming.

TEAM MEETING:
Present your suggestions in the task force meeting.
Discuss the suggestions.
Devise a priority list containing the three most important measures to be taken in the short run and the two most important measures to be taken in the long run.

[1] SUV = sports utility vehicle (e. g. BMW X3, Audi Q7 etc.)

Hinweise:
The following transcript is based on a mock exam discussion in the classroom, which
was taped for the purpose of publication in this book.
With regard to vocabulary, grammar and coherence, the transcript has been polished
a bit to make it something that can be seen as a helpful model for your exercises. So a
number of minor mistakes and pauses and "Ers" have been omitted.

Saskia: Hello everybody, I'd like to welcome you to our discussion on global warming. We have come together to talk about ideas on how to fight climate change. First of all, I'd like you to present your suggestions. Catharina, would you start, please?

Catharina: All right. Well, I do agree that we have to do something about climate change, but we shouldn't do it the hard and fast way but the slow and long way.

Daniel: Hi everybody, well, I'm also of the opinion that we must do something about climate change. In my view, we should try to force companies to reduce emissions and we must create an awareness for that issue among the population.

Tim:	I think the issue of global warming is very important. What we should do first is to change our public transport system. I think that's the way we should go.
Saskia:	In my opinion, this problem is a global problem and we have to find partner countries which will help us to attain our goals to reduce carbon dioxide emissions throughout the world. So ...
Catharina:	Well, I agree with Tim and his suggestion concerning the public transport system. When I think of the village where I live I have no opportunity to use public transport. I have to go by car. Anywhere. I've got no other possibility. There are no buses, no train stations, there is nothing.
Daniel:	I agree with you. In my village it's the same situation, there are no buses, so I have to take the car. Another problem is that the costs for the tickets are way too high. As far as I can see it's more expensive than the car, so the ticket prices have to be lowered so that public transport will be more attractive for people who usually use their cars.
Catharina:	Definitely.
Saskia:	We have a bus connection in our village, but it's only eight times a day, so if you don't catch the bus at seven o'clock, you have no chance of getting to the city before twelve. So we certainly need better connections.
Tim:	Yes, I fully agree with you, guys, but I think the big issue is the money. When you look at other cities, they are much cheaper than our public transport network. When I was in Hamburg a week ago, I learnt that their weekly or monthly tickets are cheaper than ours. So it depends on the ticket prices, it's a matter of prices.
Catharina:	That's true, but I think you need money, you must invest money to change the system. So I fear the high ticket prices will stay if they install more buses or trains.
Tim:	But some towns are able to offer lower prices. Do any of you guys know how they do this?
Saskia:	That depends on the local circumstances. In Hamburg it's the HVV network, but in Munich ...
Catharina:	Well, to get away from this ticket price discussion, we should get back to our topic of climate change ...
Tim, Daniel:	OK, yes, sure ...
Catharina:	So, improving public transport is certainly a good way to reduce CO_2 emissions if you get more people to use public transport. But I really don't know how this can be achieved, because it is really expensive to buy additional buses and underground trains and to build new bus stops and ... We even haven't got a bus stop in my village.
Saskia:	Yes, but what else can be done to reduce emissions?
Daniel:	Yeah, I'd like to introduce a new aspect. In my opinion, companies have to be forced to reduce CO_2 emissions. They have to install technology, and there have to be severe penalties if companies don't observe the rules ...

Saskia:	I totally agree with you, but in my opinion, it's a global problem because you have developing countries where you have regulations to reduce carbon dioxide emissions but all the smaller companies ... they needn't have filters in their machinery, and the same is true for private households ... they don't have to do this. That's the case in India, I think, for example.
Tim:	So maybe we have to shift the focus to private households and what they can do to reduce CO_2 emissions. I suggest we think about things like banning cars from city centres and stuff like that, which goes hand in hand with what we were talking about before – improving the public transport system.
Catharina:	That's what we have in London now, for example, or in Singapore. You are only allowed to enter the city centre by car if you pay a high price ...
Daniel:	It's called road tax or something like that, isn't it?
Saskia:	Or road pricing, I think.
Catharina:	Puh, whatever it is called, people don't use their cars in the city centre so often. If you pay so much every month for using your car in the city centre, it can be cheaper to buy a monthly ticket for the Tube or for public transport in general.
Daniel:	Yeah, that's good.
Catharina:	So why should you go there by car? And this would force politicians to improve the public transport systems which are not so perfect so far.
Daniel:	There is a relation between the use of the car, banning cars in the city centres and the use of buses and trains and making the public transport system more attractive for car drivers. So ...
Tim:	That's a great idea. There should be some pressure on people to use public transport. We should put that down as a part of our priority list.
Saskia:	Yes, of course, certainly.
Daniel:	But let's get back to the households. Environmentally-friendly behaviour should be supported by the state, maybe in the form of benefits. This could help to create more awareness for the protection of the environment.
Catharina:	Well, there are benefits already. When I think of my boyfriend's house, he's thinking of installing solar panels on his roof, and there is some kind of support from the state. In his case he would have to fell two fifty-year-old trees to have enough sunshine on those panels, but that's a different story.
Tim:	Is there enough support by the state?
Catharina:	I don't know. Maybe there could be more? As we heard from Mr Beck in Technology, it takes a long time to get the money back which you have invested.
Daniel:	I think we should not only talk about solar energy and stuff like that, we should also talk about household garbage. Part of the household garbage is burnt, and so we get a lot of emissions from burning trash.
Saskia:	That's true.

Daniel:	So we should do even more to support waste separation and recycling.
Catharina:	That's a good suggestion, I think.
Saskia:	But I think we should also focus on other countries. Germany is doing at least something, and in some of the other big industrialized countries …
Daniel:	May I interrupt you?
Saskia:	Yes.
Daniel:	I think we have to do things in the right way in our country so that we can show other countries how things work. We should first focus on our own country and then look at other countries.
Tim:	I agree with Daniel.
Saskia:	But I think if you don't show developing countries which don't use filters to reduce pollution and which don't care about CO_2 what they can do about the problem … well, they will not understand why they should do something, why they should spend money on that. We must find ways to help them to improve the situation there. And we want to sell our products there, so we must make them aware of the problem.
Tim:	I think we should sort our problems out first in our country and then have a look at the other countries …
Saskia:	But they are bigger than Germany and they produce a lot more emissions than we do, and if we don't stop them, we have no chance of stopping climate change.
Catharina:	But, sorry, we can't tell them to do it perfectly if we don't do it ourselves. I think that's something …
Daniel:	Maybe we should …
Saskia:	But we have developed so much technology and we are quite aware of the problem, and they don't have the technology and they are not so aware …
Daniel:	I think we should discuss for other countries only the things or problems which we have solved in our own country. So we can offer them the technology which we have introduced, and we can show them that it works, but we can't discuss problems which we haven't solved in Germany yet.
Catharina:	Yes, that's a good idea, that's a good step towards how to deal with it.
Saskia:	Yes, but we all live in one world, in the same world, it's not only Germany, so I think we should discuss with them. It's not about Europe alone, it's not about Germany, it's also about China and other states in Asia. Germany has strict regulations and laws, and in these countries they can do whatever they want to do. They can even throw their trash into the rivers.
Daniel:	But this is a problem we can't solve right now.
Catharina:	You have to tell the people who live there that they have to change something. So you should start with the basics there, for example, that you don't throw waste into rivers. But I think that we must start in Germany. It doesn't matter if we cause five per cent or one hundred per

	cent of the emissions. If we manage to reduce emissions only by five per cent, that's a first step.
Tim:	To a certain degree, I agree with Saskia. It's global warming, so it's worldwide. On the other hand, we are here to make up a priority list, and this has to do with our country. So let's go on with it. Maybe we can find two or three more suggestions. Does anybody have another ...?
Daniel:	The planes are a big producer of CO_2 emissions, so I've got an idea. I think planes should carry more passengers and shouldn't fly half-empty. If they are nearly empty, it should be forbidden for them to take off. We could introduce a percentage of seats which can be empty or not occupied. If this is not the case, the plane is not allowed ...
Catharina:	But Daniel, sorry, imagine you have an appointment somewhere, let's say a business meeting which is about a few million dollars, and you can't go there because your plane is not allowed to leave. I mean, sorry, this is not quite realistic.
Daniel:	But ...
Catharina:	If you book a flight from Munich to London because you have a business date there, you can't tell people, sorry, my plane didn't leave. I have to wait till tomorrow until it has enough bookings.
Tim:	You can't wait until it's fully packed.
Daniel:	But ...
Catharina:	I know what you mean ...
Daniel:	But it's a waste of kerosene if it's half-empty. I agree with you when you say it's not very realistic to do this or to introduce this within one year or so. But in the long run ...
Catharina:	Imagine you are at the airport, you want to go on holiday and they tell you, oh, you can't leave, your plane is not full enough. So you stay at the Kempinski over night?
Daniel:	But it's a fact that it's a waste of energy to fly planes with 20 passengers.
Saskia:	But I think there will be another problem or there already is another problem that the companies, the airlines, will try to reduce their prices even more so that you can fly to Hamburg for just 50 euros, let's say. So flying will be even more attractive in the future, and people will like to fly somewhere for just one or two days: Hamburg, Rome, Madrid or whatever. People will say, oh, it's so cheap, and we will have much more air traffic than we have now.
Catharina:	Well, that's fine, but I think it's high time we came to a conclusion.
Tim:	Yes, definitely.
Catharina:	So let's write down three or four points that we can suggest later on.
Daniel:	But we don't include this funny empty-planes-plan, do we?
Catharina:	OK, yes, I agree.
Tim:	It could be our very last point on the list.
Catharina:	So what about Saskia's suggestion concerning the international aspects? Do you ...?

Saskia:	We should try to find partner countries which help us, that means Germany, to help developing countries in their need to save energy and so on.
Daniel:	That means giving those countries technological support so that they can reach the technological level which we have already reached.
Saskia:	Exactly, the technological know-how.
Tim:	Alright, furthermore we had that public transport suggestion. Maybe we could write down that thing that you mentioned, Cathi, the cars in the city centres. That people must pay road taxes, so they are somewhat forced to use public transport and …
Catharina:	Yes, exactly, but this must go hand in hand with the improvement of connections and so on. We need more buses, more underground connections and so on.
Saskia:	But aren't these two different aspects? Banning cars from city centres and improving public transport?
Catharina:	We can discuss this in detail some time in the future, but there is certainly a close relation between these two aspects.
Tim:	Well, another thing to think about is … It's an idea that just came to my mind. I don't know how to explain it. It's like a bonus system for avoiding CO_2 emissions. Maybe on a smart card or something like that. Every time you do something that avoids CO_2 emissions you get bonus credits.
Catharina:	Are you thinking of a kind of Miles & More system against CO_2 emissions?
Tim:	Yes, exactly, but it should be fewer miles, of course.
Daniel:	It sounds good, but it doesn't … I don't think you can make this work in reality.
Tim:	Why not? It sounds like an illusion, but you must give people something back if you want something from them, for example, that they don't fly to Florida but stay in Germany.
Catharina:	It sounds useful for households. For example, if they give up old oil heating and install modern solar panels or pellet heating.
Tim:	It was just an idea.
Catharina:	It's a good idea. What do the others think about it?
Daniel:	Yes, that's OK.
Saskia:	We should include it as an idea, really.
Tim:	So let me make a summary of our suggestions on the priority list. First, improving international cooperation with developing countries and more technological transfer. Second, improving public transport and banning cars from city centres. And, third, a bonus system for behaviour that avoids CO_2 emissions. That's it, isn't it? Well, so thank you all, guys.

Berufliche Oberschulen Bayern – Englisch 13. Klasse
Abiturprüfung 2009

Aufgabenteil: *Reading*

Text I: David Sedaris: Go Carolina

ANYONE WHO WATCHES EVEN THE SLIGHTEST amount of TV is familiar with the scene: An agent knocks on the door of some seemingly ordinary home or office. The door opens, and the person holding the knob is asked to identify himself. The agent then says, "I'm going to ask you to come with me."

They're always remarkably calm, these agents. If asked "Why do I need to go anywhere with you?" they'll straighten their shirt cuffs or idly brush stray hairs from the sleeves of their sport coats and say, "Oh, I think we both know why."

The suspect then chooses between doing things the hard way and doing things the easy way, and the scene ends with either gunfire or the gentlemanly application of handcuffs. Occasionally it's a case of mistaken identity, but most often the suspect knows exactly why he's being taken. It seems he's been expecting this to happen. The anticipation has ruled his life, and now, finally, the wait is over. You're sometimes led to believe that this person is actually relieved, but I've never bought it. Though it probably has its moments, the average day spent in hiding is bound to beat the average day spent in prison. When the time comes to decide who gets the bottom bunk, I think anyone would agree that there's a lot to be said for doing things the hard way.

The agent came for me during a geography lesson. She entered the room and nodded at my fifth-grade teacher, who stood frowning at a map of Europe. What would needle me later was the realization that this had all been prearranged. My capture had been scheduled to go down at exactly 2:30 on a Thursday afternoon. The agent would be wearing a dung-colored blazer over a red knit turtleneck, her heels sensibly low in case the suspect should attempt a quick getaway.

"David," the teacher said, "this is Miss Samson, and she'd like you to go with her now." No one else had been called, so why me? I ran down a list of recent crimes, looking for a conviction that might stick. Setting fire to a reportedly flameproof Halloween costume, stealing a set of barbecue tongs from an unguarded patio, altering the word *hit* on a list of rules posted on the gymnasium door; never did it occur to me that I might be innocent.

"You might want to take your books with you," the teacher said. "And your jacket. You probably won't be back before the bell rings."

Though she seemed old at the time, the agent was most likely fresh out of college. She walked beside me and asked what appeared to be an innocent and unrelated question: "So, which do you like better, State or Carolina?"

2009-1

She was referring to the athletic rivalry between the Triangle area's two largest universities. Those who cared about such things tended to express their allegiance by wearing either Tar Heel powder blue or Wolf Pack red, two colors that managed to look good on no one. The question of team preference was common in our part of North Carolina, and the answer supposedly spoke volumes about the kind of person you either were or hoped to become. I had no interest in football or basketball but had learned it was best to pretend otherwise.

If a boy didn't care for barbecued chicken on potato chips, people would accept it as a matter of personal taste, saying, "Oh well, I guess it takes all kinds." You could turn up your nose at the President or Coke or even God, but there were names for boys who didn't like sports. When the subject came up, I found it best to ask which team my questioner preferred. Then I'd say, "Really? Me, too!"

Asked by the agent which team I supported, I took my cue from her red turtleneck and told her that I was for State. "Definitely State. State all the way."

It was an answer I would regret for years to come.

"State, did you say?" the agent asked.

"Yes, State. They're greatest."

"I see." She led me through an unmarked door near the principal's office, into a small, windowless room furnished with two facing desks. It was the kind of room where you'd grill someone until they snapped, the kind frequently painted so as to cover the bloodstains. She gestured toward what was to become my regular seat, then continued her line of questioning.

"And what exactly are they, State and Carolina?"

"Colleges? Universities?"

She opened a file on her desk, saying, "Yes, you're right. Your answers are correct, but you're saying them incorrectly. You're telling me that they're colleg*eth* and univer*thitieth*, when actually they're college*s* and univer*s*ities. You're giving me a *th* sound instead of a nice clear *s*. Can you hear the distinction between the two different sounds?"

I nodded.

"May I please have an actual answer?"

"Uh-huh."

"'Uh-huh' is not a word."

"Okay," – "Okay what?"

"Okay," I said. "Sure, I can hear it."

"You can hear what, the distinction? The contrast?"

"Yeah, that."

It was the first battle of my war against the letter *s*, and I was determined to dig my foxhole before the sun went down. According to Agent Samson, a "*s*tate *c*ertified *s*peech therapi*s*t," my *s* was sibilate, meaning that I lisped. This was not news to me.

75 "Our goal *is* to work together until eventually you can *s*peak correctly," Agent Samson said. She made a great show of enunciating her own sparkling *s*'s, and the effect was profoundly irritating. "I'm trying to help you, but the longer you play the*s*e little game*s* the longer thi*s is* going to take." *(951 words)*

David Sedaris: Me Talk Pretty One Day. Back Bay Books (2001).

Worksheet
Task I: Mediation Englisch – Deutsch   9 credits

1. Beantworten Sie folgende Fragen zum <u>Inhalt</u> des Textes sinngemäß <u>auf Deutsch</u>.   6

1.1 Welches spezifische Problem soll Miss Samson bei David lösen?	
1.2 Weshalb bezeichnet David Miss Samson wiederholt als „agent"?	
1.3 Was hat David im Nachhinein besonders an der Art und Weise, **wie** er von Miss Samson abgeholt wurde, geärgert?	
1.4 Welches ‚Vergehen' hat David in der Turnhalle begangen?	
1.5 Weshalb gibt es David nicht zu, dass er keines der erwähnten Teams unterstützt?	
1.6 Was meint Miss Samson mit dem Vorwurf, den sie David am Ende des Gespräches macht?	

2. Erklären Sie auf Deutsch, was die folgenden Redewendungen im
   Textzusammenhang bedeuten: 3

2.1 "doing things the hard way" (l. 8, ll. 16/17)	
2.2 "the anticipation has ruled his life" (l. 12)	
2.3 "grill someone until they snapped" (l. 54)	

Text II: It's Not Just White Girls

(A) For years, the name would haunt Rodolfo Ruiz. "Gordolfo Gelatino!" his cousins would chant, cackling at the gelatinous roll of chub peeking out from 10-year-old Rudy's T-shirt. That night, and many nights after, Ruiz would stare in the mirror and pinch that roll, vowing to avoid the fat-heavy chorizo and tacos that were staples in
5 his south Texas home. As far as border cuisine went, his family wasn't unusual: his mother melded rich Mexican cooking with the corn-syrup and trans fats of mainstream America – and, at the time, she knew no better. "Mom, is bacon good for you?" Rudy would ask. "Yes," she'd reply. "Bacon is meat."

(B) As a teen, the once chubby boy became so thin that his vision frequently blurred.
10 He guzzled gallons of diet iced tea, and jogged five miles each day, dropping – at 17 years old and 5 feet 6 inches – to 104 pounds. "Not knowing what to eat, or how to eat healthily, I opted for nothing at all," Ruiz, now 40 and a marketing executive, recalls. Even today, the two-time Harvard graduate still struggles with the obsession he'd later learn was anorexia. "I've overcome the worst, but the disease will always
15 haunt me," he tells NEWSWEEK.

(C) It's not the profile you might expect of a typical anorexic. Ruiz is not a ballerina or a model. He's not gay, or a white upper-middle-class woman. His parents never pressured him to be thin, and he's far from obsessed with his appearance. Which is part of the reason he's detailed his struggle, along with 18 other writers, in a new
20 book of essays called "Going Hungry." Edited by New York culture writer Kate Taylor, herself a recovered anorexic, the book's authors defy many of the stereotypes about eating disorders, and who suffers from them. Often assumed to be diseases of vanity (a recent UK study found that a third of the population believe those suffering from anorexia choose to do so), the struggles of these writers vary widely – from rec-
25 onciling two cultures to hiding a pregnancy and suffering for God.

(D) Of the 10 million women and 1 million men who do cope with anorexia and bulimia in this country, it is true that the majority of those documented are white. But in some cases, minorities have been excluded from samples because of this assumption – and experts say the "white girl" stereotype discourages men and minorities from coming forward.

(E) Anorexia was formalized as a diagnosis in the late 19th century, though it didn't become a household word until the 1970s, when feminists protested the rise of Twiggy[1] as the body ideal. Media attention peaked in the '90s, with Naomi Wolf's "The Beauty Myth," but has waned in recent years, perhaps overshadowed by obesity. But the number diagnosed continues to increase. In a 2003 review of the literature, researchers found that since 1930, the rate of anorexic women aged 15 to 19 years has gone up incrementally each decade. And between 1988 and 1993, bulimia in 10- to 39-year-olds tripled. Some blame skinny models and magazines that tout an often unattainable aesthetic. But for the majority of sufferers, the problem has historically been far more complicated, regardless of anorexia's popularity as a political cause.

(F) For some, like Ruiz, it has a lot to do with their cultural upbringing. Though minorities may have fewer known body issues, studies show that American thinking about size eventually seeps into immigrant communities. For others, there are religious influences: Fasting as testament of belief, punishment for perceived sin, or strict eating rituals that, when combined with other factors, can quickly become pathological. In the 1985 book "Holy Anorexia," historian Rudolph Bell describes Teresa of Avila, a Spanish saint said to have used twigs of olive trees to induce vomiting and empty her stomach – in this way, she believed she was able to truly take into herself the Host.

(G) For many of its sufferers, anorexia itself becomes like a religion. The writers describe feelings of appeasing a higher power, of gaining wisdom from starvation or strength from abstaining. They find power in tiny victories: a meal skipped or a pound lost. As one put it, it was "something to believe in." Which is a hunger that is not easy to satisfy.   *(711 words)*

Newsweek, Sep 15, 2008 (abridged).

Annotation
1 Twiggy, who was known for her thin build, was the first teenager to become a prominent model in the 1960s.

Task II: Multiple Choice Questions   8 credits
Mark the most suitable option with a cross!

1. When he was a child, Rodolfo Ruiz decided to lose weight as he ...
   A was bullied by his peers because of the kind of food he ate.
   B did not want to look like everybody else in his family.
   C was often made fun of because of his appearance.
   D realised that his mother's cooking was unhealthy.

2. As a teenager Ruiz lost so much weight that he ...
   A   could hardly be perceived by others.
   B   often could not see properly.
   C   could not focus on anything.
   D   often fainted while doing sports.

3. Rodolfo Ruiz became a co-author of the book "Going Hungry" in order to ...
   A   show that virtually anybody can be affected by anorexia.
   B   highlight how much suffering anorexia can cause.
   C   offer hope to the people who are suffering from anorexia.
   D   point out the changing circumstances in which people develop anorexia.

4. According to the text, one consequence of the notion that the typical anorexic is a white female is that other people who are affected ...
   A   refuse proper treatment.
   B   are too embarrassed to ask for help.
   C   have been given the wrong medical treatment.
   D   often feel discriminated against.

5. Which of the following statements is made in paragraph E?
   A   The fashion industry is being blamed for the growing number of anorexic women.
   B   Since the launch of a new book public interest in anorexia has increased enormously.
   C   Some women have turned eating disorders into a form of political protest.
   D   Anorexia was considered to be a disease long before it became well-known.

6. The expression "American thinking about size eventually seeps into immigrant communities" (lines 43/44) means that ...
   A   the US host culture will soon influence immigrants' attitudes towards weight.
   B   in America immigrant groups may experience the highest increase in cases of anorexia.
   C   a person's looks do not play such an important role among many immigrant groups.
   D   immigrants can sometimes not understand the American obsession with appearance.

7. According to the text, which of the following was not a religious motivation for some people do develop eating disorders? The wish to …

   A do penance.
   B express their strong religious faith.
   C follow certain religious procedures.
   D die as a martyr.

8. Towards the end of the text, the authors of the book "Going Hungry" show that many anorexics …

   A have learnt to appreciate the simple things in life.
   B can have spiritual experiences through their disease.
   C must undergo a long and painful treatment to be cured.
   D have successfully overcome their irrational beliefs.

Text III: Rule, Britannia, but maybe not over Scotland

A) LONDON: The English usually tend to regard the Scots as their slightly prickly but relatively harmless northern cousins. But lately, the English have displayed a newfound resentment that has mirrored a growing confidence and sense of nationalistic entitlement – a general flexing of the biceps – in Scotland. With relations at their uneasiest point in decades, there is even talk that unless the balance of power can somehow be renegotiated, the union is in danger of unravelling.

B) "This is about a shift in British attitudes," said Joyce McMillan, a columnist for the newspaper The Scotsman. "We've always been seen as slightly exotic or decorative. But if we start on as if we were some kind of self-determining nation, it provokes an angry atmosphere with people saying things like, 'Oh, what was wrong with the way we were ruling you? Why aren't you grateful?'"

C) Scotland has been in the inferior position since 1707, when it and its Parliament were subsumed by Britain. But three centuries is no time at all in the minds of many Scots, who have fumed in resentment and, more or less, clamoured for independence ever since.

D) The current era in Scottish-English relations began in the late 1990s, when Tony Blair's Labour government addressed the persistent irritant of Scottish nationalism by giving the Scots more power to settle their own affairs. Scotland got its own Parliament, with responsibility over areas like health, social services and education. Devolution, as this process is called, was supposed to "kill Scottish nationalism stone dead," in the saying of the time. But instead it has only magnified the Scots' difference with the English.

E) "What you've had since devolution is that England and Scotland are starting to drift apart culturally and politically, so they seem like entirely different countries," said Guy Lodge, a senior research fellow of the Institute for Public Policy Research, a left-leaning study group in London.

F) Though Scotland is an old Labour stronghold, many Scots are disillusioned with the Labour government – even though the current Prime Minister, Gordon Brown, is Scottish. Since last year, the Scottish National Party (SNP), which favours Scottish independence, has been in power in the Scottish Parliament. Its able leader, Alex Salmond, has confounded Labour by proving that the nationalists can govern plausibly at home.

G) Mr Salmond has used Scotland's budget, which comes mostly in the form of block grants from London, to enact a series of radical social-service measures. In contrast to the residents of the rest of Britain, Scots get free university tuition and free personal and nursing care for the elderly. They also pay less for National Health Service prescriptions and have access to a greater range of medicine and treatments for illnesses like cancer.

H) The Scots argue that they are merely using their available resources more effectively, but the English complain that the Scots are abusing British largess. A recent report by the Institute for Public Policy Research found that Scotland received a disproportionately larger share of money per capita, compared with other parts of Britain, and suggested that the formula for allocating the money be recalculated.

I) In the British Parliament there are rumblings that the Scots' wings must be clipped. And an age-old question about the awkwardness in having two Parliaments has raised its head again. The issue is this: Is it fair that Scottish members of the British Parliament are allowed to vote on matters that affect only England while English members of Parliament have no say over whole swaths of public policy in Scotland?

J) Another recent study, commissioned by the Conservative Party, argued that voting in the British Parliament should be reorganized so that Scottish members would have less power over bills affecting only England. That reflects another new phenomenon: the rise in English nationalism that comes with a sense that it is now the English who are not getting their fair share.

K) Mr Lodge said that historically the union between Scotland and England had always made sense. In the 18th century it was needed for security and economic stability, in the 19th century it was about empire and in the 20th century it was about defeating Hitler and building a welfare state.

L) In looking at the role of the union in the 21st century, Mr Lodge drew a comparison to Czechoslovakia. "When the Czechs and the Slovaks split, it wasn't because of a massive fight – it was because no one would put forward a good case for keeping them together," Mr Lodge said. "In the 21st century in Great Britain no one's put forward a clear, compelling case for why the union matters." *(775 words)*

Sarah Lyall: Rule, Britannia, but Maybe Not Over Scotland. From The New York Times © 18 July 2008 The New York Times. All rights reserved. Used by permission and protected by the Copyright Laws of the United States. The printing, copying, redistribution, and retransmission of the material without express written permission is prohibited.

Task III: Gapped Summary 7 credits
Fill each gap with the most suitable word from the text
(one word per line)!

Ever since Scotland became part of Great Britain, many Scots have felt
_____ against British rule. Even _____, i. e. the partial
transfer of power to Scotland, has not accomplished its aim of overcoming
Scottish nationalism. On the contrary, Scotland and England have continued to _____ _____.
English politicians have also been astonished by the SNP's ability to win
elections and _____ Scotland effectively. The popularity of
Mr Salmond, the SNP leader, can in part be explained by his social-service policies, from which many Scottish citizens have profited.
This, in turn, has led to angry demands in England that the distribution of
funds between England and Scotland should be _____. It has
also re-awakened the old dispute about whether the elected representatives of Scotland should be allowed to vote in two _____.
In the past, the Union between England and Scotland was strengthened by
a common cause, such as the British Empire, or the _____
_____ after World War II. But if current tensions are not resolved,
Britain could face the same fate as the former Czechoslovakia.

Aufgabenteil: *Writing*

Total vernetzt

Klick, klick. Jeong-Hwa loggt sich bei Nateon ein, dem beliebtesten Chatdienst in Korea – „dann kann ich mit meinen Freunden online chatten und meine Frei-SMS schonen", sagt sie. 123 von rund 200 „Freunden" sind online. Als Nächstes schaut sie nach, wer in ihrem Gästebuch Nachrichten hinterlassen hat – und dann natürlich, ob
5 es neue Fotos auf den Mini-Hompis ihrer Freundinnen gibt. „Das gehört zum guten Stil", sagt sie.
Auf viele Menschen übt das Netz eine unheimliche Anziehungskraft aus, der sie sich nur schwer entziehen können. „Die kulturpessimistische These, dass wir alle seltener persönliche Gespräche führen, weil wir häufiger online kommunizieren, ist empirisch
10 jedoch nicht haltbar", sagt der Medienforscher Klaus Beck. „Es ist nur ein Kanal hinzugekommen." Allerdings verfangen sich immer wieder einzelne Menschen im Netz. In Südkorea berichteten 2006 die Zeitungen über einen Teenager, der sich wegen einer hohen Handyrechnung das Leben nahm – er war rund um die Uhr online gewesen. Daraufhin bestimmte die südkoreanische Regierung, dass Mobilfunkfirmen Ju-
15 gendlichen monatlich nur noch umgerechnet 30 Euro berechnen dürfen.
Ein Wartezimmer südwestlich vom Zentrum Seouls, türkis bezogene Sitzreihen, dazwischen spärlich begrünte Balkonkästen, die das Linoleumboden-Ambiente freundlicher machen sollen. Hier im staatlichen „Internetsucht-Zentrum" werden Menschen

behandelt, für die moderne Medien vom Segen zum Fluch geworden sind. „Wenn jemand drei, vier Stunden täglich am Computer oder am Telefon verbringt, ständig müde und antriebslos ist, den Augenkontakt verweigert, dann kümmern wir uns um ihn", sagt Leiter Young-Sam Koh.

Meist bringen verzweifelte Eltern ihre Kinder hierher, weil die nicht mehr vom Bildschirm loskommen. „Natürlich ist Kommunikationssucht keine eigenständige Krankheit, und das Internet allein macht uns auch nicht krank," sagt Koh. Aber wenn Menschen virtuelle Welten der echten vorziehen, dann sei das ein Symptom für psychisches Leiden. „Was Korea von anderen Ländern unterscheidet, ist der hohe Grad an Vernetzung. Deshalb tritt dieses Symptom besonders häufig auf – und deshalb brauchen wir Beratungsstellen wie diese." Rund 18.000 Fälle behandelten die koreanischen Internet-Suchtzentren im Jahr 2007, einer von 59 Koreanern gehört einer Studie zufolge zur Hochrisikogruppe.

Einfach mal das Handy abzuschalten täte den meisten Menschen gut, schreibt die Sankt Gallener Kommunikationsprofessorin Miriam Meckel. Von Zeit zu Zeit müsse jeder einmal überprüfen, ob er nicht längst Opfer des „informationellen Sisyphus-Syndroms" sei, getrieben von den Informationen, die ständig via Handy und Blackberry auf ihn einströmen. Wir müssten den Aus-Knopf wieder entdecken, fordert sie, und die Phasen des Inputs mit Phasen der Kontemplation abwechseln. *Ich maile, chatte, simse, also bin ich* – dieser Satz ist eben ein verhängnisvoller Irrtum.

© *Jens Uehlecke, „Total vernetzt" in: DIE ZEIT, 28. 08. 2008 Nr. 36.*

Worksheet
Task IV: Mediation Deutsch – Englisch 12 credits
Fassen Sie den folgenden Text zusammen, indem Sie die unterstrichenen Textstellen sinngemäß ins Englische übertragen. Schreiben Sie einen zusammenhängenden Text im Umfang von ca. 150 Wörtern.

Task V: Argumentative Writing 24 credits
Choose **one** of the following topics. Write **at least 220 words**.

1. **Composition**

    "Our work on the natural environment should be timeless, (…) irrespective of the economic situation." – DONALD TUSK, Polish Prime Minister, pleading that economic worries should not affect UN climate talks.

    Discuss this statement in view of the current economic situation.

2. **Composition**

    Politics? – no thanks!

    Democracy depends on the participation of its citizens if it is to function properly. In recent years, however, many young people have lost interest in politics, stopped voting and committing themselves politically.

    What reasons do you see for this development and how can this trend be stopped?

Lösungsvorschläge

Aufgabenteil: *Reading*

Task I: Mediation Englisch – Deutsch

Hinweise:
zu 1.1: Die Antwort finden Sie in Z. 72–74.
zu 1.2: Wichtig: Der amerikanische „agent" ist ein Polizeibeamter und entspricht nicht dem deutschen Agenten. In Z. 1–7 finden Sie die Antwort.
zu 1.3: Die Antwort bezieht sich auf Z. 19–21. Schlüsselwörter im Text: „What would needle me later ..." („needle" bedeutet hier „ärgern, aufbringen") und „prearranged"
zu 1.4: Z. 27/28 liefern die Antwort. Schlüsselwörter: „gymnasium" (Turnhalle), „to alter" (verändern)
zu 1.5: Für die Antwort ist die Textpassage Z. 35–45 wichtig. Entscheidende Abschnitte: "I had no interest in football or basketball but had learned it was best to pretend otherwise." (Z. 40/41) und "... but there were names for boys who didn't like sports." (Z. 44/45)
zu 1.6: Problem bei dieser Frage: Die Fragestellung ist ein wenig irreführend, denn Miss Samson macht ihm keinen Vorwurf, sondern droht ihm, indem sie ihm Konsequenzen ankündigt für den Fall, dass er so unkooperativ bleibt (Z. 75–79).

1.1	Welches spezifische Problem soll Miss Samson bei David lösen?	David lispelt.
1.2	Weshalb bezeichnet David Miss Samson wiederholt als „agent"?	Die Szene seiner Abholung aus dem Klassenzimmer gleicht einer Festnahme durch die Polizei, wie man sie aus Filmen kennt.
1.3	Was hat David im Nachhinein besonders an der Art und Weise, **wie** er von Miss Samson abgeholt wurde, geärgert?	Seine Therapie war geplant worden, ohne ihn vorher zu informieren.
1.4	Welches ‚Vergehen' hat David in der Turnhalle begangen?	Er hat das Wort „hit" auf einem Aushang an der Turnhallentür verändert.
1.5	Weshalb gibt es David nicht zu, dass er keines der erwähnten Teams unterstützt?	Da wo David lebt, wird von Jungs erwartet, dass sie sich für Sport interessieren, sonst droht ihnen Abwertung und Ausgrenzung.

1.6 Was meint Miss Samson mit dem Vorwurf, den sie David am Ende des Gespräches macht?	Als David merkt, worauf die Logopädin hinauswill, vermeidet er krampfhaft jeden s-Laut. Miss Samson droht ihm, dass die Sache nur noch länger dauern werde, wenn er nicht kooperiert.

Hinweise: Übersehen Sie bei Aufgabe 2 nicht, dass bei der Erläuterung der Redewendungen der <u>Textzusammenhang</u> berücksichtigt werden muss.
zu 2.3: Achtung: „to grill s.o." bedeutet nicht „foltern" o. Ä.

2.1 "doing things the hard way" (l. 8, ll. 16/17)	... bedeutet hier, dass sich der Verdächtige seiner Festnahme widersetzt.
2.2 "the anticipation has ruled his life" (l. 12)	... bedeutet hier, dass der Verdächtige schon lange geahnt hat, dass er eines Tages erwischt werden wird.
2.3 "grill someone until they snapped" (l. 54)	... bedeutet hier, dass der Verdächtige so lange in die Mangel genommen oder unter Druck gesetzt wird, bis er die Beherrschung verliert bzw. alles gesteht.

Task II: Multiple Choice Questions
1 C, 2 B, 3 A, 4 B, 5 D, 6 A, 7 D, 8 B

Hinweise:
zu 1: Seine Cousins machen sich über Rodolfos Aussehen lustig: seinen dicken Bauch, der unter seinem T-Shirt hervorlugt. Der Spitzname „Gordolfo" ist eine Kombination aus dem spanischen Wort „gordo" (dick) und Rodolfo.
Option A bezieht sich in gewisser Weise auch auf das Auslachen ("He was bullied"), ist aber inhaltlich nicht zutreffend, weil als Grund für das Auslachen die Ernährung von Rodolfo angeführt wird und weil als Schikaneure die Gleichaltrigen („peers") genannt werden. Es sind aber die Cousins.
zu 2: "His vision frequently blurred" (Z. 9) bedeutet, dass er die Dinge häufig nur verschwommen gesehen hat.
zu 3: Zu Beginn des Absatzes C wird beschrieben, dass Ruiz nicht in die gängigen Klischees von Magersüchtigen passt (Balletttänzerin, schwul, schwere Kindheit etc.). Dies war ein Grund, warum er an dem Buch mitgewirkt hat („Which is part of the reason he's detailed his struggle ... in a new book" Z. 18–20).
Eine weitere Schlüsselstelle: "the book's authors defy many of the stereotypes about eating disorders, and who suffers from them" (Z. 21/22).
zu 4: Option B entspricht "the 'white girl' stereotype discourages men and minorities from coming forward" (Z. 29/30).
zu 5: Die entscheidende Textpassage findet sich in den Zeilen 31/32.
Ein „household word" ist ein Begriff oder Sachverhalt, den man überall kennt (sozusagen „in jedem Haushalt").

zu 6: Der fragliche Ausdruck bedeutet, dass die amerikanischen Vorstellungen bezüglich Körper, Körperformen und Gewicht letzten Endes („eventually" heißt nicht „eventuell") auch in die Kultur und Lebensart der Einwanderer vordringen werden. Dem entspricht Option A, auch wenn „soon" hier etwas irreführend ist.

zu 7: Option A: Buße tun („punishment for perceived sin" Z. 45)
Option B: starke Glaubensüberzeugung zum Ausdruck bringen („testament of belief" Z. 45)
Option C: bestimmte liturgisch anmutende Handlungen vollziehen („strict eating rituals" Z. 46)
Option D: Der Märtyrertod kommt im Text nicht vor.

zu 8: Hungern, nicht essen und Gewichtsabnahme bekommen eine religiöse oder spirituelle Note: Man entwickelt sich dadurch weiter (u. a. „gaining wisdom from starvation" Z. 52).

Task III: Gapped Summary

Hinweise: Entgegen der Praxis der vorangegangenen Prüfungen wurde 2009 auf den Aufgabentyp „Gapped Summary" zurückgegriffen. Grundsätzlich muss damit gerechnet werden, dass „Gapped Summary" und „Short Answer Questions" auch in der 13. Klasse Gegenstand der Prüfung sind.

Achten Sie auf die Angabe „one word per line".

Fogende Textstellen liefern die Lösung:
- „resentment": (Z. 3, Z. 14)
- „devolution": In Z. 18–20 wird beschrieben, dass und wie Schottland im Prozess der „devolution" ab den späten 90er-Jahren mehr politische Befugnisse und Eigenverantwortung erhielt. Der „Gapped Summary" greift das auf mit „i.e. the partial transfer of power to Scotland".
- „drift apart": (Z. 24)
- „govern" (Z. 32) / „rule" (Überschrift): Die Textstelle bezieht sich auf „... by proving that the nationalists can govern plausibly at home" (Z. 32/33).
- „recalculated" (Z. 44) / „renegotiated" (Z. 6): Die Textstelle bezieht sich auf „... that the formula for allocating the money be recalculated" (Z. 44).
- „Parliaments" (Z. 45)
- „welfare state" (Z. 57): Von den erwähnten Faktoren, die im Lauf der Geschichte durch die Union von England und Schottland befördert wurden, fällt laut Text nur die Etablierung des Sozialstaats in die Zeit nach dem 2. Weltkrieg.

Ever since Scotland became part of Great Britain, many Scots have felt **resentment** against British rule. Even **devolution**, i. e. the partial transfer of power to Scotland has not accomplished its aim of overcoming Scottish nationalism. On the contrary, Scotland and England have continued to **drift apart**.
English politicians have also been astonished by the SNP's ability to win elections and **govern** Scotland effectively. The popularity of Mr Salmond, the SNP leader, can in part be explained by his social-service policies, from which many Scottish citizens have profited.

This, in turn, has led to angry demands in England that the distribution of funds between England and Scotland should be **recalculated / renegotiated**. It has also re-awakened the old dispute about whether the elected representatives of Scotland should be allowed to vote in two **Parliaments**.

In the past, the Union between England and Scotland was strengthened by a common cause, such as the British Empire, or the **welfare state** after World War II. But if current tensions are not resolved, Britain could face the same fate as the former Czechoslovakia.

Aufgabenteil: *Writing*

Task IV: Mediation Deutsch–Englisch

Hinweise: In der folgenden Musterlösung werden Alternativen in Klammern angegeben. Beachten Sie aber, dass Sie in Ihrer Prüfung keine Alternativen angeben dürfen.

Many people feel a weird (incredible, mysterious) attraction to the World Wide Web – it is an attraction which is really hard to resist.

For some this attraction ends up in a tragedy (Some eventually get caught in the net).

In 2006, South Korean newspapers reported that a teenager had committed suicide because of his high cellphone bill – he had been online 24/7 (around the clock, day and night).

An "internet addiction centre" tries to cure (treat) people for whom the modern media have turned from a blessing into a curse (are no longer boon but bane, have become a nightmare).

Mr Koh, head of the centre, says that when people prefer the virtual world to the real one, it is rather obvious that they have a psychological disease.

What distinguishes (differentiates, makes different) Korea from other countries is its high rate of internet users.

According to a study, one in 59 Koreans belongs to the high risk group (is highly likely to become addicted).

In fact, it would be good for most people if they simply switched off their mobiles.

The sentence "I mail, I chat, I text (messages), therefore I am" is a tragic mistake (disastrous misapprehension). *(162 words)*

Task V: Argumentative Writing

1. **Composition**

   Hinweise: Nicht vergessen bei der Bearbeitung: Die Aufgabenstellung lautet „Discuss this statement ..." – Sie müssen sich also mit Pro und Contra auseinandersetzen. Aufbau:
   (1) eine kleine Hinführung zum Thema
   (2) Auseinandersetzung mit Pro & Contra
   – environmental issues remain important in times of financial or economic crisis

- *protecting the environment creates jobs, helps the economy*
- *neglecting the environment is much more expensive in the long run*
- *companies in financial trouble have no money for environmental issues*
- *companies have to compete with businesses from countries that ignore ecological issues*

(3) Abrunden des Aufsatzes mit einem Fazit, Ausblick, Appell o. Ä.

Remember the G 8 summit in Heiligendamm in 2007: Preventing or, at least, curbing climate change has been a top priority on the international agenda in recent years. But those were years of economic upturn. Yet, in times of economic decline, people – employees, employers, politicians – tend to ignore demands for a "timeless work on the natural environment", as Polish Prime Minister Donald Tusk put it.

It is obvious that environmental issues don't "take a break". Climate change, air pollution, soil erosion, overfishing, the extinction of certain species are pressing matters regardless of the current state of the economy. Apart from that, millions work in fields such as renewable energies, ecological research or environmental consulting. The protection of the environment creates jobs and has the potential to create even more jobs and, thus, support the economy – also in times of crisis.

Last but not least, neglecting environmental problems is detrimental from an economic point of view because ignoring such problems is likely to be much more expensive in the long run than tackling them.

On the other hand, there is no denying that companies which are losing business and have difficulty paying their employees are more concerned about surviving than about conserving the environment. In addition, having to meet environmental conditions in times of crisis can be a disadvantage when you have to compete with enterprises from countries that ignore the natural environment and its needs.

Though I can understand that politicians, managers and employees tend to reject statements like Mr Tusk's, it is my strong belief that economic worries mustn't affect our willingness to protect the environment. We will pay for it one day if we don't.

(277 words)

2. **Composition**

Hinweise: Achten Sie darauf, beide Aspekte der Aufgabenstellung zu bearbeiten: mögliche Ursachen der Entwicklung und mögliche Maßnahmen, um den Trend zu stoppen.

Aufbau:

(1) eine kleine Hinführung zum Thema

(2) Ursachen des Trends
- *negative image of politicians: incompetent, selfish, arrogant, dishonest, greedy, power-hungry*
- *politics as a hugely complex business which is hard to understand*
- *fun generation, individualism*

(3) Maßnahmen gegen den Trend
- *more democratic structures in schools*

- social studies lessons which are more practical
- youth councils with decision-making powers
- voting age 16

(4) Abrunden des Aufsatzes mit einem Fazit, Ausblick, Appell o. Ä.

Party membership figures reveal it: Figures are on the decline, and one reason is that for most young people being a member of a political party is beyond imagination. Take part in an election? – Pointless. The *Bundeswehr* in Afghanistan? – A shrug. The consequences of demographic change? – So what.

One of the major reasons behind this indifference and disinterest is that the poor image of politicians puts young people off. Politicians talk a lot, but do not listen. They argue all the time. They praise moral values, but do not live by them. They come across as incompetent, selfish, arrogant, dishonest and greedy. This is a biased view, but it is widespread.

Secondly, our times love quick and simple solutions that can be easily bought and don't involve personal efforts. But politics is an immensely complex business which people, not only the young ones, find hard to understand. So they tend to turn away from it – also because many people, again not only the young ones, have a rather individualistic approach to life. They seek fun and personal success rather than dedication to a greater cause.

Yet, democracy needs this dedication, so what can be done to revive interest and commitment?

What seems to be rather promising is to fight the impression that youngsters have no say. The best places to learn that stating one's opinion deserves respect and raising one's voice makes sense are family and school. It is within the state's power to establish more student participation in schools. Moreover, social studies lessons should focus a lot more on current affairs than on theory-based knowledge. And we should consider structural reforms: Youth councils that have decision-making powers could raise the influence of young people, a measure that could go along with lowering the voting age to 16.

Though there is no cure-all there is a variety of small steps. We've been living with the fruits of democracy for so long that we take them for granted. This is a tragic mistake.

(332 words)

**Berufliche Oberschulen Bayern – Englisch 13. Klasse
Abiturprüfung 2010**

Aufgabenteil: *Reading*

Text I (Literary Text): *Teacher Man* (by Frank McCourt)

The following text is an extract from Frank McCourt's memoir Teacher Man, *which describes and reflects on his teaching experiences in New York City high schools during the 1960s.*

Dear Mr. McCort, Mikey's grandmother who is my mother eighty years of age fell down the stairs and I kept Mikey at home to take care of her and his baby sister so I could go to my job at the coffee shop in the ferry terminal. Please excuse Mikey and he'll do his best in the future. Sincerely yours, Imelda Dolan.
5   P. S. His grandmother is OK.

When Mikey handed me the note, so blatantly forged under my nose, I said nothing. I had seen him writing it at his desk with his left hand to disguise his own handwriting. This was not his first time forging a note but I said nothing because most of the parental-excuse notes in my desk drawer were written by the boys and girls of McKee
10 Vocational and Technical High School and if I were to confront each forger I'd be busy twenty-four hours a day. It would also lead to indignation and strained relations between them and me.

I threw Mikey's note into a drawer along with dozens of others. While my class took a test that day I began to read notes I had only glanced at before. I made two piles, one
15 for the genuine notes written by mothers, the other for forgeries. The second was the larger pile, with writing that ranged from imaginative to lunatic.

I was having an epiphany. I wondered why I'd never had this particular epiphany before.

Isn't it remarkable, I thought, how they resist any kind of writing assignment in class
20 or at home. They whine and say they're busy and it's hard putting two hundred words together on any subject. But when they forge these excuse notes they're brilliant. Why? I have a drawer full of excuse notes that could be turned into an anthology of Great American Excuses or Great American Lies.

How could I have ignored this treasure trove, these gems of fiction, fantasy, creativi-
25 ty, self-pity, boilers exploding, babies and pets pissing on homework, unexpected births, robberies? Here was American high school writing at its best – raw, real, urgent, lucid, brief, lying.

The stove caught fire and the wallpaper went up and the fire department kept us out of the house all night.

30 His sister's dog ate his homework and I hope it chokes him.

We were evicted from our apartment and the mean sheriff said if my son kept yelling for his notebook he'd have us all arrested.

The writers of these notes didn't know that honest excuse notes from parents were usually dull. "Peter was late because the alarm clock did not go off."

Toward the end of the term I typed out a dozen excuse notes and distributed them to my senior classes. They read, silently and intently.

Yo, Mr. Mc Court, what's this?

Excuse notes.

Whaddya mean, excuse notes? Who wrote them?

You did, or some of you did. They're supposed to be written by parents, but you and I know the real authors. Yes, Mikey?

So, what are we supposed to do with these excuse notes?

We'll read them aloud. I want you to realize this is the first class in the world ever to study the art of the excuse note, the first class, ever, to practice writing them. You are so lucky to have a teacher like me who has taken your best writing, the excuse note, and turned it into a subject worthy of study.

They're smiling. They know. We're in this together. Sinners.

Some of the notes on that sheet were written by people in this class. You used your imagination and didn't settle for the old alarm-clock story. You'll be making excuses the rest of your life and you'll want them to be believable. Imagine you have a fifteen-year-old son or daughter who needs an excuse for falling behind in English. Let it rip.

They didn't look around. They didn't chew on their pens. They were eager, desperate to make up excuses for their fifteen-year-old children.

They produced a rhapsody of excuses, ranging from a family epidemic of diarrhea to a sixteen-wheeler truck crashing into a house.

They said, More, more. Could we do more?

I was taken aback. There was another epiphany.

I wrote on the board: "An Excuse Note from Adam to God" or "An Excuse Note from Eve to God."

The heads went down. Pens raced across the paper.

The bell rang, and for the first time in my three and a half years of teaching, I saw high school students so immersed they had to be urged out of the room by friends hungry for lunch.

Yo, Lenny. Come on. Finish it in the cafeteria.

Next day everyone had excuse notes, not only from Adam and Eve but from God and Lucifer.

There are heated discussions about the relative guilt and sinfulness of Adam and Eve. It is agreed, unanimously, that Lucifer the Snake is a bastard, a son of a bitch and no good.

I asked them to think about anyone in the world at present or in history who could use a good excuse note.

I wrote the suggestions on the blackboard: Eva Braun, Hitler's girlfriend.

I asked, How about Hitler himself?

Naw, never. No excuses there.

But maybe he had a miserable childhood.

They wouldn't agree.

On the board: Judas, Attila the Hun, Lee Harvey Oswald, Al Capone, all the politicians in America.

Mr. Mc Court, the principal is at the door.

My heart sinks.

Into the room the principal escorts the Superintendent of Schools. They don't acknowledge my existence. They don't apologize for interrupting the class. They walk up and down the aisles, peering at student papers. Superintendent shows one to the principal. Superintendent frowns and purses lips.

On their way out the principal frowns at me and whispers that the superintendent would like to see me. I know. I've done something wrong again. The shit will hit the fan and I don't know why.

There will be a negative letter in my file. You do your best. You try something that has never ever been done in the whole history of the world. But now comes the reckoning, teacher man. Down the hallway to the principal's office.

The principal is sitting at his desk, the superintendent is standing.

Ah, Mr. ... Mr. ...

McCourt.

Come in. I just want to tell you that that lesson, that project, whatever the hell you were doing in there, was top-notch. That, young man, is what we need, that kind of down-to-earth teaching. Those kids were writing at college level.

He turns to the principal and says, That kid writing an excuse note for Judas. Brilliant. But I have a reservation. I'm not sure if the writing of excuse notes for evil or criminal people is justifiable, though on second thoughts, it's what lawyers do, isn't it? And from what I've seen in your class you might have some promising future attorneys in there. So, I just want to shake your hand and tell you don't be surprised if there's a letter in your file attesting to your energetic and imaginative teaching.

(1186 words)

Abridged from Frank McCourt: Teacher Man (Chapter 6), Scribner (2005).

Worksheet
Task I: Mediation Englisch – Deutsch *(Teacher Man)*   9 credits

Lesen Sie den Text *Teacher Man* und tragen Sie die entsprechenden Antworten auf Deutsch in die folgende Tabelle ein.

1. Warum stellt Mr. McCourt seine Schüler nicht zur Rede, obwohl er weiß, dass sie Entschuldigungen fälschen?	(2)
2. Erschließen Sie die Bedeutung des Begriffs „epiphany" (Z. 17) aus dem Textzusammenhang und erläutern Sie, worauf er sich hier bezieht.	(2)
3. Was sagt das folgende Zitat über Lenny aus: "Yo, Lenny. Come on. Finish it in the cafeteria." (Z. 65)	(2)
4. Was vermutet Mr. McCourt, als ihm der folgende Gedanke durch den Kopf geht: "But now comes the reckoning, teacher man." (Z. 90/91)	(1)
5. Erklären Sie, weshalb der Schulrat am Ende des Textes zweimal Rechtsanwälte erwähnt.	(2)

Text II: The Truth about Lying

A) Ricky Gervais's new film, *The Invention of Lying*, is about a world where lying doesn't exist, which means that everybody tells the truth, and everybody believes everything everybody else says. Until one day, when Mark, a down-on-his-luck loser played by Gervais, discovers a thing called "lying" and what it can get him. Within days, Mark is rich, famous, and courting the girl of his dreams. And because nobody knows what "lying" is, he goes on, happily living what has become a complete and utter farce.

B) It's meant to be funny, but it's also a more serious commentary on us all. As Americans, we like to think we value the truth. Time and time again, public-opinion polls show that honesty is among the top five characteristics we want in a leader, friend, or lover. At the same time, deception is all around us. We are lied to by government officials and public figures to a disturbing degree; many of our social relationships are based on little white lies we tell each other. And the average person, says psychologist Robert Feldman, the author of a new book on lying, tells at least three lies in the first minutes of a conversation. "There's always been a lot of lying," says Feldman, whose new book, The Liar in Your Life, came out this month. "But I do think we're seeing a kind of cultural shift where we're lying more, it's easier to lie, and in some ways it's almost more acceptable."

C) As Paul Ekman, one of Feldman's long-time lying colleagues and the inspiration behind the Fox TV series "Lie To Me," defines it, a liar is a person who "intends to mislead," "deliberately," without being asked to do so by the target of the lie. Which doesn't mean that all lies are equally toxic: some are simply habitual –"My pleasure!" – while others might be altruistic. But each, Feldman argues, is harmful, because of the standard it creates. And the more lies we tell, even if they're little white lies, the more deceptive we and society become.

D) We are a culture of liars, to put it bluntly, with deceit so deeply ingrained in our psyches that we hardly even notice we're engaging in it. Spam e-mail, deceptive advertising, the everyday pleasantries we don't really mean – "It's so great to meet you!" "I love that dress" – have, as Feldman puts it, become "an omnipresent white noise we've learned to tune out."

E) The Josephson Institute, a non-profit organisation focused on youth ethics, concluded in a 2008 survey of nearly 30,000 high school students that "cheating in school continues to be rampant, and it's getting worse." In that survey, 64 percent of students said they'd cheated on a test during the past year, up from 60 percent in 2006. Another recent survey, by Junior Achievement, revealed that more than a third of teens believe lying, cheating, or plagiarizing can be necessary to succeed, while a brand-new study, commissioned by the publishers of Feldman's book, shows that 18- to 34-year-olds – those of us fully reared in this lying culture – deceive more frequently than the general population.

F) As Feldman notes, there is an evolutionary basis for deception: in the wild, animals use deception to "play dead" when threatened. But in the modern world, the motives of our lying are more selfish. Research has linked socially successful people to those who are good liars. Students who succeed academically get picked for the best colleges. Even lying adolescents are more popular among their peers.

G) But what's funny is that even as we admit to being liars, study after study shows that most of us believe we can tell when others are lying to us. And while lying may be easy, spotting a liar is far from it. According to one study, by researcher Bella DePaulo, we're only able to differentiate a lie from truth only 47 percent of the time, less than if we guessed randomly.

H) Ekman, meanwhile, has spent decades studying microfacial expressions of liars: the split-second eyebrow arch that shows surprise when a spouse asks who was on the phone; the furrowed nose that gives away a hint of disgust when a person says "I love you." He's trained everyone from the Secret Service to the Transport Security Administration, and believes that with close study, it's possible to identify such emoticons.

I) Which means that more often than not, we're like the poor dumb souls of *The Invention of Lying*, hanging on a liar's every word, no matter how untruthful they may be. *(761 words)*

Jessica Bennett: "The truth about Lying". From Newsweek, 8/26/2009 © 2009 Newsweek Inc. All rights reserved. Used by permission and protected by the Copyright Laws of the United States. The printing, copying, redistribution, or transmission of the material without express written permission is prohibited.

Task II: Gapped Summary – *The Truth about Lying*   7 credits
Fill each gap with the most suitable word from the text
(one word per line)!

Although _____ is one of the personal qualities Americans appreciate most, they live in a world in which lying is ubiquitous. According to psychologist Robert Feldman, being economical with the truth is by no means a new trend. What is new, however, is that Americans are experiencing a _____ _____ that encourages and socially establishes more lying. Mr Feldman believes that even well-intended lies contribute to the problem that American culture is becoming increasingly _____.

In order to find out how _____ _____ lying is in people's minds, it is sufficient to focus on the fact that very often people do not even realize that they are lying, for instance when paying a compliment.

Mr Feldman states that lying is most common among the younger generation because they have been brought up in a society that is based on it. Most people who lie do so out of _____ reasons, being eager to climb both the social and the career ladder.

Although a lot of us would disagree, Feldman thinks we have great difficulties in _____ people who do not tell the truth. This requires many years of practise and experience in examining people's _____ _____, which is a skill that most of us simply do not have.

2010-6

Text III: A return to frugality, and loving it

A) SAN FRANCISCO – Millions of Americans have trimmed expenses because they have had their jobs or hours cut, or fear they will. But a subset of savers is reducing costs not just with purpose, but with relish. These are the gleefully frugal.

B) "I'm enjoying this," said Becky Martin, 52, who has cut up her 10 credit cards, borrows movies from the library instead of renting them, and grows her own fruits and vegetables – even though her family is comfortable. Ms. Martin is a real estate investor, her husband is a plastic surgeon, and their home sits on the 12th hole of a Cincinnati country club. "It's a chance to pass along the frugal lifestyle that my mother gave to me," she says, noting that her sensibilities seem to be rubbing off not just on her sons, but also on her husband. "We're on the same page financially for the first time in years, and it's fabulous."

C) Americans' spending is down and their personal savings are up – sharply. The savings rate in the United States, which had fallen steadily since the early 1980s, dropped to less than 1 percent in August of 2008. It has since spiked to 5 percent. "It's huge," said Martha Olney, an economics professor at the University of California, Berkeley, who specializes in the Great Depression, consumerism and indebtedness. The rapid reversal is even more remarkable, she said, because in recessions consumers usually save less money. Not this time. "It implies a re-emergence of thrift as a value," she said.

D) The gleefully frugal happily seek new ways to economize and take pride in out-saving the Joneses. The mantra is cut, cut, cut – magazine and cable subscriptions, credit cards, fancy coffee drinks and your own hair.

E) In San Francisco, Cooper Marcus, 36, has canceled the family's subscription to Netflix, his premium cable package and a wine club membership. He uses a program on his phone to find the cheapest gas station and drives out of his way to save 50 cents per gallon. "It seems a little crazy," he laughs, then adds: "I'm frugal and loving it."

F) Kellee Sikes, 37, a consultant in Kirkwood, Mo., no longer uses paper napkins. Ms. Sikes uses organic cloth ones until they get threadbare and then uses them as cleaning rags. When they are no longer useful, she puts them in the in-ground waste composter in the backyard. She plans to start burying her dogs' feces there, which saves on the cost of sending refuse to a landfill. "I recently heard a phrase: 'Never waste a crisis,'" Ms. Sikes said. "I love it. This is a chance for us to re-examine what's important."

G) Indeed, the recession has given penny pinchers – once closeted in a society that valued what one had, not what one saved – license to speak up. "There is no joy in other people suffering, but this validates the choices I've made," said Vicki Robin, author of "Your Money or Your Life," a guide to saving money that was a best seller in the 1990s and was re-released last year. Currently, there are dozens of Web sites and blogs devoted to celebrating conspicuous cutting, like Dollar Stretcher, All Things Frugal, Frugal Mom and on and on.

H) "My behavior has become less strange and more of a resource," said Katy Wolk-Stanley, 41, a nurse in Portland, Ore. A practicing penny pincher for the last decade, she is now spreading her gospel. Last May, she started a blog with tips and tactics for cutting back called The Non-Consumer Advocate.

Ms. Wolk-Stanley says she is not cheap. She's sensible. Why spend on new things when there are viable alternatives? And she contends she does not judge others. "If everyone followed this advice, it would be catastrophic to the economy," she said.

I) Indeed, economists call it the Paradox of Thrift. While saving is desirable, if everyone does it then consumption falls, businesses fail and the economy grinds to a halt. Professor Olney, from Berkeley, said that the increased rate of savings would most likely slow down the pace of recovery but she also said that a higher savings rate was not inconsistent with a strong economy.

J) Ms. Martin, from Ohio, echoes other penny pinchers in hoping that the recession will inspire a new generation of frugality. Already, her 14-year-old son has picked up her lead. "He is not beyond stopping and pulling things out from someone's trash," she said. He found one sectional sofa left on the sidewalk that he resold on the Internet for $ 200. "I'm very proud of him." *(767 words)*

Matt Richtel: "Austere Times? Prefect." From New York Times © 10 April 2009 The New York Times All rights reserved. Used by permission and protected by the Copyright Laws of the United States. The printing, copying, redistribution, and retransmission of the material without express written permission is prohibited.

Task III: Mixed Reading Tasks   8 credits
Multiple Choice Questions   5 credits
Mark the most suitable option with a cross!

1. When Becky Martin says "We're on the same page financially for the first time in years", (ll. 10/11), she expresses that …
   A her family has been able to overcome their financial difficulties.
   B by cooperating her family is able to earn a reasonable income.
   C she has been able to convince her family to adopt her lifestyle.
   D her family has so far not been affected by the economic crisis.

2. In paragraph C, Professor Olney explains that …
   A consumers have reacted to the economic crisis in a predictable way.
   B American consumers have always put emphasis on saving money.
   C the American economy has always been characterized by a high level of debt.
   D current consumer behaviour can only be explained by changing attitudes.

3. The main conclusion drawn by Kellee Sikes is that American households should …
   - A regard the current recession as an opportunity.
   - B refrain from using disposable products.
   - C adopt a new approach to waste management.
   - D take advantage of every possibility of saving money.
4. Which of the following claims does paragraph G **not** make about US society?
   - A Material possessions used to be the cornerstone of American society.
   - B Wealth will always be held in higher regard than frugality.
   - C This is not the first time that Americans have taken an interest in thriftiness.
   - D Thrift used to be frowned upon by a majority of Americans.
5. Overall, the text …
   - A focuses on future social and economic developments.
   - B combines personal accounts with economic analysis.
   - C compares different economic trends in several US states.
   - D uses an example to illustrate a current trend.

Mediation Englisch-Deutsch 3 credits

Beantworten Sie die folgenden Fragen auf Deutsch.

6. Welches Verhalten wird mit dem Ausdruck „outsaving the Joneses" (ll. 20 /21) beschrieben?		(1)
7. Erklären Sie auf Deutsch, was „Paradox of Thrift" (l. 48) im Textzusammenhang bedeutet.		(2)

Aufgabenteil: *Writing*

Stirbt Englisch aus?

Die weltumspannende Sprache der Gegenwart heißt Englisch. In vielen Berufen und im Studium ist sie unverzichtbar, die Popkultur ist fest in ihrer Hand. Ein Ende der Dominanz ist nicht in Sicht. Im Zuge der Globalisierung und der zunehmenden Technisierung hat sich Englisch überall durchgesetzt. Es gibt kaum einen Winkel auf der
5 Erde, in dem man niemanden findet, der diese Sprache spricht.

Noch nie vorher gab es eine Sprache, die wirklich in jedem Land der Welt gesprochen wird", sagte David Crystal, Autor des Buches „English as a Global Language".

Es wird vermutet, dass ein Fünftel der Weltbevölkerung mehr oder weniger gut auf Englisch kommunizieren kann. In fast allen Bereichen wird es inzwischen verwendet
10 – egal ob es um die internationalen Geldmärkte, den Luftverkehr oder gar den islamischen Dschihad geht.

Es gibt zwar mehr Menschen, die als Muttersprache Chinesisch, Spanisch oder Hindi sprechen, aber viele von ihnen nutzen Englisch, um Sprachbarrieren zu überwinden. Sie werden so zu Bürgern einer immer stärker verflochtenen Welt. In manchen euro-
15 päischen Firmen wird nur Englisch gesprochen, obwohl sie beispielsweise in Deutschland beheimatet sind oder in Schweden.

Aber während Englisch sich immer weiter verbreitet, wird es immer stärker fragmentiert. Es entstehen mehrere „Englische". Nördlich und südlich der Grenze zwischen den USA und Mexiko wird „Spanglish" gesprochen, ein Mix aus Spanisch und Eng-
20 lisch, in Singapur „Singlish".

Es sei ein nie gesehenes Phänomen, so Crystal, dass Englisch von drei Mal so vielen Nicht-Muttersprachlern gesprochen wird als von Muttersprachlern. Alleine in Asien sprechen mit etwa 350 Millionen etwa genauso viele Menschen Englisch wie in den USA, dem Vereinigten Königreich und in Kanada zusammen.
25 So entstehen bereits Forderungen, die Sprache zu vereinfachen. Jean-Paul Nerrière, Franzose und ehemaliger Vizepräsident von IBM USA, forderte in der International Herald Tribune, die Zahl der Wörter zu verringern.

Er selbst hat eine eigene Variante des „Globish" entworfen, die mit lediglich 15.000 einfachen Wörtern auskommt. Zum Vergleich: Das Wörterbuch „Oxford English
30 Dictionary" beinhaltet über 600.000 Einträge.

„Wir sind die Mehrheit," sagt Nerrière und meint damit die Menschen, die Englisch nicht als Muttersprache sprechen. „Unsere Art zu sprechen sollte die offizielle Art sein, Englisch zu sprechen." *(346 Wörter)*

Marius Meyer, Süddeutsche Zeitung, 10. 4. 2007 (gekürzte Fassung)

Worksheet

Task IV: Mediation Deutsch–Englisch (Stirbt Englisch aus?) 12 credits

Fassen Sie den folgenden Artikel zusammen, indem Sie die unterstrichenen Textstellen sinngemäß ins Englische übertragen. Verfassen Sie hierfür einen zusammenhängenden Text im Umfang von ca. 150 Wörtern.

Task V: Argumentative Writing 24 credits

Choose **one** of the following topics. Write **at least 220 words**.

1. **Composition**

    Do you think that US President Obama has deserved to be awarded the Nobel Peace Prize?

    Give reasons for your opinion.

2. **Composition**

    "I woke up this morning crying, and that's not easy for a grown man to admit. The fate of my country rests in your hands."

    IAN FRY, representative of the Pacific island of Tuvalu, appealing to delegates of the Copenhagen climate summit 2009 to reach an agreement to combat global warming.

    What should the world community do to help islands like Tuvalu which are endangered by rising sea levels?

    Express your opinion and give reasons for your point of view.

Lösungsvorschläge

Aufgabenteil: *Reading*

Task I: Mediation Englisch – Deutsch

Hinweise:
- *zu 1.1: Folgende Textstellen sind relevant: „busy twenty-four hours a day", „lead to indignation", „strained relations" (Z. 11).*
- *zu 1.2: Die Antwort geht aus Z. 19–27 hervor.*
- *zu 1.3: relevante Textstelle: Z. 62–64*
- *zu 1.4: Die Vermutungen gehen aus den Z. 86–91 hervor. Schlüsselpassagen sind "the principal frowns at me" (= Stirnrunzeln), „done something wrong again", "the shit will hit the fan" (= die Kacke ist am Dampfen), "a negative letter in my file" (= negativer Eintrag in der Personalakte).*
  Weitere Antwortmöglichkeiten: Er rechnet mit Sanktionen seitens der Vorgesetzten. Er erwartet, dass er großen Ärger bekommt wegen seines Unterrichts. Wichtig: Achten Sie bei der deutschen Formulierung darauf, dass sie idiomatisch klingt. „Er erhält die Rechnung für seinen Unterricht" mag halbwegs verständlich sein, klingt aber nicht gut im Deutschen.
- *zu 1.5: Von Rechtsanwälten ist in Z. 99–102 die Rede. Entscheidende Textpassagen sind "I have a reservation [...] though on second thoughts [...] you might have some promising future attorneys."*

1. Warum stellt Mr. McCourt seine Schüler nicht zur Rede, obwohl er weiß, dass sie Entschuldigungen fälschen?	Der Lehrer wäre sonst rund um die Uhr damit beschäftigt. Die Schüler wären verärgert und die Lehrer-Schüler-Beziehung würde sich verschlechtern.
2. Erschließen Sie die Bedeutung des Begriffs „epiphany" (Z. 17) aus dem Textzusammenhang und erläutern Sie, worauf er sich hier bezieht.	Der Lehrer hat einen Geistesblitz (eine zündende Idee/eine Eingebung). Schüler, die etwas schreiben sollen, sträuben sich oft dagegen und haben keine Ideen, doch beim Fälschen der Entschuldigungen sind sie sehr kreativ. Das nutzt er für den Unterricht.
3. Was sagt das folgende Zitat über Lenny aus: "Yo, Lenny. Come on. Finish it in the cafeteria." (Z. 65)	Lenny ist so vertieft ins Schreiben, dass er von Mitschülern an die Mittagspause erinnert werden muss.
4. Was vermutet Mr. McCourt, als ihm der folgende Gedanke durch den Kopf geht:"But now comes the reckoning, teacher man." (Z. 90/91)	Er vermutet, dass er nun die Quittung für seinen unkonventionellen Unterricht bekommt.

2010-12

5. Erklären Sie, weshalb der Schulrat am Ende des Textes zweimal Rechtsanwälte erwähnt.	Der Schulrat hat zunächst Zweifel, ob es in Ordnung ist, dass die Schüler Entschuldigungen für so böse bzw. verbrecherische Menschen verfassen, doch bei näherer Betrachtung machen Rechtsanwälte ja nichts anderes. Außerdem sieht er in der Klasse einige vielversprechende Rechtsanwälte in spe.

Task II: Gapped Summary – *The Truth about Lying*

Hinweise: Achten Sie auf die Angabe „one word per line".
- honesty (Z. 10): Es geht um „qualities", also Eigenschaften, die von Amerikanern geschätzt werden. „Honesty" (= Ehrlichkeit) ist eine Elgenschaft, „truth" (Z. 9) (= Wahrheit) ist keine Eigenschaft.
- cultural shift (Z. 17): Schlüsselparallelen im Gapped Summary (GS) bzw. im Originaltext (OT) sind: „What is new, however" (GS) vs. „always been a lot of lying [...] [b]ut I do think" (OT Z. 15–17) „Americans are experiencing" (GS) vs. „we're seeing" (OT Z. 17) „encourages and socially establishes" (GS) vs. „easier to lie [...] more acceptable" (OT Z. 17/18)
- deceptive (Z. 25) bzw. untruthful (Z. 57): Schlüsselparallelen sind „well-intended lies" (GS) vs. „little white lies" (OT Z. 24/25) „American culture" (GS) vs. „we and society" (OT Z. 25) „increasingly" (GS) vs. „the more [...] the more" (OT Z. 24/25). Für „untruthful" gibt es keine Schlüsselstellen, es passt aber von der Wortbedeutung und vom Zusammenhang her (deceptive= betrügerisch, untruthful = unaufrichtig).
- deeply ingrained (Z. 26): Schlüsselparallelen sind „in people's minds" (GS) vs. „in our psyches" (OT Z. 26/27), „lying" (GS) vs. „deceit" (OT Z. 26)
- selfish (Z. 42): Im Zusammenhang der Lücke geht es darum, welcher Art die Gründe fürs Lügen sind. Die entsprechende Stelle im OT: „the motives of our lying are ..." (Z. 41/42)
- spotting (Z. 47): Die Schlüsselparallelen sind „we have great difficulties in" (GS) vs. „while lying may be easy [...] is far from it" (OT Z. 46/47), „people who do not tell the truth" (GS) vs. „liar" (OT Z. 47).
- microfacial expressions (Z. 50): Die Schlüsselparallele ist „examining" (GS) vs. „studying" (OT Z. 50).

Although **honesty** is one of the personal qualities Americans appreciate most, they live in a world in which lying is ubiquitous. According to psychologist Robert Feldman, being economical with the truth is by no means a new trend. What is new, however, is that Americans are experiencing a **cultural shift** that encourages and socially establishes more lying. Mr Feldman believes that even well-intended lies contribute to the problem that American culture is becoming increasingly **deceptive/untruthful**.

2010-13

In order to find out how **deeply ingrained** lying is in people's minds, it is sufficient to focus on the fact that very often people do not even realize that they are lying, for instance when paying a compliment.

Mr Feldman states that lying is most common among the younger generation because they have been brought up in a society that is based on it. Most people who lie do so out of **selfish** reasons, being eager to climb both the social and the career ladder.

Although a lot of us would disagree, Feldman thinks we have great difficulties in **spotting** people who do not tell the truth. This requires many years of practise and experience in examining people's **microfacial expressions**, which is a skill that most of us simply do not have.

Task III: Mixed Reading Tasks
Multiple Choice Questions
1 C, 2 D, 3 A, 4 B, 5 B

Hinweise:
zu 1: „[O]n the same page" bedeutet hier „auf der gleichen Welle liegen". Man kann den Zusammenhang erschließen aus "her sensibilities are rubbing off not just on her sons, but also on her husband" = ihre Sicht der Dinge färbt nicht nur auf ihre Söhne, sondern auch auf ihren Mann ab (Z. 9/10).
zu 2: Aus Textstellen wie "The savings rate [...] has spiked to 5 percent" (Z. 12–14) und "The rapid reversal is even more remarkable" (Z. 17) kann man erkennen, dass ein schneller und überraschender Wandel in der Einstellung der Amerikaner zum Sparen stattgefunden haben muss.
zu 3: Schlüsselstelle: "[t]his is a chance for us [the American households]" (Z. 32).
zu 4: Option A: „a society that valued what one had, not what one saved", Option C: „a guide to saving money [...] best seller in the 1990s [...] re-released last year"; Option D: „penny pinchers, once closeted in a society". Option B kommt also nicht im Text vor und ist daher die richtige Lösung.
zu 5: „Personal accounts" sind Berichte von Betroffenen, wovon sich im Text eine ganze Reihe finden (Becky Martin, Cooper Marcus, Kellee Sikes, ...). Diese Berichte sind garniert mit analytischen Beiträgen (Absätze C, G und I).

Mediation Englisch-Deutsch

6. Welches Verhalten wird mit dem Ausdruck „out-saving the Joneses" (ll. 20/21) beschrieben?	**Zwischen Nachbarn, Bekannten und Freunden herrscht eine Art Wettbewerb, wer den anderen beim Sparen übertrifft.**
7. Erklären Sie auf Deutsch, was „Paradox of Thrift" (l. 48) im Textzusammenhang bedeutet.	**Es geht um ein widersprüchliches Phänomen: Für den Einzelnen ist es vernünftig, in einer Wirtschaftskrise sein Geld zusammenzuhalten – volkswirtschaftlich verschärft sich dadurch aber die Krise, weil die Nachfrage zurückgeht.**

Hinweise:
zu 6: „*the Joneses*" *entsprechen im Deutschen den* „*Meiers*" *oder* „*Müllers*"*, damit sind Nachbarn oder Bekannte gemeint. Verben mit* „*out*" *wie* „*outnumber, outdo, outclass, outride*" *drücken häufig Überlegenheit aus.*
zu 7: Relevante Textstelle: Z. 48–52

Aufgabenteil: Writing

Task IV: Mediation Deutsch–Englisch

Hinweise: Sie dürfen hier die unterstrichenen Textstellen nicht wörtlich übersetzen. Übertragen Sie die Stellen sinngemäß ins Englische, achten Sie vor allem darauf, dass Sie einen zusammenhängenden und idiomatischen Text schreiben. In der folgenden Musterlösung sind auch Alternativen angegeben. Entscheiden Sie sich in der Abiturklausur aber stets für eine Lösung, da Alternativen zu Punktverlust führen können.

The global language of our times is English.
It is indispensable in a variety of jobs and at university, due to globalization and automation.
(Having command of it is essential / crucial / vital / absolutely necessary in many jobs and courses of study because English has come to dominate the world in the course of globalization and technological advance.)
Never before has there been (Indeed, there has never been) a language that was spoken in virtually every country of the world.
It is assumed that one in five people in the world is (Twenty percent of the world population are said to be) able to communicate in English more or less well (properly / at an acceptable level).
It is true that there are more people whose mother tongue is Chinese, Spanish or Hindi, but many of them use English to overcome language barriers.
While English continues to spread, more and more varieties (several kinds) of English are developing (arising).
There are three times more non-native speakers of English than native speakers. As a result, there are demands to simplify (people are calling for a simplification of) the language.
Mr Nerrière, from France, has developed (designed) his own version of English, called "Globish", which is based on (can do with) no more than 15,000 simple words.
He argues that the speakers of English as a foreign language are the majority and that their way of speaking should be the official way of speaking English.

(245 words)

Task V: Argumentative Writing

1. **Composition**

Hinweise: Auch wenn die Aufgabenstellung nicht „Discuss" lautet, empfiehlt sich eine Auseinandersetzung mit Pro und Contra, um den Aufsatz inhaltlich fundierter zu gestalten. Möglicher Aufbau:
1) Hinführung zum Thema
2) Auseinandersetzung mit Pro und Contra
   – new approach: multilateralism and partnership rather than solo efforts
   – Obama's move towards nuclear disarmament
   – Obama has not achieved much yet
   – well-intentioned statements rather than political action
3) Abrunden des Aufsatzes mit einem Fazit, Ausblick, o. Ä.

It was sensational front page news in October 2009 when the Nobel Peace Prize Committee announced they had picked US President Barack Obama for the mother of all international prizes. The decision immediately stirred heated discussions all over the world whether he deserved this prize or not.

Without doubt, Obama has brought change into US international policies.

His policy is profoundly different from the one of his predecessor George W. Bush. He doesn't seek conflict at any price, he is not focused on the U.S. as the one and only superpower, he pursues a partnership approach, aiming to cooperate and negotiate rather than get stuck in solo efforts. His confession that the invasion of Iraq was not justified is credible, and he has begun to withdraw the American troops from Iraq. His probably biggest achievement is his serious move towards nuclear disarmament, a step which is likely to make the world a safer place and to transform the widespread image of the U.S. as an imperialist nation.

Yet, the award has a strange taste. Is it acceptable that someone who has not achieved much yet gets this renowned prize?

Obama has given a lot of well-intentioned statements but we do not see much real political action. The U.S. is still waging war in Afghanistan, and Obama has even raised the number of U.S. troops there. So far he has not managed to bring about peace between the conflicting parties in the Middle East. Can his doings and achievements compare with what former Nobel Peace Prize winners like Mother Teresa, Willy Brandt or Nelson Mandela achieved?

In my opinion, Barack Obama does not deserve the Nobel Peace Prize, at least not yet. The change he has brought about is remarkable and he is on the right track, but the prize should go to someone who has actually put something into practice.

(310 words)

2. **Composition**

Hinweise: Sie müssen bei diesem Thema das angegebene Zitat von Ian Fry einbeziehen. Das Zitat stammt von einer internationalen Konferenz der Vereinten Nationen – im Mittelpunkt der Aufgabenstellung steht daher weniger, was der Einzelne tun kann, sondern was die Weltgemeinschaft, also die Gemeinschaft der Staaten tun kann, um Inseln wie Tuvalu zu helfen. Möglicher Aufbau:
1) Hinführung zum Thema
2) Ideelle Ebene: Dimension des Problems erfassen, Verantwortung erkennen
   – precondition: realizing the dimension of the problem, bearing the responsibility
3) Praktische Ebene: Maßnahmen ergreifen wie Energiesparen u. Ä.
   – measures: cutting CO_2 emissions, saving energy, lowering meat consumption
4) Abrunden des Aufsatzes mit einem Fazit, Ausblick, Appell o. Ä.

Ian Fry's statement reveals that global warming is not just a theory, but has an actual effect on people on this planet. For most of us it may seem far away, but for some of us it is becoming a real threat that arouses fear – fear of the loss of one's home.

An island of the size of Tuvalu depends on the support of the world community. The world community, however, as it is represented by the United Nations, can only help, if it is willing to realize the dimension of the challenge: We as the inhabitants of the world, whatever place we live in, must take on responsibility and must accept the need for radical change – otherwise we won't achieve anything.

Since the industrialized nations are most of all responsible for the greenhouse effect, they have to make the farthest-reaching changes and take short-term and long-term measures to tackle the core problem: carbon dioxide and methane emissions from heating, transport and livestock breeding. That is where we can achieve most effect.

We need more economical engines in cars, lorries, planes and ships, we need more insulation of buildings, we need more transport on the rail, by bus and by bike. We must get away from fossil fuels and we must accept that we have to change our life-style, which means less meat consumption and a reduction of food miles.

All these measures will help to restrain global warming but may not be effective enough to stop sea levels from rising. So plan B is to provide money for the building of dams around the island or the resettlement of Tuvalu inhabitants in other countries.

Global warming is not just a theory, it is real. We do not know how much we can achieve by taking action, but sitting back and doing nothing is no option.

(306 words)

Berufliche Oberschulen Bayern – Englisch 13. Klasse
Abiturprüfung 2011

Aufgabenteil: *Reading*

Text I: *The Story of an Hour* by Kate Chopin

Knowing that Mrs. Mallard was afflicted with heart trouble, great care was taken to break to her as gently as possible the news of her husband's death.

It was her sister Josephine who told her, in broken sentences; veiled hints that revealed in half concealing. Her husband's friend Richards was there, too, near her. It was he
5 who had been in the newspaper office when intelligence of the railroad disaster was received, with Brently Mallard's name leading the list of "killed." He had only taken the time to assure himself of its truth by a second telegram, and had hastened to forestall any less careful, less tender friend in bearing the sad message.

She did not hear the story as many women have heard the same, with a paralyzed ina-
10 bility to accept its significance. She wept at once, with sudden, wild abandonment, in her sister's arms. When the storm of grief had spent itself she went away to her room alone. She would have no one follow her.

There stood, facing the open window, a comfortable, roomy armchair. Into this she sank, pressed down by a physical exhaustion that haunted her body and seemed to
15 reach into her soul.

She could see in the open square before her house the tops of trees that were all aquiver with the new spring life. The delicious breath of rain was in the air. In the street below a peddler was crying his wares. The notes of a distant song which someone was singing reached her faintly, and countless sparrows were twittering in the eaves.
20 There were patches of blue sky showing here and there through the clouds that had met and piled one above the other in the west facing her window.

She sat with her head thrown back upon the cushion of the chair, quite motionless, except when a sob came up into her throat and shook her, as a child who has cried itself to sleep continues to sob in its dreams.

25 She was young, with a fair, calm face, whose lines bespoke repression and even a certain strength. But now there was a dull stare in her eyes, whose gaze was fixed away off yonder on one of those patches of blue sky. It was not a glance of reflection, but rather indicated a suspension of intelligent thought.

There was something coming to her and she was waiting for it, fearfully. What was it?
30 She did not know; it was too subtle and elusive to name. But she felt it, creeping out of the sky, reaching toward her through the sounds, the scents, the colour that filled the air.

Now her bosom rose and fell tumultuously. She was beginning to recognize this thing that was approaching to possess her, and she was striving to beat it back with her will

2011-1

35 – as powerless as her two white slender hands would have been. When she abandoned herself, a little whispered word escaped her slightly parted lips. She said it over and over under her breath: "free, free, free!" The vacant stare and the look of terror that had followed it went from her eyes. They stayed keen and bright. Her pulses beat fast, and the coursing blood warmed and relaxed every inch of her body. She did not stop
40 to ask if it were or were not a monstrous joy that held her. A clear and exalted perception enabled her to dismiss the suggestion as trivial.

She knew that she would weep again when she saw the kind, tender hands folded in death; the face that had never looked save with love upon her, fixed and grey and dead. But she saw beyond that bitter moment a long procession of years to come that would
45 belong to her absolutely. And she opened and spread her arms out to them in welcome. There would be no one to live for during those coming years; she would live for herself. There would be no powerful will bending hers in that blind persistence with which men and women believe they have a right to impose a private will upon a fellow creature. A kind intention or a cruel intention made the act seem no less a crime as
50 she looked upon it in that brief moment of illumination.

And yet she had loved him – sometimes. Often she had not. What did it matter! What could love, the unsolved mystery, count for in face of this possession of self-assertion which she suddenly recognized as the strongest impulse of her being!

"Free! Body and soul free!" she kept whispering.

55 Josephine was kneeling before the closed door with her lips to the keyhole, imploring for admission. "Louise, open the door! I beg, open the door – you will make yourself ill. What are you doing, Louise? For heaven's sake open the door."

"Go away. I am not making myself ill." No; she was drinking in a very elixir of life through that open window. Her fancy was running riot along those days ahead of her.
60 Spring days, and summer days, and all sorts of days that would be her own. She breathed a quick prayer that life might be long. It was only yesterday she had thought with a shudder that life might be long.

She arose at length and opened the door to her sister's importunities. There was a feverish triumph in her eyes, and she carried herself unwittingly like a goddess of victo-
65 ry. She clasped her sister's waist, and together they descended the stairs. Richards stood waiting for them at the bottom.

Someone was opening the front door with a latchkey. It was Brently Mallard who entered, a little travel-stained, composedly carrying his grip-sack and umbrella. He had been far from the scene of the accident, and did not even know there had been one. He
70 stood amazed at Josephine's piercing cry; at Richards' quick motion to screen him from the view of his wife. But Richards was too late.

When the doctors came they said she had died of heart disease – of the joy that kills.

(1 012 words)

Short story by Kate Chopin: The Story of an Hour

Worksheet
Task I: Mixed Reading *(The Story of an Hour)*   8 credits
Multiple Choice Questions   6 credits
Mark the most suitable option with a cross.

1. Richards …
   A   considers himself a friend of the Mallards.
   B   is a reporter seeking sensational news.
   C   is a close friend of Josephine's husband.
   D   and Brently work together in the same office.

2. According to the author, a number of women react to the news of their husbands' deaths with …
   A   hysterical crying.
   B   a physical breakdown.
   C   utter disbelief.
   D   the search for privacy.

3. Louise Mallard …
   A   is an elderly woman who had been married for years.
   B   is reminded of the freedom she enjoyed before she was married.
   C   had a husband who was capable of deep feelings for her.
   D   has always had strong feelings for Richards.

4. Which of the following is **not** true? For Mrs. Mallard marriage in general means …
   A   imprisonment.
   B   a crime.
   C   loneliness.
   D   coercion.

5. What is the "something" (l. 29) coming to Louise in her room? It is …
   A   grief.
   B   relief.
   C   surprise.
   D   confusion.

6. Josephine has reason to be worried that Louise …
   A   might suffer a heart attack.
   B   will kick her out of the house.
   C   may jump out of the window.
   D   might turn to drink.

Mediation Englisch–Deutsch 2 credits
Beantworten Sie die folgende Frage auf Deutsch.

7. Erklären Sie die Ironie im letzten Satz: "When the doctors came they said she had died … – of the joy that kills."	_____ _____ _____ _____

Text II: Arizona's Crackdown on Migrants

Arizona's governor has signed into law a tough bill aimed to stem the flow of illegal migrants into the US border state. The BBC's Rajesh Mirchandani travelled to Arizona to test the mood among local residents and also Mexicans who work there.

Nogales, Arizona, is a scruffy hotchpotch of cultures where shops sell cheap T-shirts behind signs saying "Acceptamos pesos" (We accept pesos), where men in trucks drive past blaring Mexican hip-hop and where you'll get a better deal if you haggle in Spanish. _____ **[Gap A]** _____ Rather than peter out into the desert, the
5 town – and the US nation here – ends abruptly, butted along its southern edge by a 35 ft-high (11 m) fence, rust-red iron stakes with narrow slits between them, almost taunting those on one side with glimpses of what lies on the other.

_____ **[Gap B]** _____ You might think this was one city sliced down the middle, were it not for the fact that the Mexican side looks much poorer. These are
10 two very different worlds, and the fence is the main deterrent in these parts to illegal immigration. In a state of some 6.5 m people, nearly 500,000 are here without permission. Now, with the new anti-immigration law, Arizona has an additional strategy: to make life in the US so hard for illegal immigrants that they either go home or don't come in the first place.

15 _____ **[Gap C]** _____ If that person can't prove legal immigration status they could be arrested. "It makes me sad," said an older gentleman, a US citizen with Mexican roots, "it will hurt our dignity." "Search me because my skin is brown?" a young man, also a US citizen, exclaimed. "That's bullshit!" Two young Mexican women who, like many, often cross the border for a day's shopping, said they might
20 not return to spend their money here in the future. Several law enforcement officials complain the new measure will increase their workload. Some of them are doubtful that it will be enforced. _____ **[Gap D]** _____

As you leave Nogales and head into the empty desert, buildings and people give way to spiny cactus plants and desert birds along a quiet highway that winds through beau-
25 tiful untamed hillsides. They are unusually green this spring. But soon they will be a parched furnace. This is the original Wild West, dotted with old mining towns like Bisbee and Tombstone where the actual Gunfight at the OK Corral took place. Now tourists watch daily re-enactments.

The border in this remote corner of Arizona is less heavily fortified than in the cities.
30 Despite the vigilance of the border patrol, it's a busy smuggling route for people and

drugs. And in this dusty remote corner some 25 ranchers work a million acres. They often find human debris on their vast lands, or encounter people trying to cross into America. _____ [Gap E] _____

"This was one of the last places in America to be homesteaded," says Bill McDonald, whose family has been here for 100 years. "There used to be Apaches. It was the Wild West. It's getting like that again," he says. Recently a rancher called Robert Krentz was shot dead on his property, along with his dog. Police followed tracks to the border and suspect it was an illegal entrant who killed him. One theory is that it may have been a revenge attack: shortly before, Mr Krentz's brother discovered drugs hidden on their land and alerted the police, who removed them.

_____ [Gap F] _____ On her family's ranch, Peggy Davis plays with her four-year-old grandson Zane and his pet goat Gordy. She tells me now when she goes out, she carries a gun. Peggy supports the new law. "We have been absolutely over run," she says, "and our government has not done what they need to to maintain safety … I feel this is a national security issue."

Arizona's Governor Jan Brewer, who faces a tough re-election battle this year and who signed the anti-immigration bill live on TV, agrees.

_____ [Gap G] _____ He said it was the federal government's failure to act that had opened the door to irresponsible measures like the Arizona law. He wants to reform immigration in the US, and people in border states want him to do it. But they disagree on how.

Back in Nogales, I saw a woman with her four small children huddled by the metal fence. _____ [Gap H] _____ This was a family separated by the fence. The woman said she was in the US legally, while her husband had failed once before to jump the fence. "Are you worried about the new law," I asked. "Will you try and come over again?" "Yes, of course!" he laughed.   (817 words)

Adapted from http://news.bbc.co.uk/go/pr/fr/-/2/hi/americas/8642439.stm
Published: 2010/04/25 00:51:10 GMT © BBC MMX

Task II: Multiple Matching (Arizona's Crackdown on Migrants)   8 credits
Eight sentences have been removed from the text "Arizona's Crackdown on Migrants".
In the grid below, match sentences 1 to 11 with gaps A to H.
There are three sentences that won't match.

Gap	Sentence
A	
B	
C	
D	

E	
F	
G	
H	

Sentences:
1. A US border agent watched as a man's hand poked through the iron stakes and caressed the head of one of his daughters.
2. Close by and only separated by a ridge of small hills, there is Nogales, a once flourishing Mexican city.
3. It's a frontier town on a frontline.
4. So does President Barack Obama.
5. All the same, most Arizonans support the new law.
6. And on the other side, clinging to the fence like crumbling concrete moss, is the city of Nogales, Mexico.
7. Similarly, the local representative of the Republicans is in support of the US government.
8. Police will be required to stop anyone they "reasonably suspect" is here illegally.
9. Most are tired, thirsty and looking for work, but not all.
10. Other law-abiding citizens don't like the idea of private do-it-yourself border patrols.
11. Now some here take no chances.

Text III: Demographics: The Population Hourglass by Andrew Zolli

Your future is older, browner, and more feminine than you might have realized. That will make for some major lifestyle changes ("Welcome home, Mom!") and lots of huge opportunities for business.

It's the futurist's first rule: You can't understand the future without demographics. The composition of a society shapes every aspect of civic life – politics, economics, culture and lifestyles. Demographics isn't destiny, but it's close. Our leaders, as a rule, completely miss the boat on demographics and how it informs their own organiza-
5 tions, customers, and constituencies. And it's not hard to see why: Most executives aren't trained to make sense of demographic forecasts (there are no courses on demographics at Harvard Business School or Wharton, for example), and the field itself does little to raise its own profile. Demographers frequently come across like accountants – without any sex appeal.

10 But that doesn't mean exciting and important things aren't happening. The United States of 2016 will find itself in the throes of demographic shifts that will upend our

lives. From our age distribution to the color of our skin, we will look dramatically different.

To get a sense of what lies ahead, consider a simple demographic tool: the "population pyramid." Imagine that we took all of the people in a given population and stacked them up by age, putting all the infants at the bottom and all the centenarians up top. For most stable, peacetime societies, the resulting figure would look like a pyramid, with the youngest people at the base and the oldest people up at the tip. And indeed, that is exactly what you see today in a place like India – a perfectly sloped pyramid with lots and lots of babies at the bottom and a handful of the ancient. By contrast, the current US pyramid looks like an overweight contestant on *The Biggest Loser,* with the giant baby boom billowing out from its midsection. Starting soon, however, our flabby pyramid is quickly going to slim down. It will assume the form of an hourglass, with the largest number of older people in our society's history, the quasi-retired baby boomers, up top, and the largest generation of young people since the boomers – the millennials, or echo boomers – at the bottom. The beleaguered generation-Xers will form the "pinched waist" in the middle.

It's hard to overstate the weight of the numbers: Boomers now represent about 12 % of the population, and as they move up the pyramid, the number of seniors is going to rise dramatically. By 2011, the 65-and-over population will be growing faster than the population as a whole in each of the 50 states. This will bring an avalanche of new social challenges and cultural norms. It will also change politics: We could see a multi-decade "boomerocracy" as older people tend to vote more frequently, and thus wield significant political clout.

For businesses, the huge increase in the number of older consumers, many of them backed by vast reservoirs of disposable income, represents the next American gold rush. Even today, businesses aren't confused about the opportunity that growth represents: Consumer electronics firms such as Vodafone are investing in mobile phones with designs tweaked to the requirements of older customers; IBM has developed a computer mouse that compensates for the tremors that sometimes affect seniors' hands; and Gap Inc. recently unveiled Forth & Towne, a new clothing line for women who fall into the vast retail void between the navel-pierced teen and the librarian in a twin set.

And those examples are just a foretaste. The real breakthroughs are going to come from companies helping boomers to hold on to their youth – and milk it for all it's worth. Boomers have never met a life stage they didn't want to remake in their own image, and their golden years will be no exception. Watch grandma windsurf! Pole vault! Pole *dance!*

The hourglass phenomenon will shape not only where you work but whom you work with – and how you get along with them. Some boomers, upon turning 65, will disappear in a puff of smoke from their mobile homes, retiring to a never-ending party that ends only at death. Others will find themselves fully and happily employed by companies desperate to keep them. Still others, due to lamentably low savings rates and the erosion of social services, will never be able to enter retirement.

All this will in turn create a paradox for the gen-Xers coming up behind the baby boomers. Some Xers will find themselves in the midst of an enormous job boom created by the vacating boomers, who will leave open far more jobs than there are qualified Xers to fill them. (And there will be much rejoicing.) At the same time, some Xers will find themselves trapped behind a new glass ceiling – blocked from their next career step because an all-too-healthy or all-too-indebted precursor just can't or won't retire.

Making all of this intergenerational jockeying even more complex, the millennials will soon begin showing up in the workforce en masse, carting along a mix of ravenous careerism, natural social networking and IT skills, a thirst for learning, and a rather presumptuous expectation of direct contact with senior management. How this perky generation, which is more like the boomers than any generation in between, will get along with the perennially annoyed Xers will be the fodder for sitcoms. *(890 words)*

Adapted from: http://www.fastcompany.com/magazine/l03/open_essay-demographics.html?page=O%25%2C2)

Task III: Mediation Englisch – Deutsch
(Demographics: The Population Hourglass) 8 credits
Lesen Sie den Text „Demographics: The Population Hourglass" und tragen Sie die entsprechende Information auf Deutsch in die folgende Tabelle ein.

1. Welcher Vorwurf wird unseren gesellschaftlichen Entscheidungsträgern im ersten Absatz gemacht?		(1)
2. Wie verändert sich die Form der US-amerikanischen „Alterspyramide" bis 2016?	Idealform: Pyramide Derzeit: _____ In Zukunft: _____	(1)
3. Der Autor schreibt von einer **multi-decade „boomerocracy"** (Z. 33). A) Was sagt er damit über die Babyboomer aus? B) Seine Begründung?	A: _____ B: _____	(2)

2011-8

4. Wie wird sich die Generation der Babyboomer auf das Arbeitsleben der Generation X auswirken? Begründung! (2)

5. Nennen Sie vier Aspekte, die die Millenniums-Generation zu einer Bedrohung für die Generation X machen. (2)

Aufgabenteil: *Writing*

Task IV: Mediation Deutsch – Englisch „Deutschland – kein Ziel für Top-Leute"

Deutschland ist als Einwanderungsziel für Hochqualifizierte aus dem Ausland nicht mehr erste Wahl. Im Wettbewerb um die besten Köpfe in Europa liege Deutschland inzwischen nur noch im Mittelfeld. So heißt es in einer am Dienstag veröffentlichten Studie des Bundesinstituts für Bevölkerungsforschung im Auftrag der Bertelsmann
5 Stiftung (Gütersloh). Zu ähnlichen Befunden kommt eine Umfrage des DIHK (Deutscher Industrie- und Handelskammertag)* unter 47 Außenhandelskammern.

Der Studie des Bundesinstituts für Bevölkerungsforschung zufolge verlor Deutschland zwischen 2005 und 2009 unter dem Strich jährlich etwa 1 500 Führungskräfte und Wissenschaftler an die westlichen EU-Länder (EU-15-Länder). Inzwischen seien
10 Schweden, Spanien, Österreich, Großbritannien und Belgien an Deutschland vorbeigezogen.

Ob die Öffnung des Arbeitsmarkts für die osteuropäischen EU-12-Länder im nächsten Jahr die Situation in Deutschland grundlegend verändern werde, sei ungewiss, sagte der Vorstandsvorsitzende der Stiftung, Gunter Thielen. Notwendig sei darum eine
15 neue Einwanderungspolitik in Deutschland.

„Wir können uns dabei an erfolgreichen Einwanderungsgesellschaften orientieren und das Beste aus den unterschiedlichen Systemen der Zuwanderungssteuerung übernehmen", sagte Thielen. Die Stiftung empfiehlt eine Kombination der etwa in Kanada oder Großbritannien praktizierten Modelle, die vor allem auf die Qualifikation der
20 Zuwanderer setzen, mit Modellen wie in Schweden, die sich enger an den Bedürfnissen des heimischen Arbeitsmarktes orientieren.

Ungeachtet des absehbar hohen Bedarfs an qualifizierten Zuwanderern tue die Bundesrepublik zu wenig, um Experten aus anderen Staaten anzulocken, beklagt der DIHK in seiner noch nicht veröffentlichten Studie, aus der die *Frankfurter Rundschau*
25 am Dienstag zitierte. Der Umfrage zufolge landet die Bundesrepublik auf der Skala zwischen eins („attraktiv") und fünf („unattraktiv") bei einem Wert von 2,8.

Als Hauptproblem für die sinkende Attraktivität Deutschlands wird die Sprache genannt. In vielen Ländern werde Deutsch kaum mehr als Fremdsprache gelernt; dies liege auch daran, dass aus Kostengründen viele Goethe-Institute geschlossen würden und der Deutsche Akademische Austauschdienst sowie Auslandsschulen ihre Angebote reduzierten. Problematisch seien auch die komplizierten und regional unterschiedlichen Bestimmungen für Aufenthalts- und Arbeitsgenehmigungen in Deutschland. Zudem würden sich qualifizierte Kräfte etwa aus der Türkei und Polen in Deutschland oft unerwünscht fühlen. *(346 Wörter)*

www.stern.de, 16. November 2010, bearbeitet
* Die Abkürzung DIHK kann verwendet werden.

Worksheet
Task IV: Mediation Deutsch–Englisch
(Deutschland – kein Ziel für Top-Leute) 12 credits
Fassen Sie den Artikel zusammen, indem Sie die unterstrichenen Textstellen sinngemäß ins Englische übertragen. Verfassen Sie hierfür einen zusammenhängenden Text im Umfang von ca. 150 Wörtern.

Task V: Argumentative Writing 24 credits
Choose **one** of the following tasks. Write **at least 220 words**.

1. **Composition**

    In 2010 America was confronted with the worst oil spill in US history. A 7.0-magnitude earthquake devastated Haiti. But many people have already forgotten about these events. What might be the reasons why many people seem to suffer from **disaster fatigue**?

2. **Composition**

    Despite international efforts to fight child labour, it is still commonplace in many parts of the world. Explain why.

Lösungsvorschläge

Aufgabenteil: *Reading*

Task I: Mixed Reading *(The Story of an Hour)*
Multiple Choice Questions
1 A, 2 C, 3 C, 4 C, 5 B, 6 A

Hinweise: Beachten Sie, dass die Fragen in dieser Multiple Choice-Aufgabe nicht konsequent der Textstruktur folgen. Die Fragen 5 und 6 scheren aus der Chronologie aus. Lassen Sie sich auch nicht davon verunsichern, dass bei sechs Teilaufgaben dreimal Option C die richtige Lösung ist.

zu 1: Die relevante Textstelle ist: He „had hastened to forestall any less careful, less tender friend" (Z. 7/8) – er wollte einem möglicherweise weniger achtsamen und empfindsamen Freund zuvorkommen. Das bedeutet, dass er sich als echten Freund der ganzen Familie betrachtet, und dass er nicht nur „[h]er husband's friend" (Z. 4) ist.

zu 2: Hier geht es nicht um Frau Mallards individuelles Verhalten, sondern um ein Reaktionsmuster, das auf viele Frauen zutrifft („a number of women" in der Aufgabenstellung, „as many women" im Text, Z. 9); „utter disbelief" (Option C) heißt so viel wie „völlig ungläubig" – dem entspricht im Text „with a paralyzed inability" (Z. 9/10), was bedeutet, dass jemand wie gelähmt ist und etwas nicht akzeptieren kann oder will. Optionen A und D beziehen sich nur auf Frau Mallard, Option B kommt nicht vor.

zu 3: Schlüsselstellen sind „the kind, tender hands" (Z. 42), die zärtlichen Hände ihres Mannes, und mehr noch „the face that had never looked save with love upon her" (Z. 43) („save" = hier „außer"). Ihr Mann hatte sie immer voller Liebe angesehen, hegte also tiefe Gefühle für sie. Option A stimmt nicht, da es im Text heißt „[s]he was young" (Z. 25). Option B trifft nicht zu, weil es im Text keinen Hinweis darauf gibt, dass ihre Vorfreude auf die Freiheit sich aus ihrer Erinnerung speist. Option D kommt im Text nicht vor.

zu 4: Option A trifft zu: „self-assertion [...] the strongest impulse of her being" (Z. 52/53) – Ihr Selbstbehauptungswille ist ihr stärkster innerer Antrieb, Liebe empfindet sie dagegen als einengend. Option B ebenfalls: „A kind intention or a cruel intention made the act seem no less a crime" (Z. 49) Option D stimmt ebenso: „no powerful will bending hers" (Z. 47) – „coercion" (Option D) bedeutet „Zwang, Nötigung". Sie ist der Meinung, dass Männer wie Frauen immer versuchen, dem Partner ihren Willen aufzuzwingen. Nur Option C trifft nicht zu und ist damit die richtige Antwort.

zu 5: „[S]omething" (Z. 29) steht für ein Gefühl, das die Frau ganz allmählich erfüllt. Zunächst ängstigt es sie („fearfully", Z. 29), dann macht es sie unruhig („her bosom rose and fell tumultuously", Z. 33), dann versucht sie, es zu verdrängen („striving to beat it back", Z. 34), schließlich lässt sie es zu ("she abandoned herself", Z. 35/36). Ein Gefühl von Freiheit entsteht („free, free,

free", Z. 37), sie entspannt sich (*"the coursing blood warmed and relaxed every inch of her body"*, Z. 39), sie hat eine Ahnung von gewaltiger Freude („*monstrous joy"*, Z. 40) und sie beginnt, sich auf die Zukunft zu freuen („*a long procession of years to come that would belong to her absolutely [...] she spread her arms out to them in welcome"*, Z. 44/45). Diese Entwicklung spricht für Option B („*relief"* = Erleichterung) – die weiteren Optionen beschreiben nur kurze Momente in dieser Entwicklung.

zu 6: Bereits in Zeile 1 heißt es: "*Mrs. Mallard was afflicted with heart trouble"* – es war also allgemein bekannt, dass sie herzkrank war. Einen weiteren Hinweis gibt Josephine's Ausruf "*you will make yourself ill*" (Z. 56/57).

Mediation Englisch–Deutsch

7. Erklären Sie die Ironie im letzten Satz: "When the doctors came they said she had died ... – of the joy that kills."	**Die Ironie besteht darin, dass die Außenstehenden selbstverständlich davon ausgehen, dass es die Freude über das unerwartete Auftauchen ihres Mannes ist, die sie umbringt, weil dies zu viel ist für ihr Herz. In Wahrheit ist es aber das Erschrecken über sein Auftauchen, das die soeben gewonnene Freiheit wieder zunichtemacht.**

Task II: Multiple Matching (Arizona's Crackdown on Migrants)

Hinweise:

zu A: Es geht um Nogales in Arizona, also in den USA. Nach Lücke A heißt es "*the town – and the US nation here – ends abruptly, butted [...] by a fence*" (Z. 4–6). Es handelt sich also um das US-amerikanische Nogales, das ganz nah am Zaun und damit an der Grenze liegt („*frontier town on a frontline"*).

zu B: Die Passagen „*on the other side, clinging to the fence"* (Satz 6) und „*city sliced down the middle"* (Z. 8/9) machen deutlich, dass Nogales aussieht wie eine einzige Stadt, die durch einen Zaun geteilt ist. Daher scheidet Satz 2 aus, denn er besagt, dass zwischen dem US-amerikanischen und dem mexikanischen Nogales noch Hügel liegen.

zu C: Hier braucht man für die Lösung einen Satz, der einen Bezug herstellt zu „*that person"* (Z. 15), deren möglicherweise illegalen Zuwandererstatus und einer daraus resultierenden Verhaftung (vgl. Z. 15/16).

zu D: In Absatz vor Lücke D geht es um kritische Stimmen zum neuen Gesetz und seinen Folgen – Lösungssatz Nr. 5 wischt diese Kritik für die Mehrheit der Einwohner Arizonas vom Tisch („*All the same"* = egal). Satz 4 kommt auch aus grammatikalischen Gründen nicht in Frage, denn an die vorausgehende Formulierung „*Some of them are doubtful"* (Z. 21) müsste sich anschließen "*So is Barack Obama"*, nicht "*So does Barack Obama"*.

zu E: Hier braucht man einen sinnvollen Anschluss an „*people trying to cross into America"* (Z. 32/33). Dass illegale Einwanderer, die sich vermutlich meilenweit durchs Gelände geschlagen haben, müde und durstig sind, liegt nahe.

zu F: Der Schlüssel zur Lösung ist die Bedeutung von *"Some here take no chances"* (Satz 11) = Manche Menschen hier gehen kein Risiko ein. Im Absatz vor Lücke F werden die gefährlichen Zustände im Grenzgebiet angedeutet: ein mutmaßlich von Illegalen erschossener Viehzüchter und Drogengeschäfte. Dagegen schützen sich manche Einwohner der Region, indem sie keine Risiken eingehen und, wie Peggy Davis, immer ein Gewehr dabei haben (vgl. Z. 43).

zu G: Der inhaltliche Rahmen ist hier: Arizonas Gouverneur ist wie Peggy Davis der Meinung („agrees", Z. 47), dass in der Vergangenheit die Regierung in Washington („our government has not done what they need [...] national security issue" Z. 45/45) nicht genug getan hat, um die Einwanderung in geordnete Bahnen zu lenken. Lücke G muss eine Person nennen, die zu „he" in Zeile 48 passt – dazu bieten sich die Sätze 4 und 7 an. Satz 7 besagt, dass ein Politiker der Republikaner in ähnlicher Weise die US-Regierung unterstützt. Im Kontext ist aber von Kritik an der Regierung die Rede. Mehr Sinn ergibt Satz 4: Präsident Obama teilt die Kritik des Gouverneurs und sieht die Schuld ebenfalls bei der in der Vergangenheit untätigen Regierung (d. h. bei seinem Vorgänger), wodurch es nun zu so rigiden Gesetzen wie in Arizona komme.

zu H: Schlüsselwörter und -passagen aus der Umgebung von Lücke H sind: „small children huddled by the metal fence [...] family separated" (Z. 52/53). Dazu passen in Satz 1 „man", „caressed (= streicheln)", „daughters", „through the iron stakes (= Eisenstäbe des Zaunes)".

Gap	Sentence
A	3
B	6
C	8
D	5
E	9
F	11
G	4
H	1

Task III: Mediation Englisch – Deutsch
(Demographics: The Population Hourglass)

Hinweise:

zu 1: Schlüsselstelle: Z. 3–5. Laut Text ist die Demografie ein nahezu schicksalhaftes Thema ("[it] isn't destiny, but it's close" Z. 3). Doch die Entscheidungsträger („leaders", Z. 3) versäumen es, demografische Aspekte zu berücksichtigen („miss the boat on", Z. 4 = bzgl. etwas nicht auf der Höhe der Zeit sein).

zu 2: Schlüsselstelle: Z. 20–24. Derzeit („current US pyramid", Z. 21) hat die Alterspyramide der USA nicht mehr die Idealform, sondern eine bauchige Mitte („billowing out from its midsection", Z. 22). In Zukunft wird sie die Form einer

Sanduhr annehmen („assume the form of an hourglass", Z. 23/24).
zu 3: Schlüsselstelle: Z: 32–34. Hier ist es wichtig, den Aspekt „multi-decade" nicht zu übersehen. Die Babyboomer werden auf viele Jahrzehnte politisch das Sagen haben („political clout", Z. 34 = politischer Einfluss), weil sie bzw. die älteren Leute, die sie dann sein werden, häufiger wählen gehen („tend to vote more frequently", Z. 33).
zu 4: Schlüsselstelle: Z. 55–61. Im diesem Absatz geht es um das Aufeinandertreffen von Babyboomern und Generation X im Arbeitsleben. Einerseits wird es für die Generation X viele Arbeitsplätze geben („job boom", Z. 56; „vacating boomers, who will leave open far more jobs", Z. 57; „vacating" bedeutet, dass sie ihre Arbeitsplätze räumen, also frei machen), weil viele Babyboomer in Rente gehen. Andererseits wird es für manche aus der Generation X schwierig, beruflich aufzusteigen („trapped behind a new glass ceiling", Z. 59), weil manche Babyboomer ihre Stellen eben nicht räumen („can't or won't retire", Z. 60/61) – sie sind noch so fit („all-too-healthy", Z. 60) oder brauchen das Geld („all-too-indebted", Z. 60).
zu 5: Schlüsselstelle: Z. 62–65. Mit der Millenniums-Generation werden sehr viele („en masse", Z. 63) Arbeitskräfte („workforce", Z. 63) auf den Arbeitsmarkt drängen. Folgende Eigenschaften dieser Generation könnten eine Bedrohung für die Generation X sein:
– unbändiger Karrierehunger („ravenous careerism", Z. 63/64)
– sehr gute Computerkenntnisse und selbstverständlicher Umgang mit sozialen Netzwerken (vgl. Z. 64)
– Wissensdurst („thirst for learning", Z. 64)
– keine Berührungsängste gegenüber Vorgesetzten/Management (vgl. Z. 65)

1. Welcher Vorwurf wird unseren gesellschaftlichen Entscheidungsträgern im ersten Absatz gemacht?	Die Entscheidungsträger versäumen es, demografische Aspekte zu berücksichtigen
2. Wie verändert sich die Form der US-amerikanischen „Alterspyramide" bis 2016?	Idealform: Pyramide Derzeit: **bauchige Mitte** In Zukunft: **Sanduhr**
3. Der Autor schreibt von einer multi-decade „boomerocracy" (Z. 33). A) Was sagt er damit über die Babyboomer aus? B) Seine Begründung?	A: **Die Babyboomer werden auf viele Jahrzehnte politisch das Sagen haben.** B: **Die Wahlbeteiligung ist generell bei älteren Leuten (die die Babyboomer dann sein werden) höher.**

2011-14

4. Wie wird sich die Generation der Babyboomer auf das Arbeitsleben der Generation X auswirken? Begründung!	Einerseits wird es für die Generation X viele Arbeitsplätze geben, weil viele Babyboomer in Rente gehen. Andererseits wird es für manche aus der Generation X schwierig, beruflich aufzusteigen, weil einige Babyboomer ihre Stellen eben nicht räumen – sie sind noch so fit oder sind auf das Einkommen angewiesen.
5. Nennen Sie vier Aspekte, die die Millenniums-Generation zu einer Bedrohung für die Generation X machen.	• unbändiger Karrierehunger • natürlicher Umgang mit sozialen Netzwerken und hohe IT-Kompetenz • Wissensdurst • keine Berührungsängste gegenüber Vorgesetzten

Aufgabenteil: *Writing*

Task IV: Mediation Deutsch–Englisch (Deutschland – kein Ziel für Top-Leute)

Hinweise: In folgender Musterlösung sind verschiedene mögliche Alternativen (in Klammern) angegeben. Entscheiden Sie sich in der Prüfung aber unbedingt für eine Variante, Sie riskieren sonst Punktabzug.

Germany is no longer first choice for the highly qualified from abroad (for highly qualified immigrants), according to a study by the Bertelsmann Stiftung and a survey by the DIHK.
Between 2005 and 2009 each year Germany lost approximately 1,500 executives and scientists to western EU countries.
That is why a new migration policy is essential. (Therefore, experts call for a new migration policy in Germany.)
The Bertelsmann Stiftung recommends a combination of the system which is applied in Canada or Great Britain and favours qualified immigrants and the system which is applied in Sweden and is focussed on the needs of the local labour market. (It would be of use to combine the Canadian or British approach, which puts particular emphasis on the qualifications of migrants, with the Swedish approach, which caters to the needs of the local job market.)
Despite the foreseeable lack of (high demand for) qualified immigrants, Germany (the Federal Republic) is not trying hard enough to attract (lure / entice) experts from abroad, the DIHK complains.
The main problem behind Germany's declining (diminishing) attractiveness is the fact that there are hardly any countries in which German is taught as a foreign language.
A further problem is that the German regulations for residential and work permits are very complex and differ regionally. (Another problem is that the rules which allow

people to settle and work in Germany are very complex and vary from one federal state to another.)
Apart from that, qualified staff from countries like Turkey or Poland often feel they are not welcome in Germany. *(177 words)*

Task V: Argumentative Writing

1. **Composition**

Hinweise: Bei dieser Aufgabenstellung geht es im Kern nicht um Argumente und Lösungsvorschläge, sondern um Ursachenforschung, warum Menschen Katastrophen so schnell vergessen. Möglicher Aufbau:
1) Hinführung zum Thema
2) Ursachenforschung
  – disasters seem to be far away
  – one's own life is often hard enough
  – thinking about the cruel world all the time causes depression
  – disasters may call for a change of attitude which we do not like
  – new things happen that are more important
3) Abrundung des Aufsatzes mit einem Fazit, Ausblick, o. Ä.

The 1984 famine in Ethiopia, the 1989 spill in Alaska when the oil tanker Exxon Valdez ran aground, the 2004 Indian Ocean tsunami, the 2010 earthquake devastating Haiti, the 2010 Deepwater Horizon oil spill – those disastrous events hit the headlines for weeks. Yet, except for the 1986 nuclear accident in Chernobyl, most people seem to have forgotten about them. Even the 2011 nuclear accident in Fukushima is no longer front-page news. Why is that?

Firstly, for people in the developed world, most disasters seem far away. People starve in Africa, crude oil pollutes the Gulf of Mexico: people in the developed world do not feel affected.

Secondly, we are individuals. We have our own individual joys and sorrows, and that is why, at the end of the day, we care more about ourselves than about others, even if they have a hard time.

Apart from that, thinking about the cruelty and misery of life, about what humans and the environment have to endure will get you nowhere. It will depress you, but people don't like being depressed.

Furthermore, environmental disasters often call for a change of attitude and lifestyle: switching to public transport, going by bike rather than by car, eating less meat, accepting higher prices etc. These resolutions are welcome in speeches, but when it comes to taking action people tend to hesitate and forget.

Last, but not least, there is always more recent news. After Fukushima we have had the peaceful revolutions in Tunisia and Egypt, the civil war in Libya, the killing of Osama Bin Laden, the impending bankruptcy of Greece, the first Green governor in Germany. Important things happen and replace the previously important things.

Though we should all aim to be responsible citizens of the world, we must bear in mind that we have our individual trouble to cope with, financially, on the job, in our love lives. We needn't be worried about disaster fatigue. People are moved, people care, people become indifferent ... that's the way of the world.

(335 words)

2. **Composition**

   Hinweise: Auch bei dieser Aufgabenstellung geht es im Kern nicht um Argumente, Alternativen oder Lösungsvorschläge, sondern um Ursachenforschung, warum Kinderarbeit immer noch so weit verbreitet ist. Möglicher Aufbau:
   1) Hinführung zum Thema
   2) Ursachenforschung
   *   – child labour makes products cheap*
   *   – customers often don't care about conditions of production*
   *   – families need the income generated by their children*
   *   – it's difficult enforcing laws against child labour*
   3) Abrunden des Aufsatzes mit einem Fazit, Ausblick, o. Ä.

In October 2010, the ARD, a leading German TV station, broadcast "Kinderschinder", a documentary on child labour and the dreadful living and working conditions on coffee plantations in Guatemala. Even 8-year-olds had to carry sacks of coffee beans weighing 25 kilos. For reasons like that child labour certainly has a bad reputation, but it is still commonplace. Why is that?

First of all, children usually work for far less than the legal minimum wage. Thus child labour lowers the cost of production, makes products cheaper and more competitive.

Moreover, many customers in First World countries lack awareness of poor working conditions. Though fair-trade labels such as Gepa are gaining ground in the fields of food and clothing, they are still an issue for just a minority. Most people continue to focus on low prices and mainstream appearance.

A very tricky aspect of the issue is the fact that for many Third World families the additional income generated by their children is of vital importance. They simply depend on it to make a living – this may be one reason why international efforts to fight child labour come to nothing.

Another reason is that many governments refuse to enforce international agreements. Local interest groups, lobbyism and a lack of democratic structures impair the rule of law.

International efforts to fight child labour can only be successful if the international community works on spreading the rule of law and promoting education, economic independence and sustainability. In the long run, consumers worldwide and their demand for fair-trade products have a key role. Only then can international efforts bear fruit.

(265 words)

Berufliche Oberschulen Bayern – Englisch 13. Klasse
Abiturprüfung 2012

Aufgabenteil: *Reading*

Text I: **Round Ireland with a fridge** by Tony Hawks

On arrival at Dublin Airport, I had been met by Seamus's lifelong friend Kieran and driven to Cavan. As we headed north I noticed a figure by the side of the road, hitchhiking. I looked closer, as one does with hitch-hikers, to make this split-second assessment of their appearance to judge their suitability for travel companionship. This
5 was odd. Very odd. He had something alongside him and he was leaning on it. It was a fridge. This man was hitch-hiking with a fridge.
"Kieran, was that man hitch-hiking with a fridge?" "Oh, yeah." There was nothing in Kieran's voice to suggest the slightest hint of surprise. [**Gap A** – Sentence …]

Years passed. [...]

10 The fridge incident was forgotten, banished to the recesses of my mind where matters of infinitesimal consequence belonged. It took alcohol in excess to throw it back up again. The occasion was a dinner party with some friends down in Brighton. A vast quantity of wine had been consumed and the atmosphere was, shall we say, lively. Round about midnight those present settled on a short discussion on the merits of the
15 new fridge which Kevin (another friend of Seamus's) had bought, and then, by a series of turns, our raddled attention was given to a trip he was planning to Ireland. [**Gap B** – Sentence …] Kevin's response was unambiguous. "Bollocks."
"It's not bollocks," I countered. I had hoped this would see him off, but there was more. "Yes, it is. Nobody could ever get a lift with a fridge." "They could in Ireland,
20 it's a magical place."
When I woke in the morning, in a physical condition which served as a reminder as to what had taken place the night before, I found a note by my bed: "I hereby bet Tony Hawks the sum of One Hundred Pounds that he cannot hitch-hike round the circumference of Ireland, with a fridge, within one calendar month." And there was
25 Kevin's signature, and below it, an illegible squiggle which I took to be mine. And so, the bet was made.
Now, it's no good me pretending that the gauntlet had been thrown down and that my honour was at stake if I didn't pick it up and rise to the challenge set down before me. I had been drunk and so had Kevin. I rang him up. The last thing he was going to
30 do was to hold me to something he could barely remember having taken place. So why, a month later did I find myself seriously considering taking the bet on? [**Gap C** – Sentence …]
Alas, I had been struck down with what psychoanalysts refer to as G.T.D.S.B.S. syndrome[1]. Naturally, the adopted logic of those suffering from G.T.D.S.B.S. syndrome

is flawed and can be easily exposed. I cite a short conversation I had with a mountaineer (mountaineers are probably the most common casualties of this phenomenon) as an example of how easily this may be achieved: "Why, in the bitter conditions of an Alpine winter, are you tackling the dangerous and challenging northeastern face of the fearsome Matterhorn?" "Because it's there." I think it was an American who came up with the adage "if it ain't hurting, it ain't working". It would be nice to think that shortly after he uttered those words someone smacked him in the mouth by way of demonstrating how well it was working for him. I would sit up late at night weighing up the pros and cons. All right, the cons won hands down, but there were times when I managed to make the whole thing seem glamorous. An adventure, the unknown, the chance to do something no one had done before. Wow! – something no one had done before. That's something most of us can only dream of.

I was reminded of something Nigel Walker (a former Olympic hurdler) had said: There are two words I don't want to find myself uttering as an old man, and they are "If only …" If only. We all have our own "if onlys". If only I'd studied harder, if only I'd stuck with those piano lessons, if only I'd spoken to that girl at the bus stop. The trick is to be masters of our own destiny in so far as we have control, and take the rest on the chin with a wry smile. But we must go for it! [**Gap D** – Sentence …]

And so it was that I found myself in an electric superstore looking at fridges. And there were some magnificent models on the market.

[…]

After a few weeks travelling with his fridge, Tony is about to complete his journey successfully and therefore win his bet.

As I walked out of that restaurant pulling my fridge behind me for the last time, everyone on Gerry's[2] table began applauding politely. [**Gap E** – Sentence …] Others looked up to see what was going on, and when they saw me and a fridge (we had become famous in the meantime due to the local papers and the radio stations), they applauded, possibly thinking it was somehow expected of them. I felt great. [**Gap F** – Sentence …]

This moment was a special one and I cherished it. I looked round and saw the Gerry Ryan table were still all on their feet, and others in the room were rising to theirs. Just incredible. [**Gap G** – Sentence …] Tough. They wouldn't be interested in this anyway – this happened.

So it was that a Triumphal Exit was to prove the fitting climax to this strangely moving adventure. I was glad that I was to leave Ireland exactly as I had found it over the previous four weeks. Warm, accommodating and enjoying a drink. I was leaving Ireland. The affair was over, but the friendship had just begun.

(about 938 words – abridged and adapted)

Adapted from: © Tony Hawks: *Round Ireland with a fridge*. Random House, London 1998

Annotation
1 G.T.D.S.B.S. syndrome – GOING TO DO SOMETHING A BIT SILLY syndrome
2 Anchorman of the Gerry Ryan Show, an Irish radio programme which broadcast reports on Tony's adventures.

2012-2

Worksheet
Task I: Multiple Matching *(Round Ireland with a fridge)*   7 credits

You are going to read the text "Round Ireland with a fridge". Seven sentences have been removed from the extract. Choose from the sentences 1–11 the one which fits each gap (A–G) best. There are four extra sentences which do not fit.

Gap	A	B	C	D	E	F	G
Sentence							

1	When I did get round to calling Kevin after that night, he had only a very sketchy recollection of the whole sorry saga.
2	When the Hollywood script is written, this ending might be considered too schmaltzy.
3	Astonishingly, some people on a few of the other tables started to join in.
4	It was a disheartening finale that was neither moving, uplifting nor a fitting conclusion to the whole ridiculous affair.
5	Far from being an encumbrance, the fridge became a momentary focus for the people in Ireland growing into a personality in its own right.
6	Only a fool would squander the rich opportunities which life affords us.
7	Or leave it altogether.
8	Finally, almost all the restaurant's diners were offering their spontaneous and unaffected appreciation of someone for whom they had a peculiar humble respect.
9	I had clearly arrived in a country where qualification for "eccentric" involved a great deal more than to which I had become used.
10	There was no need, no need at all, and yet there I was looking at a map of Ireland and trying to work out the mileage involved in making its coastal circuit.
11	The juxtaposition of my friends triggered a triumphal re-emergence of my fridge hitch-hiking story, which I relayed to the guests via a long-winded collection of badly slurred words.

Text II: Why I'm becoming an American by Simon Winchester

Forty years ago, this country embraced a broke Brit. On July 4, I'm giving back – with the oath of citizenship.

(A) My love affair with America began with a vast disappointment, back in 1959. My father had been offered a job as an engineer in Tulsa, Okla. My mother and I, overjoyed at the idea of exchanging our shabby little life in north London for the magic of the prairies – all high grass, sunshine, oil wells, and longhorn cattle – sold
5 the house, packed up our belongings, booked ourselves on an ocean liner. And then, the night before sailing, my father got cold feet and canceled everything.

(B) I was crushed – but vowed to go, one day, and see for myself the dream that had been so cruelly snatched away. Four years later I seized the opportunity. I took a year off before Oxford, [...] hitched 38,000 American highway miles, and it cost me just
10 $ 18. I had entered at Blaine with 200 crisp bills in my pocket; and when six months later I left for Canada by way of Houlton, Maine, I had 182 of them left. Such kindness I had never known. The experience changed me, profoundly. That summer, somewhere inside me was germinated the vague idea that one day I might make common cause with these kindly, warm, open folk, and even eventually become (as I
15 heard it was possible to do) one of them.

(C) Ten years later I was back, this time as a young reporter, and assigned to cover one of the most extraordinary episodes ever to befall the country: the resignation of a president, over Watergate. For 30 months I watched transfixed as the ponderous machinery of America's democracy cranked itself up to answer, it seemed, the ulti-
20 mate wish of the public. To get rid of British heads of state had for centuries required execution, the head on the block. Here it seemed, and more properly, it was the people who enjoyed the greater measure of sovereignty. A people I now even more urgently wanted to join.

(D) But there was more. I had come to Washington from Belfast from reporting on
25 three horror-filled years of hatred and killing. Stripped of its subtleties, the violence there stemmed from a mutual hatred between Ulster Protestants and Irish Catholics – so long as they were confined to Ulster. But then many Belfast friends moved away, to escape. I soon came to reconnect with some who had moved to America – couples who had loathed one another back in the Six Counties, but who now, in Chicago,
30 Seattle, and Dallas, far from hating one another, had married, had produced children, had quite forgotten the need to hate. And still others, people who had arrived here mired in the hostilities of other homelands – immigrants from the Balkans, the Levant[1], and Indochina were among those I came to know best – soon found their ancient animosities were fading into insignificance, too. Their experience only rein-
35 forced my feeling: the argument for my joining this extraordinary experiment in improving the human condition – an imperfect experiment at times, of course – grew steadily more powerful.

(E) The tug of home at first proved fierce, difficult to resist. It exerted an ever more powerful pull the longer I stayed away. I went off to live in India, then spent a dozen years in Hong Kong – and perhaps because I was convinced that imperial Britain, which when I lived in these outposts was still held in high esteem, had done a great deal of good for its faraway subjects, I used to feel no small sense of pride in being an Englishman. Except that once Hong Kong passed back into the hands of China, in the summer of 1997, I came back – and not to London as was expected of me, but by choice, to New York.

(F) As I settled into the rhythms of that unmatchable city, so, bit by bit my jingoistic leanings started to fade, and I began to consider what truly mattered to me, about the society in which I wanted to live out the rest of my days. I used to stroll at lunchtime down to the waterfront at the Battery, and list those attributes of Home I felt I could abandon. Though at first I felt a traitor, a heretic, I realized I would feel no qualms at all about turning my back on the notions of royalty, on the bizarre idea of an established church, on inherited privilege, on the House of Lords, on class divisions, and on the relative want of opportunity. It was this last that pushed me over the edge. By now, I was prospering, and in a way and to a degree that I felt I could never have done back home. I felt so deeply grateful to America in consequence, beholden. I now truly wanted to throw in my lot, to play in full my part in America's making and its future.

(G) Yet I couldn't: I wasn't allowed to vote. Except – what was the rallying cry, born in Massachusetts, all those years ago: no taxation without representation? Well, I told myself: I pay taxes. I demand to vote. I must vote. I must share in the right to help throw the rascals out, or keep the good ones in. And so in due course – coincident with President Obama's election, which set the capstone on it all – I submitted my application, setting in motion the formal procedure leading to the ceremony in which I will take part this Independence Day. [...]

(H) The ceremony will be held in Boston at teatime on July 4, aboard the USS Constitution, the majestic three-masted sailing frigate that is the oldest commissioned floating warship in the world. The fact that she played so heroic a role in the War of 1812 against the British invests her with a symbolism that, for me at least, is both powerful and ironic: for I will walk on to her foredeck as a Briton, swear a powerful oath before her commander, and walk back down the gangplank as a newly minted American. [...]

(988 words – abridged)

Adapted from: Copyright © 2011 by Simon Winchester. "Why I'm Becoming An American" by Simon Winchester was first published in Newsweek on June 26, 2011.

Annotation
1 The far eastern part of the Mediterranean, from the Sinai peninsula, through Israel, Lebanon and Syria, and along the Turkish coast

Task II: Mixed Reading Tasks (*Why I'm becoming an American*)   10 credits
Mediation E–D   5 credits

Beantworten Sie die nachfolgenden Fragen <u>auf Deutsch</u>.

1. Welche von ihm als positiv erlebten Ereignisse bzw. Gefühlslagen schildert der Autor in den Absätzen C–F bezüglich seiner alten Heimat Großbritannien sowie den USA? (4)

Großbritannien	•
USA	•
	•
	•

2. Erläutern Sie, was der Autor mit dem Hinweis "symbolism that … is both powerful and ironic" meint (Absatz H). (1)

_____
_____
_____
_____
_____
_____

Gapped Summary   5 credits

Fill in the gaps with words taken from the text (one word per line), but do not make any adjustments or changes.

Already early in his life, when a stay in the USA he had been looking forward to so much had to be called off, Simon Winchester _____ to himself that one day he would get to know this country better.
Later, when the British journalist was _____ to report back on a political crisis, he learned to cherish firsthand what the USA offered to its citizens.

After years in different countries, he finally moved to the USA for good. There he realized that the strong patriotic _____ he still felt towards Britain were vanishing bit by bit.

In this process of adaptation he realized that there was no need for him to have _____ about his alienation from his home country.

In the past, a famous _____ _____ voiced the people's demand to elect their own legislators. By getting the citizenship Simon Winchester was finally able to obtain this fundamental right in his new home country, too.

Text III: Why the world isn't getting smaller by Rana Foroohar

(A) It is the season to be selfish. Right after the global financial crisis exploded in 2008, many economists fretted that countries looking to hold on to their share of a shrinking pie would become more self-interested and protectionist, plunging the planet into an even sharper downturn, just as it had happened in the 1930s after the Great Depression. Thanks to panic-fueled crisis management by policymakers, it didn't happen. But after three years of pain and very little economic gain, it may be happening now.

(B) The signs are everywhere. Europeans are in the middle of a potentially calamitous debt crisis, one that threatens not only the survival of the euro zone but the idea of the European Union itself: politicians are starting to talk about rolling back visa-free travel between countries. Meanwhile, OPEC is falling apart as the Saudis and the Iranians bicker over how to control the world's energy spigots. (Result: higher oil prices for all of us.) Then there's the rise of populist politics not only in the U.S. but throughout the rest of the world. Anti-E.U. political parties are gaining support around Europe, and despite the recent overthrow of several Middle Eastern strongmen, nationalism is on the rise in places like China, Brazil and Russia.

(C) All of which underscores the point that globalization, if we define it as the free movement of goods, people and money, was never all it was cracked up to be. The world is just not as flat as pundits would have us think. More than half of global trade, investment and migration still takes place within regions – much of it between neighboring countries. Canada is the U.S.'s biggest trading partner. In his very smart book World 3.0, Pankaj Ghemawat, a professor at the IESE Business School in Spain, tallied up a few telling numbers. Some 80 % of global stock-market investment, for example, is in companies that are headquartered in the investor's home country. Exports make up only about a quarter of the global economy. Only 2 % of students attend a university outside their home country. Less than 20 % of Internet traffic crosses national borders, and so on. "It's considered very with it and modern to believe that the world is becoming more unified, but if anything, it's becoming more fragmented," says Ghemawat.

(D) Some of this reflects the fact that rich countries, especially the U.S., are still much more provincial than you might think, and the political trend in an economic downturn is to become more so – witness the rise of anti-immigrant rhetoric, China bashing and the like. Even multinational corporations, those global emissaries of American capitalism, could be a lot more diverse. Only 7% of the directors of FORTUNE 500[1] firms are foreigners.

(E) But greater economic and political fragmentation is also, ironically, a ripple effect of globalization. As wealth and power have shifted to the emerging markets, those nations now have the money and confidence to call their own shots – and their calls tend to be quite different from those we would make. Already this is reflected in company and consumer behavior. Firms like Hermès, General Motors, Levi Strauss and Coca-Cola rigorously tailor products specifically for emerging-market consumers. Pizza Hut in China is a luxury restaurant complete with white tablecloths and cutlery. For poor countries, Hewlett-Packard makes a "rural" laptop that can be set out in the dust and rain.

(F) The big-picture implications are more profound. As developing countries become wealthier and vie for a better seat on the global stage, they are often at odds not only with rich nations but also with each other. Consider Brazil's anger over a flood of cheap Chinese imports, India and China's wariness over each other's military ambitions and the uneasy regional alliances within Asia among countries vying for the same manufacturing jobs.

(G) That doesn't mean globalization's a bust. In fact, more of it – in the form of freer markets, lower trade barriers and unfettered immigration – would help alleviate tensions by growing the economic pie. Good luck with that. As they see inequality rise within individual societies (even as the world's resources taken as a whole are being more equally shared), voters have become convinced that the benefits of globalization flow mainly to the rich down the street.

(H) And it's that local scene that matters. Our sense of our own reality is shaped in relation to our neighbors, not to the state of those far away, who, in many cases, are living lives that are better, richer, happier and more prosperous than they could ever have dreamed. *(755 words – abridged)*

© *TIME, 19. Juni 2011*

Annotation
1 A ranking list of America's largest corporations

Task III: Multiple Choice *(Why the world isn't getting smaller)*   7 credits
Mark the most suitable option by crossing the appropriate letter.

1. At the end of the last decade, the global economic situation ...
   A was completely underestimated by politicians.
   B made countries put up tariffs.
   C made politicians take decisions brought about by anxiety.
   D led to an accelerating global depression.

2. Which statement ist not true according to the text? Currently …
   A political agitators are growing in popularity.
   B OPEC is about to dissolve due to mutual dissent.
   C international mobility is being questioned.
   D EU authorities are considering excluding some suffering member states.

3. According to paragraph C …
   A the world is growing together.
   B trade has become more oriented towards the domestic market.
   C globalization has not met expectations.
   D exports are being limited by trade barriers.

4. The US …
   A has become more xenophobic.
   B puts tariffs on Chinese goods.
   C limits foreigners' access to executive positions.
   D has become more capitalist.

5. According to paragraph E, the newly industrialized countries …
   A show similar consumption patterns to those of the developed countries.
   B get donations from several global players.
   C turn out to be less fragmented than before.
   D have become increasingly self-assured.

6. Which statement about some industrializing countries is not mentioned in the text?
   They …
   A envy rich countries.
   B compete against each other.
   C struggle against the industrialized world.
   D are suspicious of each other.

7. In paragraph G the author claims that …
   A only rich nations profit from globalization.
   B globalization has its virtues.
   C globalization causes an economic crisis.
   D social inequality is a myth.

Aufgabenteil: *Writing*

Task IV: Mediation Deutsch – Englisch „Atom – der totalitäre Strom"

Ist der deutsche Atomausstieg wirklich ein weltweiter Sonderweg? Nein. Wer sich die Entwicklungen genau anschaut, der stellt fest: Die Kernkraft hat in Demokratien und Marktwirtschaften keine Zukunft, sie ist die Energieform der totalitären Staaten.

Die Franzosen sind sauer auf die Deutschen. Der Ausstieg aus der Atomenergie sei ein Alleingang, der sich politisch noch nachteilig auswirken werde, so die Regierung in Paris. Auch Teile der deutschen Wirtschaft sind ungehalten. Sie glauben, die wichtigste Industrienation Europas verabschiede sich ohne Not aus einer Schlüsseltechnologie, die in anderen Teilen der Welt mit großem Aufwand und Erfolg weiterbetrieben werde. Ist es also ein Fehler, die Versorgung des Landes mit Atomstrom aufzugeben?

Nein, der Ausstieg ist richtig. Er ist zu verkraften, weil die Strommengen, die aus Uran erzeugt werden, in der Welt wie in Deutschland vergleichsweise gering sind. Wie zur Bestätigung dieser These hat sich gerade auch Italien per Referendum von der Atomkraft verabschiedet. Wenige Tage zuvor verkündete die Schweiz das Ende des Atomzeitalters.

Die Atomkraft wird in der ganzen Welt kritisch gesehen, auch wenn Länder wie China oder Russland demonstrativ am Atomstrom festhalten. Diese Technologie ist teuer und problematisch. Sie birgt langfristige Risiken für die Menschen, wie sie im Fall von Fukushima wieder deutlich wurden, und sie wird politisch immer schwerer vertretbar. Der Bau von Kernkraftwerken kostet Milliarden, er dauert Jahre. Zudem ist die Frage der Entsorgung der abgebrannten Brennelemente weltweit ungeklärt. Auch deshalb wurden in den zurückliegenden Jahren vergleichsweise wenige AKWs gebaut. Nur 84 der 440 Meiler in der Welt sind jünger als 20 Jahre. Richtig ist aber auch, dass weltweit derzeit 64 Kernkraftwerke im Bau sind.

Auffällig ist, dass vor allem in Ländern gebaut wird, die Diktaturen sind oder nur Scheindemokratien. China, der größte Energieverbraucher der Zukunft, arbeitet gerade an 27 Meilern, in Russland sind es elf neue Kernkraftwerke. In diesen Ländern ist der Energiesektor klare Staatsaufgabe. Widerstand der Menschen ist unwahrscheinlich. In demokratischen und von Marktwirtschaft dominierten Ländern dagegen, wo private Investoren die Risiken und Kosten für Energieinvestitionen schultern müssen, entstehen nur wenige Meiler. Ausnahmen sind Südkorea und Indien, wo je fünf Meiler im Bau sind, ansonsten herrscht vornehme Zurückhaltung. Selbst in Frankreich, Europas Atomland Nummer eins, ist nur ein neues Nuklearkraftwerk im Entstehen, und die Medien des Landes legen Zeugnis ab davon, dass die Skepsis der Bevölkerung in Bezug auf diese Technologie wächst.

Oder haben diejenigen recht, die behaupten, der großflächige Ausbau der Kernenergie stünde in manchen Ländern erst bevor? *(399 Wörter)*

© *Süddeutsche Zeitung vom 16.6.11, Kommentar von Karl-Heinz Büschemann*

Worksheet

Task IV: Mediation Deutsch–Englisch *(Atom – der totalitäre Strom)*   12 credits

Fassen Sie den Artikel zusammen, indem Sie die unterstrichenen Textstellen sinngemäß ins Englische übertragen. Verfassen Sie hierfür einen zusammenhängenden Text im Umfang von ca. 150 Wörtern.

Task V: Argumentative Writing   24 credits

Choose **one** of the following topics. Write **at least 220 words**.

1. **Composition**

   Good looks have obviously become a major criterion in our modern world as many people judge their fellow citizens by their outward appearance. What risks do you see in this development?

2. **Composition**

   "An eye for an eye only makes the whole world blind."
   (Mahatma Gandhi)
   Do you agree with Gandhi's words when it comes to solving problems? Give reasons.

Lösungsvorschläge

Aufgabenteil: *Reading*

Task I: Multiple Matching *(Round Ireland with a fridge)*

Hinweise:

zu A: Der Protagonist Tony Hawks ist soeben in Irland angekommen (*"On arrival at Dublin Airport"*, Z. 1) und sieht eine seltsame (*"odd"*, Z. 5) Szene: ein Anhalter steht mit einem Kühlschrank am Straßenrand. Dazu passende Schlüsselbegriffe in Satz 9 sind: *"arrived in a country where [...]"*, *"eccentric"*

zu B: Die Kühlschrankgeschichte gerät zunächst in Vergessenheit (*"banished to the recesses of my mind"*, Z. 10) und erst ein feuchtfröhlicher Abend mit Freunden bringt sie wieder hervor (*"alcohol in excess to throw it back up again"*, Z. 11/12; *"occasion [...] dinner party with some friends"*, Z. 12).
Anknüpfungspunkte in Satz 11 sind: *"juxtaposition of my friends"*, *"re-emergence of my fridge hitch-hiking story"*

zu C: Wette: Irland-Umrundung per Anhalter mit Kühlschrank innerhalb eines Monats (*"hitch-hike round the circumference of Ireland, with a fridge"*, Z. 23/24). Allerdings besteht Wettpartner Kevin nicht auf der Einhaltung, da die Wette in betrunkenem Zustand eingegangen worden war und er sich kaum erinnern kann (*"The last thing he was going to do was to hold me to something he could barely remember having taken place"*, Z. 29/30). Trotzdem denkt Tony Hawks über eine Umsetzung nach (*"seriously considering taking the bet on"*, Z. 31).
Anknüpfungspunkte in Satz 10 sind: *"There was no need [...] at all"*, *"and yet"* (= und trotzdem) *"trying to work out the mileage [...] involved in making its coastal circuit"*. Im Anschluss an Lücke C findet sich das Motiv für die Annahme der Wette: das GTDSBS Syndrom.

zu D: Es geht darum, im Alter nicht sagen zu müssen „Hätte ich doch nur" (*"two words I don't want to find myself uttering as an old man ... 'If only'"* Z. 48/49). Passender Anknüpfungspunkt in Satz 6: *"rich opportunities which life affords us"*. Satz 7 ist eine Aufforderung, es ganz bleiben zu lassen (*"Or leave it altogether"*), was nicht zur Aussage passt, dass man sein eigenes Schicksal in die Hand nehmen soll (*"masters of our own destiny [...] have control"*, Z. 51).

zu E: Höflicher Applaus am Tisch (*"table applauding politely"*, Z. 59), den Tony verlässt; weitere Gäste fallen ein (Satz 3: *"other tables started to join in"*), wieder andere werden aufmerksam und klatschen dann auch (Z. 60–62).

zu F: Tony fühlt sich großartig (*"felt great"*, Z. 62) und genießt den besonderen Moment (*"This moment was a special one and I cherished it"*, Z. 64), dass so viele Gäste im Restaurant durch ihren Applaus ihre Wertschätzung zeigen (*"almost all diners were offering [...] appreciation"*, Satz 8).

zu G: Die ganze Szene ist so unglaublich und rührend, dass sie in einem Hollywood-Film zu schmalzig wirken würde (Satz 2). Satz 4 erweckt dagegen den Eindruck, dass der Autor selbst seine Geschichte und ihr Ende enttäuschend finden würde, was aber nicht der Fall ist.

Gap	A	B	C	D	E	F	G
Sentence	9	11	10	6	3	8	2

Task II: Mixed Reading Tasks *(Why I'm becoming an American)*
Mediation E–D
Hinweise: Bei dieser Aufgabe geht es darum, Textstellen in den Absätzen C bis F herauszufiltern, die positive Ereignisse und Gefühlslagen in Bezug auf die USA und Großbritannien beinhalten.

1.	Großbritannien	• Das Erbe des britischen Empire weckt im Autor patriotische Gefühle. "[...] I was convinced that imperial Britain, which when I lived in these outposts was still held in high esteem, had done a great deal of good for its faraway subjects, I used to feel no small sense of pride in being an Englishman." (Z. 41–44)
	USA	• Bewunderung für das politische System der USA, das dem Volk mehr Macht einräumt als seiner Meinung nach das britische System. Ein Schlüsselerlebnis war für ihn der Rücktritt des Präsidenten im Watergate-Skandal. "[...] the resignation of a president, over Watergate. [...] America's democracy cranked itself up to answer, it seemed, the ultimate wish of the public. [...] it was the people who enjoyed the greater measure of sovereignty. A people I now even more urgently wanted to join." (Z. 17–23)
		• Begeisterung des Autors für das friedliche Zusammenleben von Menschen unterschiedlicher ethnischer Herkunft, die sich in ihren Heimatländern befehden würden. "[...] people who had arrived here mired in the hostilities of other homelands [...] soon found their ancient animosities were fading into insignificance." (Z. 31–34)
		• Begeisterung/Dankbarkeit für die Chancen, welche die USA den Menschen bieten "By now, I was prospering, and in a way and to a degree that I felt I could never have done back home." (Z. 55–56)

2012-13

2. Genau auf dem Schiff, das im britisch-amerikanischen Krieg von 1812 eine bedeutende Rolle gespielt hatte, wird der Autor, bislang britischer Staatsbürger, ein Amerikaner.

Gapped Summary

Hinweise: Achten Sie auf die Angaben „one word per line" sowie „no adjustments or changes". Die Wörter, die Sie einsetzen sollen, erscheinen im Text in chronologischer Reihenfolge.

vowed (Z. 7): "I was crushed – but <u>vowed</u> to go, one day, and see for myself the dream that had been so cruelly snatched away."

assigned (Z. 16): "Ten years later I was back, this time as a young reporter, and <u>assigned</u> to cover one of the most extraordinary episodes ever to befall the country: the resignation of a president, over Watergate."

leanings (Z. 48): "[...] bit by bit my jingoistic (= hurrapatriotisch, chauvinistisch) <u>leanings</u> started to fade [...]"

qualms (Z. 51): "[...] I would feel no <u>qualms</u> at all about turning my back on the notions of royalty, on the bizarre idea of an established church, on inherited privilege, on the House of Lords, on class divisions, and on the relative want of opportunity."

rallying cry (Z. 59): "[...] the <u>rallying cry</u>, born in Massachusetts, all those years ago: no taxation without representation [...]"

Already early in his life, when a stay in the USA he had been looking forward to so much had to be called off, Simon Winchester **vowed** to himself that one day the would get to know this country better.

Later, when the British journalist was **assigned** to report back on a political crisis, he learned to cherish firsthand what the USA offerd to its citizens.

After years in different countries, he finally moved to the USA for good. There he realized that the strong patriotic **leanings** he still felt towards Britain were vanishing bit by bit.

In this process of adaptation he realized that there was no need for him to have **qualms** about his alienation from his home country.

In the past, a famous **rallying cry** voiced the people's demand to elect their own legislators. By getting the citizenship Simon Winchester was finally able to obtain this fundamental right in his new home country, too.

Task III: Multiple Choice *(Why the world isn't getting smaller)*

Hinweise:

zu 1: Die relevante Textstelle lautet: "Thanks to panic-fueled crisis management by policymakers, it didn't happen." (Z. 5/6) – Die Politik hat, von Sorge und Panik getrieben, Krisenmanagement betrieben, sodass es nicht zu einer wirtschaftlichen Katastrophe kam wie in den 1930er Jahren.

zu 2: Option A: "the rise of populist politics" (Z. 13); Option B: "OPEC is falling

2012-14

apart" (Z. 11); Option C: "Politicians are starting to talk about rolling back visa-free travel [...]" (Z. 10/11)

zu 3: Schlüsselstellen sind "[...] globalization [...] was never all it was cracked up to be" (Z. 17/18) – d. h., die Globalisierung hat sich nicht in allem als das erwiesen, was man erwartet hat – und *"It's [...] modern to believe that the world is becoming more unified, but [...] it's becoming more fragmented." (Z. 27–29)* – d. h. die Welt wächst nicht zusammen, wie man allgemein glaubt.

zu 4: Grundlage der richtigen Antwort ist *"[...] rise of anti-immigrant rhetoric, China bashing and the like" (Z. 32/33).*

zu 5: *"[...] the emerging markets, those nations now have the money and confidence to call their own shots ..." (Z. 37/38)* – d. h., dass die aufstrebenden Märkte/ Nationen mittlerweile selbstbewusst (= *"self-assured"*) genug sind, um ihre eigenen Trümpfe auszuspielen (= *"to call their own shots"*).

zu 6: Option A: Die *"industrializing countries"* der Fragestellung sind die *"developing countries"* im Text (Z. 45); Option B: *"often at odds with each other* (= untereinander uneins sein)*" (Z. 46/47), "... Brazil's anger over a flood of cheap Chinese imports" (Z. 47/48);* Option C: *"[...] vie for a better seat on the global stage" (Z. 46);* Option D: *"India and China's wariness* (= Vorsicht) *over each other's military ambitions" (Z. 48/49), "uneasy regional alliances within Asia" (Z. 49)*

zu 7: Die relevanten Textstellen sind: *"That doesn't mean globalization's a bust."* und *"In fact, more of it [...] would help alleviate tensions [...]" (Z. 51–53).* Die Globalisierung ist also nicht notwendigerweise ein „Reinfall" (= *"bust"*), sondern hat auch ihre positiven Seiten (= *"has its virtues"*).

1 C, 2 D, 3 C, 4 A, 5 D, 6 A, 7 B

Aufgabenteil: *Writing*

Task IV: Mediation Deutsch–Englisch

Is it a mistake to pull out of nuclear energy (or: to quit supplying the country with nuclear energy)?
No, the nuclear power phase-out is the right thing to do.
This technology involves many long-term risks and it is becoming more and more difficult to politically justify its use (or: to find political support for it).
Building nuclear power plants costs billions and takes years.
Apart from that, the disposal of nuclear waste is a global problem which has yet to be solved (or: no country in the world has yet found an answer to the question of how to get rid of nuclear waste).
That is why comparatively few nuclear power stations have been built in recent years.
It is striking that those power plants are being built primarily in countries which are dictatorships or pseudo (or: bogus) democracies.
In those countries the energy sector is the explicit responsibility of the state (or: it is

the state only that is in charge of the energy sector). Public resistance is not likely to happen. Yet, in democratic countries with market economy conditions, where private investors have to bear the risks and the costs of energy investments, only few nuclear power plants are built. *(170 words)*

Task V: Argumentative Writing

1. **Composition**

Hinweise: Bei dieser Aufgabenstellung geht es im Kern darum, dass gutes Aussehen offensichtlich in zunehmendem Maße als Kriterium für die Beurteilung von Menschen dient, was die Frage aufwirft, mit welchen Risiken diese Entwicklung verbunden ist.
Aufbau:
(1) Kurze Hinführung zum Thema
(2) Risiken und Konsequenzen
   – blinded by appearances, often lack of substance
   – inferiority complexes
   – contradiction to equality of man
(3) Abrunden des Aufsatzes mit einem Fazit, Ausblick, o. Ä.

Whatever a new trend is about, almost always it has to do with good-looking people who promote the trend. We are surrounded, for example, by stunning, perfect beauties like Rihanna, by celebrity supercouples like Brangelina, by models in casting shows like GNTM. No wonder good looks have become a kind of standard, something we expect in people though we all know that "fine feathers make fine birds" is no suitable attitude. There are a number of risks involved.

Firstly, people who are easily blinded by impressive appearances may fail to see that someone or something lacks substance. Remember the hype about Baron zu Guttenberg. A good-looking politician with casual elegance, manners and a winning smile impressed the German public in a way that a critical look at the substance of his policy was almost impossible.

Secondly, people who do not meet the standards (or who simply believe they do not or cannot meet them) may feel flawed. It requires a good deal of self-assurance to overcome that. People with low self-esteem may desperately attempt to meet the standards by emulating the celebrities en vogue. So they buy fashionable clothes and accessories and even have cosmetic operations. Some people might even develop an inferiority complex and feel excluded from the mainstream, from what is accepted and popular.

Finally, the hype about good looks contradicts a core value in democratic societies. People are born equal, no matter what their race, sex or state of health is. A society which places too much value on good looks runs the risk of being split into the good-looking, successful, influential "winners" and the "losers", who have a narrower range of opportunities and are looked down upon.

Without doubt, appearance matters and will always matter. But it is up to parents and teachers to raise a critical awareness among young people and to help build a high level of self-assurance and independence. With such awareness good looks will not obtain more importance than is appropriate. *(330 words)*

2. **Composition**

Hinweise: Bei dieser Aufgabenstellung ist es wichtig, Gandhis Aussage in Bezug zu setzen zum Thema „Lösung von Problemen/Konflikten".
Aufbau:
(1) Kurze Hinführung zum Thema
(2) Argumente, die Gandhis Sichtweise stützen
  – *solution of problems requires willingness to compromise*
  – *"an eye for an eye" leads to vicious circle of mistrust and suspicion, hatred and revenge, breakdown of communication*
  – *examples: Northern Ireland, Near East*
(3) Abrunden des Aufsatzes mit einem Fazit, Ausblick, Appell o. Ä.
  – *Gandhi's statement is without alternative*

In a certain way, Gandhi's words "An eye for an eye only makes the whole world blind" are an equivalent of Jesus's call for non-violent behaviour: "If anyone slaps you on the right cheek, turn to him the other also". Gandhi and Jesus want us to respond to an aggression without using violence.
Though this kind of attitude and behaviour may be hard to achieve and realize, it is essential when it comes to solving problems. Problems usually mean conflict and no conflict can ever be solved without a sincere willingness to compromise. In the long run an "eye-for-an-eye" attitude will undermine any attempt to work out a compromise. Instead, it will lure people into a vicious circle of mistrust and suspicion. Communication will break down and, eventually, people on either side will end up with feelings of hatred and thoughts of revenge.
This development could be seen in the so-called "Troubles" in Northern Ireland, for example, and can still be observed in the Near East conflict. For a long time the motto in Northern Ireland was "It's payback time" when Catholic and Protestant groups counted their dead, their injured and their sufferings and sought revenge. And the same goes for the ongoing conflict between Israelis and Palestinians.
It goes without saying that a non-violent attitude is hard to realize. But as long as politicians, governments and ordinary people are driven by the desire to pay others back what they had done to them, there is no chance to find a peaceful way out of conflicts. Obviously, it is essential to overcome thoughts of revenge, so at the end of the day, there is no alternative to Gandhi's words. *(279 words)*

Berufliche Oberschulen Bayern – Englisch 13. Klasse
Abiturprüfung 2013

Aufgabenteil: *Reading*

Text I: **Joseph** by Etgar Keret
The following short story by Tel Aviv-born writer Etgar Keret is set in contemporary Israel.

There are conversations that can change a person's life. I'm sure of it. I mean, I'd like to believe it. I'm sitting in a café with a producer. He's not exactly a producer, he never produced anything, but he wants to. He has an idea for a film and he wants me to write the screenplay. I explain that I don't write for films and he accepts that
5 and calls the waitress over. I'm sure he wants to ask for the check, but he orders himself another espresso instead. The waitress asks me if I want something else and I order a glass of water. The wannabe-producer's name is Yossef, but he introduces himself as Joseph. "_____ [Gap A] _____," he says, "is really called Yossef. It's always Sefi or Yossi or Yoss, so I went for Joseph." He's sharp, that Joseph.
10 Reads me like a book. "You're busy, right?" he says when he sees me glance at my watch, and immediately adds, "very busy. Traveling, working, writing emails." _____ [Gap B] _____. It's a statement of fact, or at the most, an expression of sympathy. I nod. "Not being busy scares you?" he asks. I nod again. "Me too," he says and gives me a yellow-toothed smile. "There must be something down there.
15 Something frightening. If not, we wouldn't be grinding our time so thin on all kinds of projects. And you know what scares me most?" he asks. I hesitate for a second, thinking about what to answer, but Joseph doesn't wait. "_____ [Gap C] _____," he continues, "what I am. You know that nothingness that fills you up a second after you …? Not with someone you love, just with some girl, … You know it? That's what
20 scares me, looking into myself and finding nothing there. Not your average nothingness, but the kind that totally bums you out, I don't know exactly what to call it …"
Now he's quiet. I feel uncomfortable with his silence. If we were closer, maybe I could be silent with him. But not at our first meeting. Not after a comment like that. "Sometimes," I try to return his frankness, "life seems like a trap to me. _____ [Gap D]
25 _____. And when you're inside, inside life I mean, there's no escape, except maybe suicide, which isn't really an escape, it's more like surrender. You know what I mean?"
"It's fuck-all," Joseph says. "It's just fuck-all that you won't write the screenplay." There's something very weird about the way he talks. He doesn't even curse like
30 other people. I don't know what to say after that, so I keep quiet. "Never mind," he says after a minute. "_____ [Gap E] _____. And that's the best part of this business. I don't think the actual producing is for me." I must have nodded because he reacts to it. "You think I don't have it, right? That I'm not really a producer, that

2013-1

I'm just some guy with a little money from his parents who talks a lot." I must still be nodding, unintentionally, from the pressure, because now he's laughing. "_____ [Gap F] _____," he says, "or maybe not, maybe I'll surprise you. Maybe I'll surprise myself." Joseph asks for the check and insists on paying. "What about our waitress?" he asks while we wait for his credit card to be swiped, "You figure she's trying to escape too? From herself, I mean?" I shrug. "And that guy who just walked in, with the coat? Look how he's sweating. He's definitely running away from something. Maybe we'll form a start-up. Instead of the film – a program that finds people who are trying to run away from themselves, who are afraid of what they might find out. It could be a hit." I look at the sweaty guy in the coat. _____ [Gap G] _____. Afterwards, in the hospital, foreign journalists will ask me to describe him and I'll say I don't remember. Because I'll think it's something kind of personal, something I should keep between me and him. Joseph will survive the blast too. But not so the waitress. Not that there's any culpability on her part. In terrorist attacks, character is not a factor. In the end, it's all a matter of angle and distance. "That guy who just came in is definitely running away from something." _____ [Gap H] _____. "Maybe he'll agree to write the screenplay for me or at least meet for coffee." Our waitress, laminated menu in hand, dances her way over to the sweaty guy in the coat.   *(about 738 words)*

Adapted from: Keret, Etgar: "Joseph", slightly adapted, in: Suddenly, a knock on the door. Chatto & Windus: London 2012, pp. 146–148 [translation by Sondra Silverston].

Worksheet
Task I: Multiple Matching *(Joseph)* 8 credits

Eight pieces of conversation have been removed from the story "Joseph". Choose from sentences 1–10 the one which fits each gap (A–H) best. There are two extra sentences which do not fit.

Gap	A	B	C	D	E	F	G	H
Sentence								

1	I'm glad you'll be doing the job
2	It's the first time in my life I see a suicide bomber
3	Joseph laughs, rummaging around in his pockets for some change for the tip
4	Myself
5	No one
6	So they told me
7	Something you walk into unsuspectingly and then it snaps closed around you
8	There's nothing malicious or sarcastic in the way he says it
9	You're right
10	Your saying no just gives me the chance to meet with other people, drink more coffee

Text II: Europe's Immigration Challenge
by Peter Sutherland and Cecilia Malmstrom

Europe faces an immigration predicament. Mainstream politicians, held hostage by xenophobic parties, adopt anti-immigrant rhetoric to win over a fearful public, while the foreign-born are increasingly marginalized in schools, cities, and at the workplace. Yet, despite high unemployment across much of the continent, too many em-
5 ployers lack the workers they need. Engineers, doctors, and nurses are in short supply; so, too, are farmhands and health aides. And Europe can never have enough entrepreneurs, whose ideas drive economies and create jobs.

The prevailing skepticism about immigration is not wholly unfounded. Many communities are genuinely polarized, which makes Europeans understandably anxious.
10 But to place the blame for this on immigrants is wrong, and exacerbates the problem. We are all at fault.

By not taking responsibility, we allowed immigration to become the scapegoat for a host of other, unrelated problems. The enduring insecurity caused by the global economic crisis, the rise of emerging powers and the endless political debates about
15 what will become of Europe is too often expressed in reactions against migrants. Not only is this unjust, but it distracts us from crafting solutions to the real problems.

European countries must finally and honestly acknowledge that, like the United States, Canada, and Australia, they are lands of immigrants. The percentage of foreign-born residents in several European countries – including Spain, the United Kingdom, Ger-
20 many, the Netherlands, and Greece – is similar to that in the US.

Yet, despite this, we do not make the necessary investments to integrate newcomers into our schools and workplaces. Nor have we done enough to reshape our public institutions to be inclusive and responsive to our diverse societies. We need to acknowledge the nature and composition of the societies in which we already live.

25 It is ironic – and dangerous – that Europe's anti-immigrant sentiment is peaking just when global structural changes are fundamentally shifting migration flows. The most important transformation is the emergence of new poles of attraction. Entrepreneurs, migrants with PhDs, and those simply with a desire to improve their lives are flocking to places like Brazil, South Africa, Indonesia, Mexico, China, and India. In the
30 coming decade, most of the growth in migration will take place in the global south. The West is no longer the Promised Land, placing at risk Europe's ability to compete globally.

The aging of Europe's population is historically unprecedented. The number of workers will decline considerably, and could shrink by almost one-third by mid-century,
35 with immense consequences for Europe's social model, the vitality of its cities, its ability to innovate and compete, and for relations among generations as the old become heavily reliant on the young. And, while history suggests that countries that welcome newcomers' energy and vibrancy compete best internationally, Europe is taking the opposite tack by tightening its borders.

But all is not lost. Europe got itself into this situation through a combination of inaction and short-sighted policymaking. This leaves considerable room for improvement and some countries have already taken promising steps. […] Yet international cooperation on migration is also needed. No country is an island, and none can address the issue alone. We have a long way to go, probably in a climate that will not turn favorable to immigration for many years. How much progress we can make will hinge on our ability to break through the myths about migration. *(551 words)*

Peter Sutherland/Cecilia Malmstrom: Europe's Immigration Challenge. In: Project Syndicate, Jul 20, 2012. © 2012 Project Syndicate – www.project-syndicate.org

Task II: Gapped Summary *(Europe's Immigration Challenge)* — 9 credits

Fill the gaps in the summary with appropriate words or expressions (one word per line) from the corresponding sections of the text. Note that the summary does not exactly follow the order of the text! Please also provide the number of the line in which you have found the word/expression.

Nowadays many Europeans think we already have too many immigrants and are worried about more immigration. In an attempt not to leave the field to extremist parties, even **mainstream politicans** (l.) have begun to hold the immigrants responsible for Europe's problems. But it is not at all helpful to use immigration as a **scapegoat** (l.), because this keeps us from making Europe fit for the future. One thing we should do is _____ (l.) that immigration is part of European reality. We should accept the fact that the populations in many European countries are very _____ (l.). And we should act to adapt to this fact. In other words, we should no longer hesitate to make the _____ (l.) needed to finance better education for immigrants and to improve their employment prospects. Another reality we should take into account is that Europe cannot do without additional immigrants. The workforce is shrinking _____ (l.) due to demographic change. This has to be counterbalanced, at least to some degree, by attracting more immigrants instead of _____ (l.) immigration laws. Our real problem is that this is getting increasingly difficult since international _____ (l.) are changing direction. More and more migrants seem to prefer other regions to Europe. This endangers our _____ (l.) to keep up economically with the rest of the world.

Text III: The John Lewis Economy: Why Is Downing Street Looking to Britain's Most Beloved Department Store? by Thomas K. Grose

(A) In Britain, big department stores tend to be as concerned about social background as the country's consumers. Ultra-posh stores like Harrods and Harvey Nichols cater to luxury lovers, while cheaper stores like BHS serve the budget-minded. But John Lewis, the country's largest and most successful department store, has become a national institution by doing both. At the 148-year-old chain, which has 29 department stores and eight smaller home stores around the country, members of the 1 % drooling over $ 6,200 Maurice Lacroix crocodile-leather watches commingle with value shoppers angling for $ 31 unisex plastic Casios. Imagine wrapping a Bloomingdale's, Macy's and J.C. Penney into one in the U.S. "In class-conscious Britain, it manages to be fairly democratic," says Michael Poynor, founder of the consulting firm Retail Expertise. "No one is ashamed to be seen with a John Lewis bag." John Lewis' high-low strategy has paid off throughout the recession even though the U.K.'s retail sales have been falling or flat since 2009 and shopping districts and malls are littered with vacant shops.

(B) Through it all, John Lewis has maintained an unbroken 10-year streak of outsize sales growth. In an ailing economy, John Lewis' group sales – generated by the department store chain and its upscale grocery chain, Waitrose – jumped 6.4 % to a record $ 13.48 billion in its last fiscal year, beating competitors like Marks & Spencer and House of Fraser, whose sales rose a meager 2 % and 1.5 %, respectively. The company wasn't immune to the downturn: profits dipped nearly 9 % to $ 607 million last year, partly because it invested more in its businesses. But the move didn't hurt sales, which surged 11 % in the first 24 weeks of the year from the same period a year earlier.

(C) One of John Lewis' secret weapons is its unusual structure: it's 100 % owned by its 81,000 full-time employees. That makes its shareholders – who have a bigger stake in the company's success than those of public companies – acutely focused on the long haul. "Our ownership model creates the right conditions for success," says Charlie Mayfield, John Lewis' chairman since 2007. Research shows that employee-owned businesses fare as well as or better than traditionally owned enterprises in good times and bad. They're more profitable, they create jobs faster than other companies, and they shed less staff, according to a recent study by London's Cass Business School. And they're out-pacing rivals: business at worker-run shops is growing 50 % faster than the British economy as a whole, according to new figures from the U.K. government.

(D) Amid news of exorbitant bonuses and a barrage of high-profile corporate scandals – Rupert Murdoch's phone-hacking affair and the interest rate manipulations of Barclays Bank being the latest – Downing Street has found a champion in John Lewis. Deputy Prime Minister Nick Clegg calls for a "John Lewis economy," one that encourages a more responsible brand of capitalism through employee-owned businesses. In July, days after the Barclays scandal broke, Clegg announced plans for a government office that will advise businesses on how to become employee-run, along with tax breaks to sweeten the deal. Barclays, he said in a speech, is "a timely reminder that our economy desperately needs an injection of responsibility, greater checks on unaccountable power, power in more hands."

(E) John Lewis employees – or partners, as they're called – don't actually own shares individually. It's rather a profit-sharing arrangement, so when the company performs well, workers pocket a fat annual bonus. Last year it was worth 14 % of their yearly salary, or roughly seven weeks' pay. Each store has an employee forum that elects representatives all the way up ending in a 14-member partnership board chaired by Mayfield, which meets four times a year. There, twice yearly, Mayfield puts his job up to a vote that could have him sacked. "And that's real power," says Mayfield, 47, who earned the same 14 % bonus – for a total of $ 179,000 – as the rest of his staff last year. The equivalent bonus for Mare Bolland, CEO of Marks & Spencer, totaled $ 1.03 million.

(F) Ceding power and pay is a lesson learned from the company's history. Founded by John Lewis as a curtain store in London in 1864, the shop quickly grew into a successful department store. As communist thinking spread in the early 20th century, John Spedan Lewis, the founder's son, began to fear for the business. He viewed the vast sums that his father, his brother and he earned – which totaled more than the pay of all their employees combined – as a tinderbox. The more reticent father turned down his son's designs on improving working conditions and offering paid holidays. Instead he tasked him with turning around a smaller family-owned shop, the Peter Jones department store. When the elder Lewis died in 1928, Spedan Lewis took over the namesake store and set up an initial profit-sharing scheme. In 1950, he handed full ownership to the employees in a trust tied to a constitution. It promotes the virtues of "worthwhile and satisfying employment" for the "happiness of all its members." […]

(G) Of course, the model isn't a fix-all. Partnerships tend to work best for small-to-medium-size companies. John Lewis' recent expansion abroad could fail if the cultural advantages are lost on foreign franchisers. Unlike with publicly traded firms, employee-owned companies are also less regulated, which can make raising outside capital harder, since banks and bond buyers have less data to assess risk. […] Still, investors in employee-run firms tend to be more patient about returns. And employees are often better keepers of a founder's vision than outsiders. John Lewis employees overruled a push to sell the company to outside investors in 1999 – which promised a windfall payout of roughly $ 150,000 per employee – fearing that cutbacks by any new owner would destroy company culture. "Since that wobble," says Poynor, "the business has gone from strength to strength." […] *(980 words – abridged)*

Thomas K. Grose: The John Lewis Economy. Why Is Downing Street Looking to Britain's Most Beloved Department Store? In: Time Magazine, Aug 13, 2012.

Task III: Multiple Choice *(The John Lewis Economy)* 7 credits
Mark the most suitable option by crossing the appropriate letter.

1. John Lewis department stores …
   A are almost as exclusive as places like Harrods.
   B mainly appeal to small budgets.
   C are run by Retail Expertise.
   D cater for a wide variety of people.

2. John Lewis' profits have recently been …
   A fluctuating.
   B falling.
   C floating.
   D surging.

3. Which advantage of John Lewis' ownership model is **not** mentioned in **paragraph C**?
   A Coping better with economic fluctuations.
   B Greater job security for employees.
   C Improved competitiveness of the company.
   D Extra payments for employees and management.

4. Deputy Prime Minister Nick Clegg wants more of a John Lewis Economy in Britain because he thinks …
   A the economic system so far has been too open to misuse.
   B economic power is in too many hands.
   C the concept promises higher tax revenues.
   D British business should be a model in the EU.

5. The special thing about the John Lewis ownership model is that the employees …
   A hold stocks which pay out substantial dividends.
   B get bonuses while the chairman doesn't.
   C ultimately have their say about who runs the firm.
   D are represented on a partnership board twice a year.

6. John Spedan Lewis …
   A was more interested in communist ideas than in the family business.
   B had to postpone his plans due to his father's reservations.
   C turned his father's curtain store into a department store.
   D was forced by his father to try out his concept in the Peter Jones department store.

7. Which downside of a John Lewis-like company structure is **not** mentioned in **paragraph G**?

   A   Investors are deterred because the employees can reject company decisions.
   B   Foreign franchisers might not follow John Lewis' company philosophy.
   C   The scheme could be problematic for bigger companies.
   D   It's difficult for outside investors to determine how profitable the business is.

Aufgabenteil: *Writing*

Task IV: Mediation Deutsch – Englisch „Internet und Demokratie: Zu viel der Freiheit" von Alexandra Borchardt

Schmäh-Videos, die verirrte Hass-Prediger um den Globus schicken; der arabische Frühling, aus dem nun ein YouTube-Herbst werden könnte – was lässt sich aus den Entwicklungen dieser Tage lernen? Auf der Hand liegt zum einen die simple Erkenntnis: Das Internet selbst schafft keine Demokratie. Die entsteht nur über starke
5 Institutionen wie konkurrierende politische Parteien, unabhängige Gerichte und in sorgsam erdachten Wahlverfahren bestimmte Parlamente. Und starke Medien, die aufklären, Themen setzen, Interessen bündeln und allzu radikalen Kräften keine Bühne geben.

Völker, die sich von Diktatoren befreit haben, können das Netz zwar nutzen, um sol-
10 che Institutionen aufzubauen, denn keine Technologie bietet so viele Möglichkeiten zum Lernen, zur Information und Rückkoppelung mit den Bürgern. Aber ohne den unbedingten Willen aller wichtigen Akteure, das Abenteuer Demokratie wagen zu wollen, wird sich auch keine entwickeln. Jede Gesellschaft muss in der realen Welt um ihre Werte ringen.

15 Zweite Erkenntnis: Das Internet ist zunächst nur ein neutrales Medium. Es ist offensichtlich weitaus wirkungsvoller, als Druckpressen, Radiosender oder Fernsehkanäle dies für die Widerstandsbewegungen früherer Zeiten waren. Informationen, Meinungen und Bilder lassen sich darüber praktisch kaum gefiltert in Echtzeit und weltweit verbreiten. Freiheitssuchende können es für ihre Mobilisierung nutzen. So
20 haben die Aufständischen im Nahen Osten stark von den Möglichkeiten des Netzes und mobiler Geräte profitiert. Jedoch bietet das Netz auch radikalen Interessenvertretern, Extremisten und Verrückten eine Plattform, die sie auf anderen Kanälen nie bekommen hätten. „Das Internet dient eben nicht nur den ‚Guten', sondern auch den ‚Bösen'", resümiert Professorin Marianne Kneuer, die an der Universität Hildesheim
25 den Forschungsschwerpunkt Politik und Internet leitet.

Dieser Grundsatz gilt nicht nur für zündelnde Randgruppen, sondern auch für repressive Regime. Denn das Netz ermöglicht Diktatoren und Autokraten ganz neue Möglichkeiten, ihr Volk zu überwachen, zu manipulieren und Gegner zu identifizieren. In Syrien zum Beispiel wurde schon manch ein Oppositioneller über die Ortung seines
30 Mobilfunkgeräts aufgespürt. Und niemand weiß, ob vermeintliche Internet-Rebellen Lockvögel der Regierung sind.

Während hierzulande über die Verfügbarkeit von Kinderpornografie per Mausklick diskutiert wird, sieht die scheinbar so offene Netz-Welt in einigen Diktaturen schon so aus, wie deren Mächtige sich das wünschen. Dies geschieht übrigens auch mithilfe
35 westlicher IT-Firmen, die den Unterdrückern gerne Soft- und Hardware zur Unterdrückung liefern. *(357 Wörter)*

© *Süddeutsche Zeitung vom 19.9.2012, gekürzt und bearbeitet.*

Worksheet

Task IV: Mediation Deutsch–Englisch (*Internet und Demokratie: Zuviel der Freiheit*) 12 credits

Geben Sie zentrale Aussagen des Textes in englischer Sprache wieder. Stützen Sie sich auf die unterstrichenen Textstellen und fertigen Sie daraus einen zusammenhängenden Text im Umfang von ca. 150 Wörtern an.

Sie beginnen mit dem folgenden Satz:

What can we learn from hate videos on the Internet and an Arab Spring that could turn into a "YouTube autumn"? ...

Task V: Argumentative Writing 24 credits

Choose **one** of the following topics. Write **at least 220 words**.

1. **Composition**

    We urgently have to rethink the way we produce and consume food. Comment on this statement.

2. **Composition**

    The use of regional and local dialects used to be frowned upon. Now, however, it is officially encouraged in schools. What do you think about this development?

Lösungsvorschläge

Aufgabenteil: *Reading*

Task I: Multiple Matching *(Joseph)*

Hinweise:
zu A: Hier wird ein Subjekt für die Satzfortsetzung „is really called Yossef" (Z. 8) gesucht.
zu B: Satz 8 enthält die Formulierung „in the way he says it". Es muss also vorher eine Äußerung des Gesprächspartners geben. Auf diese Äußerung bezieht sich auch "It's a statement of fact" (Z. 12).
zu C: Die Lösung muss eine Antwort auf Josephs Frage geben: "You know what scares me most?" (Z. 16). „Myself" (auf deutsch: ich selbst) ist die einzig sinnvolle Antwort.
zu D: Dem Sprecher erscheint das Leben wie eine Falle („trap" Z. 24). In Satz 7 findet sich eine Beschreibung dessen, was eine Falle tut; sie schnappt zu („it snaps closed around you"), wenn man dann drinsteckt („when you're inside, inside life I mean" Z. 25).
zu E: Lücke E ist der Beginn einer direkten Rede von Joseph. Er bezieht sich dabei auf seine vorhergehende Äußerung „fuck-all that you won't write the screenplay" (Z. 28). In Satz 10 findet sich hierzu der Bezug „Your saying no" (wörtlich: „Ihr Nein-Sagen").
Gleichzeitig muss die Lösung zur Fortsetzung seiner Äußerung passen („that's the best part of this business" Z. 31/32). Mit „best part of this business" meint er, dass man als Produzent andere Menschen trifft, mit ihnen Kaffee trinkt und quatscht usw.
zu F: Joseph bringt zum Ausdruck (Z. 33/34), dass er sich wohl zum Produzenten nicht wirklich eignet. In seiner Antwort in Lücke F bezieht er sich auf das bestätigende Nicken des Erzählers ("I must still be nodding", Z. 34/35).
zu G: Die Lösung muss mit dem vorher erwähnten „sweaty guy in the coat" (Z. 43) und mit der später im Krankenhaus gewünschten Beschreibung dieses Typen (Z. 44/45) zu tun haben. Der „suicide bomber" verbindet sozusagen den „sweaty guy" und das Krankenhaus.
zu H: Lücke H steht zwischen zwei Äußerungen in direkter Rede, die nur Joseph zugeordnet werden können. Hier wäre theoretisch auch Satz 8 denkbar, aber dieser muss definitiv in Lücke B eingesetzt werden.

Gap	A	B	C	D	E	F	G	H
Sentence	5	8	4	7	10	9	2	3

Task II: Gapped summary *(Europe's Immigration Challenge)*
Hinweise:
Achten Sie auf die Angaben „one word per line" sowie „the summary does not exactly follow the order of the text"!
Erstmals muss man bei dieser Prüfung die Zeile angeben, in der man die jeweilige Lösung gefunden hat.

- mainstream politicians (Z. 1): Bezugspunkte zwischen Gapped Summary (GS) und Originaltext (OT) sind: „attempt not to leave the field to extremist parties" (GS) vs. „held hostage by xenophobic parties" (OT Z. 1/2); „have begun to hold the immigrants responsible" (GS) vs. „adopt anti-immigrant rhetoric to win over a fearful public" (OT Z. 2)
- scapegoat (Z. 12): Bezugspunkte zwischen GS und OT sind: „to use immigration as" (GS) vs. „we allowed immigration to become" (OT Z. 12); „making Europe fit for the future" (GS) vs. „debates about what will become of Europe" (OT Z. 14/15)
- acknowledge (Z. 17): Bezugspunkte sind: „One thing we should do is" (GS) vs. „European countries must finally" (OT Z. 17); „is part of European reality" (GS) vs. „they are lands of immigrants" (OT Z. 18)
- diverse (Z. 23): Bezugspunkte sind: „We should accept" (GS) vs. „We need to acknowledge" (OT Z. 23/24); „populations" (GS) vs. „societies" (OT Z. 23)
- investments (Z. 21): Bezugspunkte sind: „needed to finance" (GS) vs. „necessary investments" (OT Z. 21); „education [and] employment prospects" (GS) vs. „schools and workplaces" (OT Z. 22)
- considerably (Z. 34): Bezugspunkte sind: „The workforce is shrinking" (GS) vs. „The number of workers will decline" (OT Z. 33/34)
- tightening (Z. 39): Bezugspunkte sind: „counterbalanced" (GS) vs. einen Ausgleich schaffen für die all die problematischen Begleiterscheinungen der Alterung in Europa (OT Z. 33–35); „immigrations laws" (GS) vs. „tightening its borders" (OT Z. 39)
- migration flows (= Migrationsströme, Z. 26) : Bezugspunkte sind: „changing direction" (GS) vs. „shifting" (OT Z. 26)
- ability (Z. 31): Bezugspunkte sind: „More and more migrants seem to prefer other regions" (GS) vs. „those [...] are flocking to places like Brazil" (OT Z. 28/29); „endangers" (GS) vs. „placing at risk" (OT Z. 31); „to keep up economically with the rest of the world" (GS) vs. „to compete globally" (OT Z. 31/32)

Nowadays many Europeans think we already have too many immigrants and are worried about more immigration. In an attempt not to leave the field to extremist parties, even **mainstream politicians (l. 1)** have begun to hold the immigrants responsible for Europe's problems. But it is not at all helpful to use immigration as a **scapegoat (l. 12)**, because this keeps us from making Europe fit for the future.
One thing we should do is **acknowledge (l. 17)** that immigration is part of European reality. We should accept the fact that the populations in many European countries are very **diverse (l. 23)**. And we should act to adapt to this fact. In other words, we should no longer hesitate to make the **investments (l. 21)** needed to finance better education for immigrants and to improve their employment prospects.

Another reality we should take into account is that Europe cannot do without additional immigrants. The workforce is shrinking **considerably** (l. 34) due to demographic change. This has to be counterbalanced, at least to some degree, by attracting more immigrants instead of **tightening** (l. 39) immigration laws. Our real problem is that this is getting increasingly difficult since international **migration flows** (l. 26) are changing direction. More and more migrants seem to prefer other regions to Europe. This endangers our **ability** (l. 31) to keep up economically with the rest of the world.

Task III: Multiple Choice *(The John Lewis Economy)*

Hinweise:

- *zu 1:* Die feinen Kaufhäuser („Ultra-posh stores", Z. 2) sind für die Betuchten („luxury lovers", Z. 3), die weniger teuren Geschäfte („cheaper stores", Z. 3) sind für die Preisbewussten („budget-minded", Z. 3). John Lewis Kaufhäuser wenden sich an beide Zielgruppen („by doing both" Z. 5 – Option D: „cater for a wide variety of people").
- *zu 2:* „[S]ales [...] surged 11 % in the first 24 weeks of the year", (Z. 22) entspricht „John Lewis' profits have recently been surging."
- *zu 3:* Option A: „employee-owned businesses fare as well or better [...] in good times and bad" (Z. 28–30)
  Option B: „they shed less staff" (Z. 31)
  Option C: „they're outpacing rivals" (Z. 32)
- *zu 4:* Der Text erwähnt diverse Wirtschaftsskandale in den Zeilen 35 bis 37. Clegg ist der Meinung, dass das Geschäftsgebaren von John Lewis verantwortungsvoller ist („encourages a more responsible brand of capitalism", Z. 39).
- *zu 5:* Der Chef von John Lewis, Charlie Mayfield, ist einem 14-köpfigen Gremium aus Beschäftigten des Unternehmens verantwortlich, von dem er entlassen werden kann („a vote that could have him sacked", Z. 51).
- *zu 6:* John Spedan Lewis hielt das ausgeprägte Profitstreben seines Vaters für gefährlich („tinderbox" = Pulverfass Z. 60), wollte die Arbeitsbedingungen der Beschäftigten verbessern („improving working conditions" Z. 61), wurde aber von seinem Vater daran gehindert („turned down his son's designs" Z. 60/61), indem er ihm stattdessen die Verantwortung für die Peter Jones Läden übertrug („Instead he tasked him with turning around a smaller family-owned shop", Z. 62).
- *zu 7:* Option B: "John Lewis' recent expansion abroad could fail if the cultural advantages are lost on foreign franchisers," (Z. 69/70)
  Option C: "Partnerships tend to work best for small-to-medium-size companies." (Z. 68/69)
  Option D: „banks and bond buyers have less data to assess risk" (Z. 72)

1 D, 2 D, 3 D, 4 A, 5 C, 6 B, 7 A

Aufgabenteil: *Writing*

Task IV: Mediation Deutsch–Englisch

What can we learn from hate videos on the Internet and an Arab spring that could turn into a "You Tube autumn"?
The Internet alone does not bring about (or: establish / set up a) democracy.
What it takes to develop democracy is the strong (or: unbending / indomitable) will of all important activists involved to try out democracy (or: to take a chance on democracy). (Alternative: Democracy can only develop if all important groups of society are willing to try out democracy.)
Apart from that, the Internet is a neutral medium. Obviously, it is far more effective (or: powerful) than the printing press, radio and TV stations. Information, opinions and pictures can be spread worldwide, immediately (or: in real time) and virtually (or: practically) unfiltered. Those seeking freedom (or: striving for freedom) can use it for mobilization. Yet, the Internet provides a platform also for extremists, madmen and repressive regimes. Moreover, the Net gives dictators absolutely new options to look at what their people do, to manipulate them and to identify opponents. By the way, this is possible also because Western IT companies supply oppressors with the soft- and hardware needed. *(about 146 words)*

Task V: Argumentative Writing

1. **Composition**

   Hinweise: Beachten Sie bei dieser Aufgabenstellung, dass Sie sich sowohl zur Produktion als auch zum Konsum von Nahrungsmitteln äußern.
   Aufbau:
   (1) Kurze Hinführung zum Thema
   (2) Aspekte der Produktion und des Konsums
   *   – convenience food, fast food*
   *   – working conditions on plantations etc.*
   *   – intensive livestock farming, battery farming*
   *   – overproduction*
   *   – deforestation for agricultural use*
   (3) Abrunden des Aufsatzes mit einem Fazit, Ausblick, o. Ä.

   Every few months another food-safety scandal outrages the German public: horse meat in frozen lasagne, rotten meat in doner kebab, dioxin in eggs. Obviously, there is something wrong about the production and consumption of food in industrialised societies.
   It is true that weekly markets with their fresh offers enjoy a good reputation. Yet, it is a fact that you also find more and more shelves and chest freezers in supermarkets stocked with a continually growing variety of convenience food products. The same goes for the fast food industry: KFC, McDonald's and Burger King are highly profitable and still expanding. And we, the members of an affluent society, throw away more edible food than any generation before.

What, to my mind, is even more appalling is the way we produce food for mass consumption. In order to keep the cost of production down and to raise profits, cattle, pigs and hens are kept in intensive farming. Animals suffer in conditions that are far from what could be a near-natural environment, they receive prophylactic doses of antibiotics which potentially harm human health in the long run.

Not only do we treat animals badly, we also show disrespect for humans working for the food industry. Working conditions on, for instance, coffee plantations often are beyond description. Though it is officially disapproved of in Western countries, child labour is rather commonplace there.

As we love to have full shelves in our supermarkets at any time of the day, we produce more food than we need. To do so we are not reluctant to destroy the environment. We cut down the rain forest in South America to create new areas for agricultural use, giant monocultures with a large-scale use of insecticides and pesticides, e. g. for the soybeans that are fodder for cattle in European barns.

But it is obvious that the way we produce and consume food is a huge burden for our natural resources which threatens biodiversity, encourages exploitation in general and child labour in particular, and ignores animal rights. Without doubt, food must be affordable for all classes of society, not only for the better-off. But we must not strive to achieve this to the cost of humans and animals alike.

(369 words)

2. **Composition**

> **Hinweise:** *Auch wenn die Aufgabenstellung es nicht explizit erwähnt, ist es sinnvoll, sich auf die Situation in Deutschland zu konzentrieren.*
> *Aufbau:*
> *(1) Kleine Hinführung zum Thema*
>   *– wide variety of regional and local dialects in Germany and in Bavaria*
> *(2) Aussagen zum Wesen, zur Verbreitung und zur Bedeutung von Dialekten*
> *(3) Vor- und Nachteile*
>   *– importance of dialects with regard to culture, sense of belonging, identity, expressiveness*
>   *– need for command of standard German in various situations*
> *(4) Abrunden des Aufsatzes mit einem Fazit, Ausblick, Appell o. Ä.*

There is an impressive variety of regional and local dialects in Germany and in Bavaria in particular, but the use of these dialects used to be frowned upon in the higher education classroom in grammar schools and universities. Apparently, some upper-class people consider dialect speakers to be ill-educated and backward. But is such an attitude outdated?

In contrast to their bad reputation in education, dialects have always enjoyed tremendous success in all fields of art: Gerhard Polt, Kurt Krömer, Monika Gruber – there is a large number of highly-popular German cabaret artists, comedians, singer-songwriters and authors etc., whose trademark is that they perform "in dialect". The local dialect can be seen as a key element of local identity, it gives people a sense of belonging, it enriches cultural life. Imagine a lorry driver from Passau expressing his anger about a car driver blocking his way. Think of those little Bavarian mocking verses called "Gstanzl" which can hit out at dignitaries and celebrities in a way standard German could never do. In many contexts of everyday life, saying something in dialect is much more expressive than saying it in standard German.

Still it is important that all Germans, whatever their local origin is, must be in command of standard German in its written form. And they must be able to express themselves orally in a way that is understandable for every German. But this does not mean that the use of dialects in schools must be oppressed. As long as pupils are able to speak standard German when necessary, it does not do any harm when they speak dialect in class.

Only recently there seems to have been a trend towards a mild encouragement of local dialects in Bavarian schools. In my view, this is a favourable development. Nevertheless, I doubt that this will lead to a real revival, because among teenagers and people in their twenties the use of Bavarian has disappeared almost completely, at least in the area around Munich. And once you have lost your dialect, you cannot teach it to the next generation. *(345 words)*

| Berufliche Oberschulen Bayern – Englisch 13. Klasse |
| Abiturprüfung 2014 |

Aufgabenteil: *Reading*

Text I: **The Inspiration** by Dorothy L. Sayers

£ 500 – REWARD The Evening Messenger has decided to offer the above reward to any person who shall give information leading to the arrest of the man, William Strickland, who is wanted by the police in connection with the murder of the late Emma Strickland at 59, Acacia Crescent, Manchester.
5 *DESCRIPTION OF THE WANTED MAN The following is the official description of William Strickland: Age 43; height 6 ft 1 or 2; complexion rather dark; hair silver-grey and abundant, may dye same; full grey moustache and beard, may now be clean-shaven; eyes light grey; left upper eye-tooth stopped with gold; left thumb-nail deformed by a recent blow. Disappeared, may have left, or will try to leave the country.*

10 Mr Budd read the description through carefully once again and sighed. It was most unlikely that William Strickland should choose his small and unsuccessful saloon, out of all the barbers' shops in London, for a haircut or a shave, still less for dyeing. Nevertheless, Mr Budd committed the description, as well as he could, to memory.
_____ **[Gap A]** _____ – and Mr Budd's eye was always fascinated by head-
15 lines with money in them. However, even razor in hand, he would hardly be a match for William Strickland, height six feet one or two, who had so fiercely beaten his old aunt to death.
Shaking his head doubtfully, Mr Budd advanced to the door, and nearly ran into a large customer who dived in rather suddenly. "I beg your pardon, Sir," murmured
20 Mr Budd, fearful of losing nine pence; "just stepping out for a breath of fresh air, Sir, a shave, Sir?"
The large man tore off his overcoat without waiting for Mr Budd's helping hands. "Are you prepared to die?" he demanded abruptly. _____ **[Gap B]** _____ that for a moment it quite threw him off his professional balance. "I beg your pardon,
25 Sir," he stammered, and in the same moment decided that the man must be a preacher of some kind. _____ **[Gap C]** _____, with his odd, light eyes, his bush of fiery red hair and short chin-beard. "Do you do dyeing?" said the man impatiently. "Oh!" said Mr Budd, relieved, "yes, Sir, certainly, Sir." A stroke of luck, this dyeing meant quite a big sum.
30 "Fact is," said the man, "my young lady doesn't like red hair. She says it attracts attention. Dark brown, now – that's the colour she has a fancy for. And I'm afraid the beard will have to go. My young lady doesn't like beards." "Will you have the moustache off as well, Sir?" "Well, no, no, I think I'll stick to that as long as I'm allowed to!" He laughed loudly, and Mr Budd approvingly noted well-kept teeth and a gold
35 stopping. _____ **[Gap D]** _____, Mr Budd gave his customer's hair the examination of trained eye and fingers. Never, never in the process of nature could hair of

2014-1

that kind have been red. It was naturally black hair, prematurely grey. However, that was none of his business. He received the information he really needed – the name of the dye formerly used, and noted that he would have to be careful. Some dyes do not mix kindly with other dyes.
Chatting pleasantly, Mr Budd worked on, and as he used the roaring drier, talked of the Manchester murder. "The police seem to have given it up as a bad job," said the man. "Perhaps the reward will liven things up a bit," said Mr Budd, the thought being naturally uppermost in his mind. "Oh, there's a reward, is there? I hadn't seen that." "It's in tonight's paper, Sir. Maybe you'd like to have a look at it." The stranger read the paragraph carefully and Mr Budd, watching him in the glass, saw him suddenly draw back his left hand, which was resting carelessly on the arm of the chair. Many people had such an ugly mark, Mr Budd told himself hurriedly. "Well," said Mr Budd, "the man is safe out of the country by now, I reckon. They've put it off too late." The man laughed, "I reckon, they have," he said. Mr Budd wondered whether many men with smashed left thumbs showed a gold upper left eye-tooth. Probably there were hundreds of people like that going about the country. Likewise with silver-grey hair ("may dye same") and aged about forty-three.
"Be as quick as you can, won't you?" said the man, a little impatiently, but pleasantly enough. "It's getting late. I'm afraid it will keep you overtime." "Not at all, Sir," said Mr Budd. "It doesn't matter at all." No, if he tried to rush out of the door, his terrible customer would jump upon him, drag him back, and then with one frightful blow like the one he had given his aunt […].
Yet surely Mr Budd was in a position of advantage. A decided man would do it. He retreated to the back of the shop, collecting his materials. If only he had been quicker – more like a detective in a book – he would have observed that thumbnail, that tooth and put two and two together. _____ [**Gap E**] _____, Mr Budd didn't have to arrest the man himself.
"Information leading to arrest" – those were the words. He would be able to tell them the wanted man had been there, that he would now have dark brown hair and moustache and no beard.
It was at this moment that the great inspiration came to Mr Budd. As he fetched a bottle from the glass-fronted case he remembered an old-fashioned wooden paper-knife that had belonged to his mother. Hand-painted, it bore the inscription "Knowledge is Power". Mr Budd now felt a strange freedom and confidence; he removed the razors with an easy, natural movement, and made light conversation as he skillfully applied the dark-brown tint.
The streets were less crowded when Mr Budd let his customer out. He watched the tall figure cross Grosvenor Place and climb on to a 24 bus.
He closed the shop door, and in his turn made his way, by means of a 24, to the top of Whitehall.
Mr Budd was interviewed by an important-looking inspector in uniform, who listened very politely to his story and made him repeat very carefully about the gold tooth and the thumbnail and the hair which had been black before it was grey or red and was now dark-brown.

"But there's one thing more," said Mr Budd – "and I'm sure to goodness," he added, "I hope, Sir, it is the right man because if it isn't it'll be the ruin of me."
Nervously he crushed his soft hat into a ball as he leant across the table, breathlessly uttering the story of his great professional betrayal.

The Miranda, a huge ferry boat, docked at Ostend at 7 a.m. A message was delivered to the English police: "Man on board answering to description. Ticket booked name of Watson. Has locked himself in cabin and refuses to come out. Insists on having hairdresser sent out to him because of his green hair."

_____ [**Gap F**] _____ had Mr Budd studied the complicated reactions of chemical dyes. In the pride of his knowledge he had set a mark on his man. Was there a port in the world where a murderer might slip away, with every hair on him green as a parrot?

Mr Budd got his £500. The Evening Messenger published the full story of his great inspiration. More customers than ever began to flock to his saloon. *(about 1,263 words)*

Dorothy L. Sayers: "The Inspiration of Mr Budd", (about 1,263 words – abridged and adapted) from: Dorothy L. Sayers: In the Teeth of the Evidence (1939).

Worksheet
Task I: Mixed Reading Tasks *(The Inspiration)*   8 credits

1. **Multiple Matching**   6 credits

   You are going to read the text "The Inspiration". Six sentences have been removed from the extract. Choose from sentences 1–9 the one which fits each gap (A–F) best. There are three extra sentences which do not fit.

Gap	A	B	C	D	E	F
Sentence	4	5				

1	He had taken conscious note of the mark
2	Not for nothing
3	He looked rather like it
4	It was a chance
5	The question fitted in so alarmingly with Mr Budd's thoughts about murder
6	But after all
7	In fancy
8	In vain
9	Lightly talking about the feminine mind

2. **Mediation Englisch–Deutsch**   2 credits

   Beantworten Sie die nachfolgende Frage <u>auf Deutsch</u>.

   Worin bestand der geniale Einfall des Mr Budd und was ermöglichte er damit?

   _____
   _____
   _____
   _____
   _____

2014-4

Text II: Myth of the Teenager by Lucy Maddox
Does the stroppy adolescent exist?

(A) Teenagers often get a bad press. There are easy stories to be mined here: ASBOs[1], underage drinking, drug use – even, recently, the teenager who drugged her parents to access the internet. These are not new stereotypes. As a shepherd in Shakespeare's *A Winter's Tale* puts it, "I would there were no age between 10 and
5 three-and-20, or that youth would sleep out the rest; for there is nothing in the between but getting wenches with child, wronging the ancientry, stealing, fighting." Change the language, and this description could easily fit in many newspapers today.

(B) Are the stereotypes fair? Is the idea of wild adolescence rooted in evidence? There are two sorts of arguments. On the one hand, neuroscientific evidence seems
10 increasingly to suggest that this is a true developmental phase of its own – teenagers behave differently because their brains are different. On the other hand, some argue that teenagers behave differently because they are learning to handle so many new situations, and if we hold stereotypical ideas about their behaviour, we risk underestimating them.

15 (C) Take the latter argument first. Philip Graham, a professor of psychiatry who has written extensively on what he perceives to be a misconception, believes that although hormonal and physical changes are occurring, most teenagers are not risky or moody. Graham sees teenagers as a stigmatised group, often highly competent yet treated as if they were not. He argues that teenagers need to be acknowledged as po-
20 tentially productive members of society and that the more independence and respect they are given, the more they will rise to the challenge.

(D) "Once young people reach the age of 14, their competence in cognitive tasks and their sexual maturity make it more helpful to think of them as young adults," says Graham. "Media coverage is almost uniformly negative. Adolescence is a word used
25 to describe undesirable behaviour in older adults. Young people of 14, 15 or 16 are thought to be risk-takers ... they are people who are experimenting. They are doing things for the first time and they make mistakes. Would you call a toddler who is learning to walk and who falls over all the time a risk-taker? These people are just beginning something."

30 (E) However, neuroscientific evidence suggests a basis for the teenage stereotype. Sarah-Jayne Blakemore, a professor at University College London, has specialised in researching the adolescent brain using a variety of techniques, including functional brain scanning. Although also concerned that teenagers can be vilified in the media, Blakemore rejects the idea that adolescence is entirely a social construct: "If you look
35 throughout history at the descriptions of adolescence you will notice they are similar, and this also applies to cultures all around the world. Of course, this is not to say that all adolescents are the same, but there is quite a lot of evidence that during this period of life there's an increase in risk-taking, peer influence and self-consciousness." Blakemore's research suggests that during the teenage years the brain is still devel-
40 oping the capacity for certain sophisticated skills, including problem-solving, social skills and impulse control. Blakemore and other researchers describe a gradual devel-

opment of brain areas related to planning, inhibiting inappropriate behaviour and understanding other points of view. [...]

(F) Despite their different views, both academics conclude that teenagers could benefit from being treated according to their development. Graham suggests friendly advice-giving. It is important to "recognise their desire for autonomy," he says. [...] Blakemore thinks that we should adjust the way we try to motivate teenagers: "Anti-smoking campaigns, for example, might be more effective if they used short-term social negatives like bad breath as a disincentive, rather than longer-term health consequences." [...]

(G) Whether you attribute adolescent differences in decision-making to brain development or lack of experience, educational aims could include the handling of social dilemmas. Parents might be able to help by being explicit about the pros and cons of a situation, considering other people's views or negotiating a transparent way. We should also bear in mind that teenagers are often uniquely affected by economic and political challenges such as high unemployment levels.

(H) In my view, adolescence is a tricky time, where individuals often struggle to find their own identity in the face of a sometimes hostile outside world, whilst needing peer support. Both Blakemore and Graham are more phlegmatic. "Every time's a tricky time," says Graham. "You try being my age."

(727 words)

Lucy Maddox: In: Prospect Magazine, March 20, 2013 (about 727 words, abridged)

Annotation
1 Anti-social behaviour orders = Orders of the Court which restrict behaviour in some way, e.g. by prohibiting a return to a certain area or shop, or by restricting swearing or drinking alcohol.

Task II: Mixed Reading Tasks *(Myth of the Teenager)* 8 credits

1. **Mediation Englisch – Deutsch**

    Beantworten Sie die folgenden Fragen auf Deutsch.

    a) Warum zitiert der Autor Shakespeare, wenn er über Teenager spricht?

    1 credit

    b) Philip Graham legt im Text seine Sichtweise auf Jugendliche und ihr Verhalten dar. Erläutern Sie, was er im Textzusammenhang unter „misconception" (Absatz C) versteht.

    2 credits

2. **Gapped Summary** 5 credits

Fill the gaps in the summary with appropriate words or expressions (one word per line) from the corresponding sections of the text (paragraphs E to H). Do not make any changes or adjustments. Please also provide the number of the line in which you have found the word/expression.

In contrast to Philip Graham, Sarah-Jayne Blakemore draws completely different conclusions regarding the reasons for teenage behaviour. Even if she is also worried about the fact that adolescents may be ___vilified___ (l.   ) in the public eye, for example by the press, she disapproves of the notion that teenage behaviour is a phenomenon completely created by society. She points out that this is something that has always existed and can be found in diverse culture groups today.

To adolescents, people of the same age and their opinions suddenly gain far more relevance. This so-called ___peer influence___ (l.   ) is one important characteristic of adolescent development Blakemore mentions.

In addition, numerous researchers agree that between 12 and 20, young people improve important skills. Adolescents become increasingly able to see things from other people's perspective or to manage bad and ___inappropriate___ (l.   ) conduct like fighting or lying.

What is the best way to motivate and teach youngsters then? Blakemore argues that instead of explaining future effects it is better to give a ___disincentive___ (l.   ) like pointing out the immediate negative consequences of a certain behaviour.

According to the author, parents, for example, should support their offspring by helping them to think about other people's opinions or by ___negotiating___ (l.   ) openly and comprehensibly.

2014-7

Text III: Secure Enough

(A) EIGHT "carpet shoes" outside Jim Chilton's house testify to the frugal innovation of Mexico's people-smuggling industry. These shoes, bound pieces of denim with soft soles designed to leave no trace in the Arizona desert, have been lost or abandoned by illegal immigrants traversing Mr Chilton's 50,000-acre cattle ranch, which stretches to the Mexican border. Mr Chilton displays them to help convince visitors that, whatever the politicians in Washington may say, America's southern border is far from secure.

(B) Whether the country gets a long-overdue reform of its immigration system, including a route to citizenship for the 11m illegal migrants now living there, may hinge on this question. The bill currently being debated in the Senate devotes $4.5 billion to border security, including yet more drones, fences and guards with guns. But many Republicans, recalling the multitudes that arrived after Ronald Reagan's amnesty in 1986, want even more. John Cornyn, a Texas Republican senator, says no illegal alien should be granted a green card (i.e. permanent residency) until the southern border is 90 % secure. It is not clear that this target makes sense. Driving back late from the border fence through Mr Chilton's ranch, the difficulties of measuring security become clear. A passing agent explains that a ground sensor has detected movement; he is on his way to investigate. Asked how he will spot anyone in the dark, he agrees that it is hard; he will use a torch and try his best. An agent encountered a little later hopefully mentions a helicopter, but none appears.

(C) To bolster its argument that the border is secure, Barack Obama's administration points to the drop in apprehensions at or near it. These bottomed out in 2011, and as the once-porous Tucson sector has tightened, there are signs that the action may be moving east, to Texas. Apprehension numbers are a poor proxy for border security, but few dispute that, compared with the free-for-all of the late 1990s and early 2000s, today's border is calm.

(D) Why might this be? Economics probably matters more than enforcement. America's downturn cost many illegal migrants their jobs, just as opportunities were blossoming back home in Mexico. In the past two years Mexico's economy has grown at a healthy 3.9 % annually, creating jobs (albeit at much lower pay than in America). In the longer term, demography is also likely to slow the flow of migrants. The number of 15–24-year-olds in Mexico and El Salvador will start declining between 2015 and 2020. Since illegal crossers tend to be young men, this will surely ease the pressure on the border. And over the next 40 years fertility rates in both countries are forecast to drop below America's.

(E) Walls and drones do make a difference. Gordon Hanson, an economist at the University of California, San Diego, credits tighter security for one-third of the drop in migration between the late 1990s and 2010. Spending yet more money could reduce crossings further, he says – although he believes that America is already inflicting economic self-harm by spending so much to keep workers out.

(F) Tighter security also pushes border-crossers to more remote areas. Out in the desert, dozens of miles from Nogales's steel-and-concrete fence, the chances of detection are slimmer. But so are the odds of survival; the number of bodies recovered by border agents has remained stable even as apprehensions have plummeted. Nor is a lonely death from exposure the only risk. Once, migrants would slip $ 300 to a *coyote* in a border town who would guide them across. Today illegal crossings are controlled by criminal gangs, which charge more and care less. People- and drug-smuggling routes have merged, and many migrants carry bales of dope to fund their journey. Their guides may assault or abandon them, or they may be robbed of their cargo. Mr Chilton and his wife, Sue, encounter fewer crossers these days, but those they do see sometimes carry AK-47 rifles.

(G) Fortifying the border has two immediate effects: it makes it easier to catch illegal migrants and it deters others from trying. Raising the cost of crossing must keep out some economic migrants. But the record number of deportations under Mr Obama has created a giant class of expelled foreigners with deep roots in the United States. One survey of recent deportees found that 22 % had offspring who were American citizens. Parents separated from their children are unlikely to be put off by extra helicopters or double fencing. The policy often forces people to choose between social death and the risk of physical death.

(H) Today, most of America's 2,000-mile southern border is tighter than it has ever been. Greater use of surveillance technology may reduce crossings further. Yet the growth in numbers of migrants from countries such as Guatemala and Honduras shows how strong the "push" factors behind migration remain. America's politicians may or may not find a way to declare the border "secure". But if Mexico's economy stutters, or violent crime soars again, the magnets of high wages, jobs and security across the border will prove too powerful for many to resist. *(842 words)*

The Economist, Jun 22nd, 2013 (about 842 words, adapted and abridged).

Task III: Multiple Choice *(Secure Enough)* 8 credits
Mark the most suitable option by crossing the appropriate letter.

1. Mr Chilton …
   A cares about illegal immigrants.
   B thinks the Mexican-American border is tough to cross.
   C disagrees with many US politicians.
   D hardly ever sees any signs of immigrants on his land.

2. Many Republicans …
   A are satisfied with the current border policy.
   B demand tougher legislation to cordon off the US.
   C still comply with President Reagan's immigration policies.
   D believe that green cards are a good way of keeping immigrants away.

3. According to paragraph C, which of the following statements is not correct?
   A Obama's government claims to have made some progress on the immigration agenda.
   B There have been fewer arrests near the Mexican-American border than before.
   C The Tucson area used to have a big problem with illegal immigrants.
   D One cannot draw any conclusions at all from the number of arrested illegals.

4. Which statement is true according to paragraphs D and E?
   A In Latin America there will always be a higher number of births than in the US.
   B America might fare better with more immigrants.
   C Financial funding and border protection are not directly connected to migration numbers.
   D Unemployment figures don't play a role for immigration.

5. Illegal immigration today …
   A is still organized by the same people as in the past.
   B is often related to other types of crime.
   C has become cheaper but more dangerous.
   D appears in more or less the same places as in the past.

6. President Obama's immigration policies have …
   A had no effect whatsoever on people willing to leave their countries.
   B solely focused on technological improvements.
   C been counterproductive when trying to detect illegal immigrants.
   D led to a large number of uprooted Latin Americans.

7. The key message of the last paragraph is that …
   A America's politicians cannot ultimately influence the number of arrivals.
   B new border policies have had an effect on immigration figures.
   C people from Guatemala and Honduras are the new main issue.
   D Mexico has a huge problem with crime and its economic development.

8. In the given text, the author wants to state that …
   A illegal immigrants often lead a horrible life.
   B all American politicians tackle immigration in the wrong way.
   C immigration is no longer the problem it used to be.
   D immigration is an almost uncontrolled social development.

Aufgabenteil: *Writing*

Task IV: Mediation Deutsch – Englisch „Soziale Ungleichheit in den USA"

Land begrenzter Möglichkeiten

Die Börse boomt, der Immobilienmarkt erholt sich und selbst vom Arbeitsmarkt gibt es gute Nachrichten: In den USA läuft derzeit alles nach Plan, so scheint es. Doch der Aufschwung hat eine negative soziale Komponente. Die Gegensätze zwischen den Superreichen und dem Rest verschärfen sich.

Es war Präsident John F. Kennedy, der die Flut als Fortschrittsmetapher populär gemacht hat. „A rising tide lifts all boats", sagte er 1963, als Wohlstandsgewinne in den USA noch von der gesamten Gesellschaft geteilt wurden. Lange her.

Die vergangene Woche war voller guter Nachrichten. An der Börse kletterte der Dow-Jones-Index von Rekord zu Rekord, und auch vom Immobilienmarkt wurden Fortschritte gemeldet. Die Häuserpreise steigen wieder. Selbst die Beschäftigungslage verbessert sich, 236 000 Jobs hat die US-Wirtschaft im Februar geschaffen, deutlich mehr als erwartet. Das Drehbuch für den Aufschwung stammt von Notenbankchef Ben Bernanke. Er setzt wie Kennedy auf die Kraft der Flut, der Geldflut um genau zu sein. Und siehe da: Bernankes Aufschwung gewinnt an Fahrt. Soweit die gute Nachricht. Die schlechte: Das Primat der Geldpolitik hat eine soziale Schlagseite, es verschärft die Gegensätze zwischen den Superreichen und dem Rest.

Das Durchschnittseinkommen ist, berücksichtigt man die Inflation, seit 2000 um acht Prozent gesunken. Und der Arbeitsmarkt steckt weiter in der Krise, auch der unerwartet positive Jobreport ändert nichts daran, dass zwölf Millionen Amerikaner keine Beschäftigung finden. Das Heer der Langzeitarbeitslosen wächst und immer mehr Amerikaner brauchen Zweit- und Drittjobs, um ihren Lebensstandard zu halten.

Das Land der unbegrenzten Möglichkeiten ist zum Mythos verkommen. Die Aufsteigerbiografien, die als Lumpenexistenz beginnen und im Luxusleben enden, werden immer weniger. In kaum einer anderen Industrienation ist die soziale Mobilität inzwischen so gering wie in Amerika. Es geht um die Chance, von Chancengleichheit zu profitieren: funktionsfähige Familien, die ihren Kindern Wissensdurst vermitteln; und soziale Einrichtungen, die eingreifen, wenn Familien versagen. Ausgerechnet hier wird jedoch mit eiserner Hand gespart, seit der Kongress seinen Gestaltungsanspruch aufgegeben und sich einem Sanierungsdiktat unterworfen hat. Neben den Militärausgaben kürzt das Rotstiftregiment Hilfsprogramme wie Head Start, das einkommensschwache Kinder auf die Schule vorbereitet. Wann, wenn nicht jetzt, soll die Frühförderung ausgebaut, wann, wenn nicht jetzt, die soziale Kluft bekämpft werden?

Leider findet die Vernunft in Washington keine Mehrheit. Die Flut kommt. Viele Amerikaner können nicht schwimmen.

(382 Wörter)

Moritz Koch, New York, Süddeutsche Zeitung, 11. März 2013.

Worksheet
Task IV: Mediation Deutsch–Englisch
(Soziale Ungleichheit in den USA) 12 credits
Fassen Sie den folgenden Artikel zusammen, indem Sie die unterstrichenen Textstellen sinngemäß ins Englische übertragen. Verfassen Sie hierfür einen zusammenhängenden Text im Umfang von ca. 150 Wörtern. Beginnen Sie mit dem folgenden Satz:

It seems that in the US things are working out as expected, but ...

Task V: Argumentative Writing 24 credits
Choose **one** of the following topics. Write **at least 220 words**.

1. **Composition**

   In 2008, for the first time in history, more than half the world's population lived in urban areas. According to a recent study published in the *"Proceedings of the National Academy of Sciences"*, urban territory will cover about 10 % of the planet's land area by 2020. What are the consequences of these growing cities?

2. **Composition**

   A single person can change the world. Discuss.

Lösungsvorschläge

Aufgabenteil: *Reading*

Task I: Mixed Reading Tasks *(The Inspiration)*

1. **Multiple Matching**

   Hinweise:
   zu A: Mr Budd rechnet zwar nicht damit („*It was most unlikely*" Z. 10/11), dass der Gesuchte in seinem Salon auftaucht, aber ihn lockt trotzdem („*Nevertheless*" Z. 13) die Chance auf Belohnung. Darum prägt er sich die Beschreibung des Gesuchten ein („*committed the description [...] to memory*" Z. 13)
   zu B: Vor Lücke B wird eine Frage gestellt (*"Are you prepared to die?"* Z. 23), die in Option 5 aufgegriffen wird.
   zu C: Mr Budd stellt Vermutungen an („*must be a preacher of some kind*" Z. 25/26) und stützt diese Vermutungen auf das Erscheinungsbild des Fremden („*odd, light eyes, his bush of fiery red hair and short chin-beard*" Z. 26/27).
   zu D: Der Fremde begründet seine Änderungswünsche zu Haarfarbe und Bart mit den Vorlieben seiner Freundin („*my young lady doesn't like red hair*" Z. 30) und den Vorschriften, die sie ihm macht („*as long as I'm allowed to*" Z. 33/34). Mr Budd reagiert darauf mit dem typischen Smalltalk unter Männern über das, was sich die Frauen so einbilden („*the feminine mind*").
   zu E: Mr Budd hat erkannt, dass er den Gesuchten vor sich hat, überlegt, was er tun soll, und wird sich dann bewusst, dass er den Gesuchten ja gar nicht selber festnehmen muss („*after all*" = schließlich).
   zu F: Mr Budd kennt sich mit chemischen Reaktionen beim Haarefärben aus, er hat sich nicht umsonst (= „*Not for nothing*") damit befasst.

Gap	A	B	C	D	E	F
Sentence	4	5	3	9	6	2

2. **Mediation Englisch–Deutsch**

   Mr Budd färbte die Haare des Gesuchten mit einer dunkelbraunen Tinktur, die erst später, als der Gesuchte schon längst nicht mehr im Salon war, die Farbe Grün annahm.
   Dadurch war der Gesuchte leicht zu identifizieren und konnte festgenommen werden.

Task II: Mixed Reading Tasks *(Myth of the Teenager)*

1. **Mediation Englisch–Deutsch**

    a) Das Zitat zeigt, dass die Vorurteile, die in unserer Gesellschaft heute gegenüber Jugendlichen und jungen Erwachsenen bestehen, nicht neu sind, sondern schon seit Jahrhunderten bestehen.

    b) Graham beschreibt eine verbreitete Fehleinschätzung („misconception"), nämlich, dass man landläufig der Meinung ist, dass die meisten Teenager aufgrund der hormonellen und körperlichen Veränderungen risikofreudig oder launisch werden. Das stimmt aber so nicht.
    (Alternative Antwort: Teenager werden in der Regel falsch wahrgenommen (= „misconception") und stigmatisiert. Sie werden nämlich als Menschen behandelt, denen man nichts zutrauen kann, obwohl sie in Wirklichkeit oft vielfältige Kompetenzen mitbringen.)

2. **Gapped summary**

    Hinweise:
    Achten Sie auf die den Zusatz im Arbeitsauftrag „one word per line"!
    vilified (Z. 33): Bezugspunkte zwischen Gapped Summary (GS) und Originaltext (OT) sind: „Even if she is also worried" (GS) vs. „Although also concerned" (OT Z. 33); „in the public eye, for example by the press" (GS) vs. „in the media" (OT Z. 33)
    peer influence (Z. 38): Blakemore erwähnt mehrere bedeutende Veränderungen in der Entwicklung von Jugendlichen („there's an increase in risk-taking, peer influence and self-consciousness." Z. 38). Der GS hebt die zunehmende Bedeutung der Gleichaltrigen hervor. Bezugspunkte zwischen GS und OT sind: „people of the same age" (GS) vs. „peer" (OT Z. 38); „and their opinions suddenly gain far more relevance" (GS) vs. „influence" (OT Z. 38)
    inappropriate (Z. 42): Bezugspunkte sind: „numerous researchers agree" (GS) vs. „Blakemore and other researchers" (OT Z. 41); „improve important skills" (GS) vs. „gradual development of brain areas" (OT Z. 41/42); „see things from other people's perspective" (GS) vs. „understanding other points of view" (OT Z. 43); „conduct" (GS) vs. „behaviour" (OT Z. 42)
    disincentive (Z. 49): Bezugspunkte sind: „instead of explaining future effects it is better" (GS) vs. „might be more effective if" (OT Z. 48); „pointing out the immediate negative consequences" (GS) vs. „short-term social negatives" (OT Z. 48/49)
    negotiating (Z. 54): Bezugspunkte sind: „parents [...] should support their offspring by helping" (GS) vs. „Parents might be able to help" (OT Z. 53); „think about other people's opinions" (GS) vs. „considering other people's views" (OT Z. 54); „openly and comprehensibly" (GS) vs. „a transparent way" (OT Z. 54)

    In contrast to Philip Graham, Sarah-Jayne Blakemore draws completely different conclusions regarding the reasons for teenage behaviour. Even if she is also worried about the fact that adolescents may be **vilified (l. 33)** in the public eye, for example by the press, she disapproves of the notion that teenage behaviour is a phenomenon completely created by society. She points out that this is something that has always existed and can be found in diverse culture groups today.

To adolescents, people of the same age and their opinions suddenly gain far more relevance. This so-called **peer influence (l. 38)** is one important characteristic of adolescent development Blakemore mentions.

In addition, numerous researchers agree that between 12 and 20, young people improve important skills. Adolescents become increasingly able to see things from other people's perspective or to manage bad and **inappropriate (l. 42)** conduct like fighting or lying.

What is the best way to motivate and teach youngsters then? Blakemore argues that instead of explaining future effects it is better to give a **disincentive (l. 49)** like pointing out the immediate negative consequences of a certain behaviour.

According to the author, parents, for example, should support their offspring by helping them to think about other people's opinions or by **negotiating (l. 54)** openly and comprehensibly.

Task III: Multiple Choice *(Secure Enough)*

Hinweise:

zu 1: *Mr Chilton ist der Ansicht, dass die Grenze zwischen den USA und Mexiko alles andere als sicher ist („far from secure" Z. 7 – damit scheidet Option B aus). Die amerikanischen Politiker mögen das Gegenteil behaupten oder beschwichtigen („whatever the politicians in Washington may say" Z. 6), von seiner Einschätzung ist Mr Chilton überzeugt.*

zu 2: *Obwohl der diskutierte Gesetzentwurf in mehr Sicherheit investieren soll (weitere Drohnen, Zäune, bewaffnete Posten – vgl. Z. 11), genügt das vielen Republikanern nicht („want even more" Z. 13). Sie wollen z. B. strengere Auflagen bei der Vergabe der Greencard an illegale Einwanderer, fordern also eine Verschärfung der Gesetzeslage („demand tougher legislation").*

zu 3: *Die folgenden Textstellen zeigen, dass A, B und C nicht zutreffen:*
Option A: "Obama's administration points to the drop in apprehensions" (Z. 21/22)
Option B: „drop in apprehensions […]. These bottomed out in 2011" (Z. 22)
Option C: „the once-porous Tucson sector has tightened" (Z. 23)

zu 4: *Der zu Option B passende Satz ist "America is already inflicting economic self-harm by spending so much to keep workers out" (Z. 39/40).*
Option A: Falsch, denn die Zahl der Geburten in Mexiko und El Salvador wird in den kommenden 40 Jahren unter die Geburtenrate der USA fallen (vgl. Z. 34/35).
Option C: Falsch, denn Mittel zur Abwehr von Migranten, wie Drohnen und Mauern, zeigen Wirkung (vgl. Z. 36–38).
Option D: Falsch, denn das Wirtschaftswachstum in Mexiko hat dort Arbeitsplätze geschaffen und Menschen im Land gehalten (vgl. Z. 27–30).

zu 5: Menschen- und Drogenschmuggel verlaufen mittlerweile auf denselben Routen. Die illegalen Migranten finanzieren ihre Reise durch Drogenschmuggel (vgl. Z. 47/48).

zu 6: Unter der Obama-Regierung werden illegale Einwanderer häufiger als früher des Landes verwiesen („deportations" Z. 54, „deportees" Z. 56). Deren in den USA geborene Kinder sind aber amerikanische Staatsbürger, sodass durch die Ausweisungen Familien zerrissen werden (Z. 56/57; „uprooted" = entwurzelt).

zu 7: Auch ein immer ausgefeilteres Grenzregime kann die Wanderungsbewegungen nicht verhindern, wenn die Auswanderungsgründe bedeutend genug sind („‚push' factors" Z. 63: „if Mexico's economy stutters, or violent crime soars again, the magnets of high wages, jobs and security across the border will prove too powerful for many to resist" Z. 64–66).

zu 8: Der Tenor des Artikels ist, dass man die Migration nicht in den Griff bekommen kann, so sehr sich auch die Politik durch sicherheitstechnische und andere Maßnahmen darum bemühen mag.

1 C, 2 B, 3 D, 4 B, 5 B, 6 D, 7 A, 8 D

Aufgabenteil: *Writing*

Task IV: Mediation Deutsch–Englisch *(Soziale Ungleichheit in den USA)*

It seems that in the US things are working out as expected, but ... ... the economic boom involves (or: comes with) drawbacks for society. (Alternative: ... there is something negative about the economic upturn as far as social justice is concerned.) The gap between the very rich and the rest of the population is becoming wider and wider.

It is true that the Dow Jones Index is breaking all records (or: is climbing to record heights/is beating record after record), house prices (real estate prices) are on the rise again and the job market (or: employment situation) is improving. However, since 2000 the average income has declined by eight per cent. 12 million Americans are jobless (or: are unemployed/do not have a job), and more and more Americans need a second or third job to maintain (or: keep) their standard of living.

So the land of opportunity (or: land of unlimited/endless possibilities / land of boundless opportunities / land of plenty / American Dream) has become a myth, as fewer and fewer people manage to make it from rags to riches. (Alternative: ... as people who struggle hard but then make it from the bottom to the top have become a rare thing.)

Meanwhile social mobility in America is lower than in almost any other industrial nation. So it is now that the social divide must be fought. (Alternative: Now, if ever, efforts must be made to bridge the wealth gap. / So this is the right time to tackle social inequality.)

(about 145 words)

Task V: Argumentative Writing

1. Composition

Hinweise: Beachten Sie bei dieser Aufgabenstellung, dass es im Kern um die Folgen geht, die sich aus dem anhaltenden Trend zu Megastädten ergeben. Maßnahmen zur Linderung der Folgen spielen bei dieser Themenstellung, wenn überhaupt, nur eine untergeordnete Rolle, z. B. im Fazit/Ausblick.
Möglicher Aufbau:
(1) Kleine Hinführung zum Thema
 – Germany: booming metropolitan areas, megacities in China, Mexico, Brazil etc.
(2) Mögliche positive und negative Konsequenzen
 – potentially positive consequences: synergies in infrastructure (traffic, energy etc.), wide range of opportunities (culture, childcare, education, job market etc.)
 – potentially negative consequences: complex management of infrastructure, environmental impact, social inequality, depopulation in rural areas etc.
(3) Abrunden des Aufsatzes mit einem Fazit, Ausblick, o. Ä.

Urban territories are growing throughout the world. They are growing in Germany with its booming metropolitan areas – and they keep spreading around dozens of megacities in China, Brazil, India, Nigeria, Indonesia and so forth. Is this ongoing trend a boon or a bane?

On the one hand, to a certain extent big cities can provide synergies in the infrastructure. In all likelihood, the water and electricity supply, the waste management or the telecommunications system are cheaper and easier to organise in a smaller area, where distances are relatively short and the number of customers and users is high. Similarly, basic needs in the fields of culture, education or childcare can be met quite easily because it pays to establish a wide range of corresponding facilities.

Yet, on the other hand, life in a megacity can turn into a nightmare for the majority of inhabitants. Above a certain level, infrastructure management can become quite impossible: Providing affordable housing for the poor who are flocking into these cities in the hope of finding work, establishing a decent public transport system, or supplying millions with clean drinking water and functioning sewage management etc.

How can you make sure that in a Moloch like Mexico City or Lagos children can grow up in a way that satisfies their needs? Is it possible to curb the environmental impact that is almost inevitable in megacities: smog that forces people to wear dust masks, unbearable traffic noise, the loss of natural land resources needed for roads, rails, airports, industrial estates and housing?

Last, but not least, megacities are often a hotbed for violence and crime, which is no surprise considering the dimensions of social inequality, the gap between the rich in their gated communities and the poor in their slums, and the exploitation of those who hope to be able to live a better life some day.

A look at the development during the past 50 years reveals that, unfortunately, the trend towards megacities seems to be unstoppable. The politicians and administrations in charge of their management are not to be envied. *(345 words)*

2. **Composition**

   Hinweise:
   Möglicher Aufbau:
   (1) Kleine Hinführung zum Thema
   (2) Beispiele, die zeigen, dass man als Einzelner wenig wirklich bewegen kann
   – in the following fields an individual doesn't make much of a change: meat consumption, factory farming ...
   (3) Beispiele, die zeigen, was sich durch das Engagement Einzelner bewegen kann
   – examples of people who changed the world: M. Gandhi, N. Mandela, R. Parks, W. Brandt ...
   (4) Abrunden des Aufsatzes mit einem Fazit, Ausblick, Appell o. Ä.

"It's not fair." We humans dispose of a well-developed sense of fairness, in the minor things in life as well as in the big issues like child labour, political oppression or hunger crises. Sometimes we demand that there must be a change but at the same time we feel that, at least as individuals, we are not powerful enough to change the world.

Take factory farming, for instance. It is not fair, it is cruelty to animals and if you want to change the world on this issue, there are three things you can do: vote for political parties which stand for more natural animal farming, become an activist, or reduce your meat consumption. However, this is not going to end factory farming – none of these options will lead to a visible change because it takes millions to bring about change.

The same goes for the fight against political oppression. Repressive regimes intimidate and threaten their opponents, and for an individual there is not much you can do about it, especially without putting yourself in danger.

Yet, we know from history that there are people who have changed the world. South Africa would not have overcome apartheid without Nelson Mandela, the American civil rights movement needed the courage and willpower of Rosa Parks, and peace in Europe after 1945 was only possible because men like Willy Brandt did not give up their vision of reconciliation despite stiff opposition.

These men and women were individuals, but they set an example, inspiring others and becoming so influential that we can rightly say that they changed the world.

Furthermore, at the end of the day, it depends on how you define "change". Not everyone is born a Mandela, not everyone has the talents that you need to achieve far-reaching effects. But change can also be the little steps that you take when you go by bike or put solar panels on your roof. *(320 words)*

Berufliche Oberschulen Bayern – Englisch 13. Klasse
Abiturprüfung 2015

Aufgabenteil: *Reading*

Text I: **Sightseeing in Louth** by Bernadette M. Smyth

1 The whole thing is to help John. This is the reason why I have to light the sitting room fire every evening, and squash in beside Julie every night, it's the reason why Mammy and Granny and Patricia have made the house into a circuit of tea and sandwiches – it's all in the name of Helping John.

5 John is a third cousin once removed, or a first cousin three times removed, well he's some kind of relation anyway, some shoot of some twig of some branch of the family tree which has found itself growing, by accident, in America.

He's coming to Louth to explore his roots, i.e. us, and the plan is to feed him and warm him and give up your bed for him, it's to generally help him, so that he can go
10 back to America and tell them all how wonderful the Irish are, _____ [Gap A] _____. Thanks be to Jesus, the Yank who imposed on us for two full weeks in April.

He's wearing an orange raincoat when he arrives, like the ones you see on all the tourists in Dublin, and this is my first picture of John, _____ [Gap B] _____, then blazing after her towards the front door. "You're very welcome John," Granny says,
15 marshalling him into the kitchen, "You must be starved after your journey, are you?" "Well actually I got dinner on the plane ..." But it's too late, she's already sliding a plate in front of him, made tall with rashers and eggs.

John is from Boston. He's a teacher there, and has a beard to show that he's serious about it. He's quiet and polite, and we're all relieved about this, relieved that al-
20 though John is American, he's not too American, you know, _____ [Gap C] _____. John does have some American habits though, like an ex-wife in Seattle, and an accent that slides over some sounds and stretches out others, _____ [Gap D] _____.

Julie stares at John and giggles as he chases the eggs around his plate. She's only ten, but what's Patricia's excuse? She sits there smiling at him in a kind of daze, twirling
25 her hair stupidly. Granny and Mammy are busy making orbits of the table and each other with teapots. Is anyone going to say anything to this man?
"Did you really use to live in Seattle?" I ask.
"Yeah."
"So do you know Kurt Cobain then?"
30 "No, not personally," he says, a smile sneaking into his beard, "Nirvana are pretty cool though, right?"
And now it's my turn to smile.

"I hear you're interested in finding out a bit about the family tree," Granny says, "Patricia here did a project on it for school, didn't you, love? I'm sure she'd love to
35 show it to you."

"Oh, that would be great," he says, and Patricia beams, letting me know with a slanted look that despite my good start, she has already won.

I don't try to compete with Patricia in this, or in anything else, because even though I'm a year older, it's a given that *she's* the prize of the family, and that everything
40 bad that ever happened to us is all *my* fault.

It's my fault that Daddy left us years ago, because I was the difficult child who terrorised him into going, and then wee Francis died, and that was my fault too, because everyone loved Francis, he was a little angel so he was, and it should have been me who died instead.

45 So I just watch, _____ **[Gap E]** _____, and spills out boxes of photos for him after school, blathering on about our ancestors, like she knew them or something, like what they got up to was the least bit interesting.

I don't know much about what they have in America, but I know what they don't have by the pictures John takes with his camera. They don't have crumpled cottages
50 with flowers growing out of their roofs, or lanes with runners of moss colouring their middles, they don't have weather that's upside down – clouds that start on the ground and grow upwards, _____ **[Gap F]** _____. And they don't have grannies, well like Granny – ones who wear fat woollen skirts, and thick shoes laced up to the ankle.

John is fascinated by Granny, by how *authentic* she is. I see him watching her in the
55 evenings, marvelling at the nooks and crannies of her face, and the knots of her legs; the veins that wriggle blue routes out under the gleam of her tights.

But what John really loves about Ireland is the history. He loves the tragedy of it, _____ **[Gap G]** _____. He loves the way the Irish own it, and how it becomes urgent when we're drunk. He loves how the Stone Age happened back when it was sup-
60 posed to, that the Stone Agers gradually copped themselves on over the centuries, without having to be shocked into modernity by cowboys with guns.

He's got a booklet from the tourist office called: *Sightseeing in Louth*. There's a list of local attractions on the back, _____ **[Gap H]** _____. Myself and Patricia are even allowed to skip school for the day-trips which result. I miss a home economics test,
65 and Patricia foregoes a debating contest, but for once it doesn't matter, because education is only a poor second to the primary goal of Helping John. *(about 879 words)*

Bernadette M. Smyth: Sightseeing in Louth (879 words, abridged and slightly adapted), from: The Fish Anthology 2010. Cork University Press (2010)

Task I: Multiple Matching *(Sightseeing in Louth)* 8 credits

You have read the short story "Sightseeing in Louth" by Irish write Bernadette M. Smyth. Now choose which of the below (1–11) fit into the numbered gaps (A–H). Please note: there are three extra options which do not fit in any of the gaps.

Gap	A	B	C	D	E	F	G	H
Part of Sentence	5	1	8	9	2	4	7	11

	Parts of Sentences for Multiple Matching
1	emerging from Mammy's car like a flame
2	as Patricia stalks John with cups of tea
3	offering them triangles of toast, made sweaty with butter
4	in mists that blur the countryside into a fairytale
5	and we can breathe a collective sigh of relief that he's gone
6	as I trudge across to the bathroom
7	all of the things that nearly happened
8	not like the people you'd see on *Baywatch*[1] and that
9	until we're all nearly mesmerised by his sentences
10	where he clicks pictures of the round tower
11	and it becomes the family's mission to see that John gets through all of them

Annotation
1 American TV series

Text II: Can't Start, Won't Start: Getting Over Procrastination
by Maria Konnikova

"Want to hear my favorite procrastination joke? I'll tell you later." Piers Steel, a psychologist at the University of Calgary, has saved up countless such lines while researching the nature of procrastination. Formerly a terrible procrastinator himself, he figures a dose of humor can't hurt. It's certainly better than continually building up anxieties about work you should do now but put off until later and later, as your chances of completing it grow ever slimmer, and the consequences loom ever larger.

The tendency to procrastinate dates back to the very beginnings of civilization. As early as 1400 B.C., Steel told me, ancient Egyptians were struggling with basic time management. "Friend, stop putting off work and allow us to go home in good time," read some hieroglyphs, translated by the University of Toronto Egyptologist Ronald Leprohon.

The twenty-first century seems no different. Students procrastinate instead of doing their schoolwork. In one study, thirty-two per cent of surveyed university students were found to be excessive procrastinators – meaning that their procrastination had gone from being an annoyance to an actual problem – while only one per cent claimed that they never procrastinated at all. Employees procrastinate instead of taking care of their office tasks. The average employee, one survey found, spends about an hour and twenty minutes each day putting off work; that time, in turn, translates to a loss of about nine thousand dollars per worker per year. In a study conducted in 2007, about a quarter of surveyed adults reported that procrastination was one of their defining personality traits.

"It's a common pulse of humanity," Steel told me. We've all likely experienced it: There's that project we have to finish, that email we have to send, that phone call we need to make. But somehow, despite our best intentions, we never seem to get any closer to doing it. "One thing that defines procrastination isn't a lack of intention to work," Steel said. It's the difficulty of following through on that intention. For most of us, procrastination isn't a pleasant experience. It's not like blowing off a meeting or a class and sensing the freedom of rebellion; we feel growing discomfort as we know we'll have to deal eventually with whatever it is we're putting off. As Steel writes in his book, "The Procrastination Equation," procrastination leads to lower over-all well-being, worse health, and lower salaries. Why, then, is procrastination so common? If we don't particularly want to procrastinate, and if we find it so unpleasant, why do we persist in doing it?

This was the question that preoccupied Steel as he began his research into procrastination in the nineties. When he completed his analysis, one finding in particular jumped out: excessive procrastinators were worse at self-regulating. From that connection came Steel's main insight: individuals who were prone to impulsiveness also tended to be excessive procrastinators.

If we think of procrastination as the flip side of impulsiveness – as a failure of self-control rather than a failure of ambition – then the way we approach it shifts. When it comes to self-control, one trick that tends to work well is to reframe broad, ambitious

goals in concrete, manageable, immediate chunks, and the same goes for procrastination. "We know there is a lot of naturally occurring motivation as deadlines approach," Steel pointed out. "Can you create artificial deadlines to mimic the same
45 thing?" So, set the goal of working on a task for a short time, and then reassess. Often, you'll be able to stay on task once you've overcome that initial jump.

The other approach involves eliminating the roadblocks you may encounter on the way to achieving your goal. Identify the "hot" conditions for impulse control – those moments when you're most prone to give in to distraction – and find ways to deal
50 with them directly. "One of the easiest things to do is to realize that maybe it's your distractions, not your goals, that are the problem," said Steel. "So you make the distractions harder to get to. Make them less obvious." He points to an Android app that makes it more difficult for people to access the games on their phones. Steel's own team has designed a phone and desktop app that adds a simple delay mechanism to
55 distracting programs.

Of course, if you are an excessive procrastinator you may be unlikely to install such a program. "The ironic thing is that procrastinators put off dealing with their procrastination," Steel said. So I have an idea: instead of doing whatever you're supposed to be doing right now, take a look at Steel's online procrastination test. There are few
60 things we like more than online personality assessments – and this one might even help you beat your procrastination. Just you wait and see. *(793 words)*

Maria Konnikova, in: The New Yorker, July 22, 2014 (793 words, abridged and slightly adapted).

Task II: Gapped Summary
(Can't Start, Won't Start: Getting Over Procrastination) 8 credits

Fill the gaps in the summary with appropriate words or expressions (one word per line) from the underlined corresponding sections of the text. Do not make any changes or adjustments. Please also provide the number of the line in which you have found the word / expression.

Although procrastination is very widespread nowadays, it is by no means a new phenomenon: Even in former times, people had difficulties with __time__ __management__ (l. 8). Now the topic has come under the spotlight of scientific research again: In a recent survey a considerable number of students stated that their inclination to procrastinate was so __excessive__ (l. 14) that it was beginning to cause concern. For the majority of people, being unable to complete work one is actually willing to do is a negative __experience__ (l.   ). Procrastination causes increasing __discomfort__ (l.   ) and can result in health problems. With all these detrimental effects it has been interesting for the psychologist Piers Steel to find out what motivates people to __persist__ (l.   ) in postponing work.

2015-5

Further research on the topic unveiled that procrastinators have deficiencies in self-regulation, which has led to the conclusion that procrastination and __impulsiveness__ (l.   ) are interconnected. Based on the findings, Steel recommends two approaches to overcome procrastination: One method is to set short-term __goals/deadline__ (l.   ) within which procrastinators must complete their tasks. Secondly, in a situation in which a procrastinator is __prone__ (l.   ) to inattention, it is advisable for him to avoid diversions when possible.

Text III: The World Can't Hide From Pandemics by Lawrence Summers

(A) Epidemics and pandemics are like earthquakes. Tragic, inevitable and unpredictable. It starts as a random event. A virus jumps species from a bird, bat or other animal to "patient zero" – who passes it on to other human beings. More likely than not, over the course of this century we will face an influenza pandemic similar to the one in 1918 that killed an estimated 50 million people.

(B) President Obama's first chief of staff, Rahm Emanuel, said in the wake of the global economic meltdown that "you never want a serious crisis to go to waste." Crises point to measures that will prevent the collapse of institutions when they are under extreme pressure.

(C) While the focus now is understandably on responding to Ebola, it is equally important that the crisis serves as a wake-up call with respect to inadequacies that threaten not just tragedy on an unprecedented scale but also the basic security of the United States and other wealthy nations. As with climate change, no part of the world can insulate itself from the consequences of epidemic and pandemic.

(D) The Global Health 2035 report by the Commission on Investing in Health, which I co-chaired, points up three crucial lessons. First, collective action must be taken to build strong health systems in every corner of the globe. In West Africa, Ebola was a "stress test" on national health systems, and in Sierra Leone, Liberia and Guinea the systems could not cope. There were too few trained health professionals, too little equipment and supplies, and too little capacity for public health surveillance and control.

(E) Nigeria's success in containing the virus after the first case was diagnosed there in July is instructive. Its success, hailed by the World Health Organization (WHO) as a piece of "world-class epidemiological detective work," is explained by its aggressive, coordinated surveillance and control response. It already had a polio surveillance system, with skilled outbreak specialists who could be quickly put to work tackling Ebola. While much of Nigeria's health system, such as primary care services, remains very weak, on Ebola the surveillance and control system worked.

(F) Every country needs this kind of system. Prevention is cheaper than cure, and leads to better outcomes. Building these systems takes time and money. Our research, conducted with an international team of economists and health experts and published last year in the medical journal the Lancet, suggests that the price of this "systems strengthening" would be about $30 billion a year for the next two decades. The good news is that we have the funds to pay for this through a combination of aid and domestic spending. The cost is well under 1 percent of the additional gross domestic product that will be available to low- and lower-middle-income countries due to increased GDP growth over the next 20 years.

(G) The second lesson is that the lack of investment in public health is a global emergency. The WHO's slow response to Ebola was not surprising, given its recent staff cuts. For that, we all share the blame. Since 1994, the WHO's regular budget has declined steadily in real terms. Even before the Ebola crisis, it struggled to fund basic functions. Its entire budget for influenza was just $7.7 million in 2013 – less than a third of what New York City alone devotes to preparing for public health emergencies. It takes just one infected airline passenger to introduce an infection into a country. We need the WHO more than ever. It alone has the mandate and legitimacy to serve as a health protection agency for all countries, rich and poor. Starving it of funds is reckless.

(H) The third lesson concerns scientific innovation. When it comes to discovering and developing medicines, vaccines and diagnostic tests, we have largely ignored the infectious diseases that disproportionately kill the world's poor. Consequently, we still have no medicines or vaccine for Ebola. All we can do is provide basic life support, such as fluids and blood pressure treatment. For prevention, we have to rely on old-fashioned measures such as quarantine. Margaret Chan, the WHO's director-general, has explained the reason for this neglect. Doctors were "empty-handed," she said, because "a profit-driven industry does not invest in products for markets that cannot pay." Ebola affects poor African nations, so drug companies see no profit in working on it. Nor is there an adequate incentive to invest in prevention. No society will allow companies to reap huge profits when disease is spreading rapidly.

(I) Rich governments and donors need to step up. Investing several billion dollars a year, less than 0.01 percent of global GDP, could be decisive in preventing tragedy on the scale of world war.

(J) Some issues are even more important than recessions and elections. Ebola is a tragedy. Let us hope that it will also be a spur to taking the necessary steps to prevent the far greater one that is nearly inevitable if there is no change in current policies. The next Ebola is just around the corner. *(840 words)*

Lawrence Summers in: The Washington Post, November 9th, 2014 (840 words, slightly abridged and adapted). Lawrence Summers is a professor at Harvard University and was economic adviser to President Obama from 2009 through 2010.

Task III: Mixed Reading Tasks *(The World Can't Hide From Pandemics)* 8 credits

1. **Mediation Englisch – Deutsch** 2 credits

   Beantworten Sie die folgenden Fragen auf Deutsch.

   Erläutern Sie das Zitat *"you never want a serious crisis to go to waste"* (Z. 7) von Rahm Emanuel. Wie wird seine Aussage in Paragraph B verdeutlicht?

   _____
   _____
   _____
   _____
   _____
   _____
   _____
   _____
   _____
   _____
   _____
   _____

2. **Multiple Choice** 6 credits

   Mark the most suitable option by crossing the appropriate letter.

   a) Which statement is **not** in accordance with paragraph A?
   - ~~A~~ The flu pandemic of the 20th century was a unique event.
   - B The outbreak of worldwide diseases cannot be prevented.
   - C In a pandemic, the chain of infection is usually not restricted to a single species.
   - D Mankind will probably be struck by a disastrous flu pandemic in the 21st century.

   b) Which heading summarizes paragraph C best?
   - A No way out
   - B A third world problem
   - C Global survival at stake
   - ~~D~~ All in the same boat

   c) Nigeria could successfully fight the spread of Ebola because …
   - ~~A~~ it had a well devised emergency system for another epidemic.
   - B its general medical services were well funded.
   - C the country was heavily supported by the WHO.
   - D it could draw on the experience of other West African countries.

2015-8

d) Which statement concerning the WHO is true according to paragraph G?
   A It is supported by all countries according to their financial means.
   B It is responsible for the coordination of safety measures in case of pandemics.
   C It lacked the personnel required to deal with the Ebola virus quickly.
   D It had little difficulty financing operations prior to the Ebola outbreak.

e) The key message of the last paragraph is that …
   A the world is heading towards an international political crisis.
   B action must be taken to avert a devastating future pandemic.
   C economic and political problems must not be neglected today.
   D mankind cannot avoid the next tragic Ebola pandemic.

f) Which advice does the author **not** give in the text? We need to …
   A strengthen the WHO and supply it with sufficient financial resources.
   B spend more effort on developing drugs against epidemics.
   C boost the morale of medical staff in developing countries.
   D establish efficient health care infrastructures all over the world.

Aufgabenteil: *Writing*

Task IV: Mediation Deutsch – Englisch „Verloren und trotzdem gewonnen"

Fassen Sie den folgenden Artikel zusammen, indem Sie die unterstrichenen Textstellen sinngemäß ins Englische übertragen. Verfassen Sie hierfür einen zusammenhängenden Text im Umfang von etwa 150 Wörtern.

Die Befürworter der schottischen Unabhängigkeit haben verloren und sind gleichwohl die Gewinner. Denn schon vor der Abstimmung sah sich der britische Premierminister David Cameron gezwungen, Schottland deutlich mehr Macht zu versprechen.

Nach diesem Votum wird nichts mehr sein wie es war, nicht in Schottland, nicht in Großbritannien und vielleicht auch nicht in Europa. Mit der Abstimmung über die Unabhängigkeit hat Schottland sich verändert. Die Kampagne, ob sich das Land von Großbritannien abspalten soll, hat eine ebenso emotionale wie hochpolitische Debatte über die eigene Kultur, Politik und Identität entfacht.

Jetzt, nach dem Ja zum Vereinigten Königreich, stehen die Schotten selbstbewusster da als zuvor. Sie haben sich, allen Briten und auch dem Kontinent gezeigt, dass es möglich ist, zugleich leidenschaftlich und doch fair miteinander über Politik zu streiten. Die Schotten haben bewiesen, dass Politik eine Sache aller ist, dass sie alle interessieren, ja begeistern kann – vorausgesetzt, die Menschen werden gefragt. Die hohe Wahlbeteiligung und der weise Ausgang sind ein Beleg für die Reife und Attraktivität von Demokratie und widersprechen allen, die über Politikmüdigkeit und Populismus lamentieren. […]

Schon vor dem Referendum sah sich der britische Premierminister David Cameron gezwungen, Schottland mehr Rechte und mehr Selbstständigkeit, kurz: mehr Macht zu versprechen. Gut möglich, dass dies zuletzt viele bewogen hat, mit Nein zu stimmen und das ökonomische Risiko der Unabhängigkeit nicht zu wagen. Cameron jedenfalls sichert es sein politisches Überleben. Die Verhandlungen über mehr Eigenständigkeit werden schnell beginnen. Die Yes-Kampagne kann sich also, obwohl sie verloren hat, als Gewinner betrachten. Viele ihrer Ziele wird sie, wenn sie klug verhandelt, erreichen.

Was die europäische Frage betrifft, so zeigt diese Wahl, dass der Wunsch nach mehr nationaler oder regionaler Identität nicht zwangsläufig einhergeht mit anti-europäischen Motiven. Gerade die Schotten wollen in der EU bleiben und fürchten das Referendum über die EU-Mitgliedschaft, das Cameron für 2017 versprochen hat. Für Rest-Europa, das mit den Briten zusammenbleiben will und auf weniger statt mehr Grenzen hofft, ist das schottische No ein gutes Signal. Die wichtigsten Europa-Freunde der Inseln bleiben dabei. Und für Cameron und seine EU-Skeptiker könnte es ein Auftrag sein: *Better together* – das gilt auch für das Vereinigte Königreich und Europa. *(352 Wörter)*

Jutta Kram, Berliner Zeitung, 20. September 2014 (gekürzte Fassung, 352 Wörter)

Task V: Argumentative Writing 24 credits
Choose **one** of the following topics. Write **at least 220 words**.

1. **Composition**

    In a recent speech Pope Francis criticized the rather selfish lifestyles in Europe. Do you think that Germany has turned into a society of self-centered individuals?

2. **Composition**

    Egg freezing, also called social freezing, is a novel technology in which a woman's eggs are extracted, frozen and stored until she is ready to become pregnant.

    Social freezing has been criticized as being immoral, particularly if employers offer to pay their female employees to make use of this practice.
    Discuss this criticism.

Lösungsvorschläge

Aufgabenteil: *Reading*

Task I: Multiple Matching *(Sightseeing in Louth)*

Hinweise:

- zu A: John, der Yankee, kommt nach Irland zu Besuch und wird mit einer Portion Skepsis („feed him and warm him and give up your bed for him" Z. 8/9) empfangen. Seine irische Familie, die ihn noch überhaupt nicht kennt, dankt dem Herrn („Thanks be to Jesus" Z. 11), wenn er endlich wieder weg ist („sigh of relief that he's gone").
Satz 8 passt zwar grammatikalisch in Lücke A, ergibt aber keinen Sinn.
- zu B: „[B]lazing" (Z. 14 = leuchtend, lodernd) bezieht sich auf die leuchtend orangen Regenjacken der Touristen und genauso leuchtend („like a flame") entsteigt John Mammy's Auto. „[A]fter her" (Z. 14) bezieht sich auf „Mammy", kein anderer der 11 angebotenen Sätze bietet einen Bezug zu „her".
- zu C: Der entscheidende Bezug ist: „not too American" (Z. 20) = „not like the people you'd see on Baywatch".
- zu D: Die einzige Option, die einen Bezug zur Wirkung von Johns amerikanischem Akzent herstellt („accent that slides [...] and stretches" Z. 21/22), ist „mesmerised by his sentences". Aus dem Begriff „sentences" geht auch hervor, dass es hier um einen sprachlichen Aspekt („accent" Z. 21/22) gehen muss.
- zu E: Im Abschnitt von Z. 33 bis 35 wird deutlich, dass Patricia, die Schwester der Protagonistin, dem amerikanischen Gast den Familienstammbaum („family tree" Z. 33) näherbringen wird („Patricia here did a project on it", „she'd love to show it to you" Z. 34/35). Nur Option 2 bietet dazu einen Bezug.
- zu F: Der Bezug wird gestützt durch die wetterbezogenen Begriffe in der Umgebung der Lücke: „weather" (Z. 51), „clouds that [...] grow upwards" (Z. 51/52), „mists" (= Nebel).
- zu G: Es geht um die Bedeutung von Irlands Geschichte („history" Z. 57), also um „things that nearly happened". Satz 7 ist auch der einzige Satz, der grammatikalisch in die Lücke passt.
- zu H: „[T]hem" in Satz 11 bezieht sich auf die „local attractions" (Z. 63).
Die Familie macht es sich zur Aufgabe („mission"), dem amerikanischen Gast diese Attraktionen näherzubringen, Patricia und die Erzählerin werden dafür sogar vom Unterricht befreit („allowed to skip school" Z. 64).

Gap	A	B	C	D	E	F	G	H
Sentence	5	1	8	9	2	4	7	11

Task II: Gapped Summary (*Can't Start, Won't Start: Getting Over Procrastination*)

Hinweise:
- Achten Sie auf den Zusatz im Arbeitsauftrag: „one word per line"!
- time management (Z. 8/9): Bezugspunkte zwischen Gapped Summary (GS) und Originaltext (OT) sind: „by no means a new phenomenon" (GS) vs. „dates back to the very beginnings of civilization" (OT Z. 7); „had difficulties with" (GS) vs. „were struggling with" (OT Z. 8)
- excessive (Z. 14): Bezugspunkte zwischen GS und OT sind: „considerable number of students" (GS) vs. „thirty-two percent of surveyed university students" (OT Z. 13); „their inclination [...] was beginning to cause concern" (GS) vs. „procrastination had gone from being an annoyance to an actual problem" (OT Z. 14/15)
- experience (Z. 27): Bezugspunkte sind: „being unable to complete work one is actually willing to do" (GS) vs. „isn't a lack of intention to work" (OT Z. 25/26); „negative" (GS) vs. „isn't a pleasant" (OT Z. 27)
- discomfort (Z. 28): Bezugspunkte sind: „increasing" (GS) vs. „growing" (OT Z. 28); „result in health problems" (GS) vs. „leads to lower over-all well-being, worse health" (OT Z. 30/31)
- persist (Z. 33): Bezugspunkte sind: „find out what motivates people" (GS) vs. „Why, then, is procrastination so common?" (OT Z. 31/32); „in postponing work" (GS) vs. „in doing it" (OT Z. 33) = „procrastinate" (OT Z. 32)
- impulsiveness (Z. 37 oder 39): Bezugspunkte sind: „procrastination and [...] are interconnected" (GS) vs. „individuals who were prone to impulsiveness also tended to be excessive procrastinators" (OT Z. 37/38)
- deadlines (Z. 43 oder 44): Bezugspunkte sind: „short-term" (GS) [= kurzfristig] vs. „approach" (OT Z. 43/44) [= näherkommen]; „set" (GS) vs. „create" (OT Z. 44)
- prone (Z. 49): Bezugspunkte sind: „to inattention" (GS) vs. „to give in to distraction" (OT Z. 49)

Although procrastination is very widespread nowadays, it is by no means a new phenomenon: Even in former times, people had difficulties with **time management** (**ll. 8/9**). Now the topic has come under the spotlight of scientific research again: In a recent survey a considerable number of students stated that their inclination to procrastinate was so **excessive** (**l. 14**) that it was beginning to cause concern. For the majority of people, being unable to complete work one is actually willing to do is a negative **experience** (**l. 27**). Procrastination causes increasing **discomfort** (**l. 28**) and can result in health problems. With all these detrimental effects it has been interesting for the psychologist Piers Steel to find out what motivates people to **persist** (**l. 33**) in postponing work.

Further research on the topic unveiled that procrastinators have deficiencies in self-regulation, which has led to the conclusion that procrastination and **impulsiveness** (**l. 37** or **39**) are interconnected. Based on the findings, Steel recommends two approaches to overcome procrastination: One method is to set short-term **deadlines** (**l. 43** or **44**) within which procrastinators must complete their tasks. Secondly, in a situation in which a procrastinator is **prone** (l. 49) to inattention, it is advisable for him to avoid diversions when possible.

Task III: Mixed Reading Tasks *(The World Can't Hide From Pandemics)*
1. **Mediation Englisch–Deutsch**
   Erläuterung:
   Eine Krise bietet immer auch Chancen, die man nicht ungenutzt lassen soll.
   Verdeutlichung in Absatz B:
   Aus dem Krisengeschehen lassen sich Maßnahmen ableiten, wie man den Zusammenbruch von Institutionen, die unter starken Druck geraten sind, verhindern kann.

2. **Multiple Choice**
   Hinweise:
   zu a): *"More likely than not, [...] we will face an influenza pandemic similar to the one in 1918"* (Z. 3–5) besagt, dass die Grippeepidemie vom Anfang des 20. Jahrhunderts kein einmaliges Ereignis (*"unique event"*) war, sondern sich wohl (*"More likely than not"* Z. 3) wiederholen wird (*"we will face"* Z. 4).
   Option B: *"cannot be prevented"* entspricht *"inevitable"* (Z. 1).
   Option C: *"is [...] not restricted to a single species"* entspricht *"a virus jumps species"* (Z. 2).
   Option D: *"will probably be struck"* drückt eine hohe Wahrscheinlichkeit aus, dass etwas passiert, das Gleiche gilt für *"more likely than not"* (Z. 3).
   zu b): *"All in the same boat"* findet seine Entsprechung in *"no part of the world can insulate itself from"* (Z. 13/14).
   Option C ist unzutreffend, weil es im Absatz C zwar schon um *"global"*, also globale Probleme geht, der Begriff *"survival"* aber über das hinaus geht, was im Text als Gefahr dargestellt wird.
   zu c): Das *"well devised emergency system for another epidemic"* findet seine Entsprechung in *"a polio surveillance system, with skilled outbreak specialists who could be quickly put to work tackling Ebola"* (Z. 25–27).
   zu d): *"It lacked the personnel required"* entspricht *"given its recent staff cuts"* (Z. 39/40).
   zu e) *"Action must be taken to avert"* entspricht *"a spur to taking the necessary steps to prevent"* (Z. 64).
   zu f): Option A: In Absatz G thematisiert der Autor die mangelnde finanzielle Ausstattung der WHO (*"starving it of funds is reckless"* Z. 46/47).
   Option B: In Absatz H wird für mehr Anstrengung bei der Entwicklung von Medikamenten und Impfstoffen plädiert.
   Option D: In Absatz F tritt der Autor dafür ein, die Gesundheitsversorgung wirksam zu stärken (*"systems strengthening"* Z. 32/33), wobei Prävention eine bedeutende Rolle spielen soll (*"Prevention is cheaper than cure"* Z. 29).

   a) A, b) D, c) A, d) C, e) B, f) C

Aufgabenteil: *Writing*

Task IV: Mediation Deutsch – Englisch *(Verloren und trotzdem gewonnen)*

With the referendum (vote, ballot) on its independence, Scotland has changed.
Saying yes to the UK, the Scottish appear more self-confident than ever before.
(Alternative: After saying yes to the UK, the Scots appear more self-assured than ever.)
They have proved that political issues matter whoever you are; that political issues can be interesting, even exciting for everybody.
(Alternative: They have demonstrated that politics concerns us all; that it can be interesting and even fascinating for everybody.)
Additionally, the high voter turnout and the wise result (outcome) are indeed proof of the maturity and appeal of democracy.
Even before the referendum David Cameron, the British Prime Minister, felt (found himself) forced to promise Scotland more political power.
Negotiations (talks) on more independence will start soon.
So the Yes-campaign can consider itself the winner, even though it lost the ballot.
At the end of the day the result is a positive signal for the rest of Europe:
"Better together" is a good motto (slogan, message) that goes for both the UK and Europe. *(about 130 words)*

Task V: Argumentative Writing

1. **Composition**

   Hinweise:
   Papst Franziskus geht es in seiner Kritik an „selfish lifestyles in Europe" nicht um Deutschlands Einstellung zu anderen Ländern und Kontinenten und darum, ob man diesen helfen oder nur auf sich selbst schauen will. Ihm geht es um die die angebliche oder tatsächliche Ichbezogenheit des Einzelnen („self-centered individuals").
   Aufbau:
   (1) Kleine Hinführung zum Thema
   (2) Aspekte, die Franziskus' Einschätzung stützen
   – *People who consciously try to take selfish advantage: tax evasion, competition in business or sport etc.*
   – *Declining interest in volunteering and charity*
   (3) Aspekte, die Franziskus' Einschätzung widersprechen
   – *People in tough jobs who do not focus on personal benefits: Doctors, nurses, teachers, soldiers*
   – *Still widespread interest in volunteering and charity*
   (4) Abrunden des Aufsatzes mit einem Resümee, einer persönlichen Einschätzung oder etwas Ähnlichem

The Facebook status line asks you: "What's on your mind?". Instagram pages overflow with selfies. Online food delivery services offer "custom pizza" with a huge variety of toppings for you to choose from. So are we a society of self-centered individuals?

At first sight, it seems that Pope Francis is right.

Many people consciously take their selfish advantage with little regard for rules, social standards or consequences for others. People evade paying taxes although they know that this is at the expense of the honest taxpayer. Students insist on getting a better mark although they know they do not deserve it. Footballers go down in the penalty box in order to get a penalty kick for their team although there was no foul.

Apart from these attempts to get personal benefit from selfish practice, there seems to be a rather obvious tendency for people to rely on others: "Somebody else is going to do that, I needn't care." As a result, many organisations – citizen groups, charities, political parties, all kinds of clubs and so on – suffer from a declining interest in volunteering and charity. Many people prefer to enjoy a relaxed time after work than to be committed to public welfare.

Yet, on closer examination, there is a lot of evidence which suggests that Francis is not right.

Hundreds of thousands of citizens in Germany dedicate their free time to working for a good cause and one of the motives that drives them is a sense of duty. They volunteer for the fire brigade, a political party, nature or animal protection, the local sports club etc. The most striking example in this context is the impressive commitment of many Germans who volunteer for local initiatives to support the refugees flocking into Germany.

Taking all these aspects into account, I am of the opinion that Germany cannot generally be considered a society of self-centered individuals. But there is an obvious tendency towards more individualism and less of a sense of responsibility for the public welfare. I must admit that to a certain degree I am concerned about that.

(347 words)

2. **Composition**

   Hinweise:
   Im Zentrum der Themenstellung steht nicht die Auseinandersetzung mit Chancen und Risiken von Social Freezing *im Allgemeinen, sondern die Diskussion der Frage, ob* Social Freezing *gegen moralische Grundsätze verstößt, vor allem wenn Arbeitgeber die Kosten dafür übernehmen. Die Argumente müssen sich also immer wieder auf die Frage von Moralität und Immoralität beziehen.*
   Der Aufgabentyp „Discuss" verlangt die Auseinandersetzung mit Pro und Contra.
   Aufbau:
   (1) Kleine Hinführung zum Thema
   (2) Argumente gegen die These, dass es sich um eine moralisch fragwürdige Methode handelt

- Up to the women to decide whether they accept the offer or not
- Social freezing gives women opportunities they might never have if they get children early

(3) Argumente für die These, dass es sich um eine moralisch fragwürdige Methode handelt
- Women who give birth at the age of 50: against nature and carries huge health risks
- Basic idea behind employers paying the costs of social freezing: business, not equality of opportunity
- A practice that puts huge pressure on women who refuse to comply

(4) Abrunden des Aufsatzes mit einem Fazit, Ausblick, Appell oder etwas Ähnlichem

Although females constitute more than 50 percent of those who hold an A-level certificate or an academic degree in Germany, there is still the glass ceiling when it comes to having a successful professional career. To promote real gender equality, American companies like Apple or Citibank have been offering their female employees company-paid egg freezing lately – a practice which is regarded as immoral by critics. Is this criticism justified?

On the one hand, it is still a woman's own decision whether she accepts her employer's offer or not. If she is not forced to make use of it, there is nothing immoral about social freezing.

Apart from that, social freezing can give female employees particular job opportunities. The first ten or fifteen years on the job are crucial for a successful career. That is when your employer wants you to be fully focussed on pursuing your career, on gaining expertise and gathering experience in a way that the company can profit from in the long run. Thus, a woman who can put off having a baby can have it all: career growth, a top job and – later – children. Is this supposed to be immoral?

On the other hand, giving birth at the age of 45 or 50 is against nature. There is a reason why women have children at a younger age. One of the reasons is that the older an expecting mother is the more severe the health risks are for the mother and the newborn. Exposing one's employees to such risks is truly immoral.

Even worse, it seems that the basic motive behind the employers' offer to cover the cost of egg freezing is pure business interest. Facebook and Google do not care about gender equality, they want employees who are willing to meet company needs whatever these needs are. Consequently, this practice puts huge pressure on women who refuse to comply, because their refusal can be understood as damaging to the company. An offer based on such an attitude is, morally, debatable.

Considering all this, I hold the view that the arguments against social freezing outweigh the arguments in favour of the procedure. The employers' offer may be tempting for women, but particularly because it is so tempting I conclude that it is immoral. *(377 words)*

Berufliche Oberschulen Bayern – Englisch 13. Klasse
Abiturprüfung 2016

Aufgabenteil: *Reading*

Text I: **The Devil Wears Prada** by Lauren Weisberger

I knew nothing when I went for my first interview and stepped onto the infamous Elias-Clark elevators, those transporters of all things en vogue. I had no idea that the city's most well-connected gossip columnists and socialites and media executives obsessed over the flawlessly made up, turned-out, turned-in riders of those sleek and quiet lifts. I had never seen women with such radiant blond hair, didn't know that those brand-name highlights cost six grand a year to maintain or that others in the know could identify the colourists after a quick glance at the finished product. I had never laid eyes on such beautiful men. They were perfectly toned – not too muscular because "that's not sexy" – and they showed off their lifelong dedication to gym work in finely ribbed turtlenecks and tight leather pants. Bags and shoes I'd never seen on real people shouted Prada! Armani! Versace! from every surface. I had heard from a friend of a friend – an editorial assistant at Chic magazine – that every now and then the accessories get to meet their makers in those very elevators, a touching reunion where Miuccia, Giorgio, or Donatella can once again admire their summer '02 stilettos or their spring couture teardrop bag in person. I knew things were changing for me – I just wasn't sure it was for the better.

I had, until this point, spent the past twenty-three years embodying small-town America. My entire existence was a perfect cliché. Growing up in Avon, Connecticut, had meant high school sports, youth group meetings, "drinking parties" at nice suburban ranch homes when the parents were away. We wore sweatpants to school, jeans for Saturday night, ruffled puffiness for semi-formal dances. And college! Well, that was a world of sophistication after high school. Brown[1] had provided endless activities and classes and groups for every imaginable type of artist, misfit, and computer geek. Whatever intellectual or creative interest I wanted to pursue, regardless of how esoteric or unpopular it may have been, had some sort of outlet at Brown. High fashion was perhaps the single exception to this widely bragged-about fact. Four years spent muddling around Providence in fleeces and hiking boots, learning about the French impressionists, and writing obnoxiously long-winded English papers did not – in any conceivable way – prepare me for my very first post college job.

I managed to put it off as long as possible. For the three months following graduation, I'd scrounged together what little cash I could find and took off on a solo trip. I did Europe by train for a month, spending much more time on beaches than in museums, and didn't do a very good job of keeping in touch with anyone back home except Alex, my boyfriend of three years. He knew that after the five weeks or so I was starting to get lonely, and since his Teach for America training had just ended and he had the rest of the summer to kill before starting in September, he surprised me in Amsterdam. I'd covered most of Europe by then and he'd traveled the summer before, so after a not-so-sober afternoon at one of the coffee shops, we pooled our traveler's checks and bought two one-way tickets to Bangkok.

40 Together we worked our way through much of Southeast Asia, rarely spending more than $10 a day, and talked obsessively about our futures. He was so excited to start teaching English at one of the city's underprivileged schools, totally taken with the idea of shaping young minds and mentoring the poorest and the most neglected, in the way that only Alex could be. My goals were not so lofty: I was intent on finding a
45 job in magazine publishing. Although I knew it was highly unlikely I'd get hired at *The New Yorker* directly out of school, I was determined to be writing for them before my fifth reunion. It was all I'd ever wanted to do, the only place I'd ever really wanted to work. I'd picked up a copy for the first time after I'd heard my parents discussing an article they'd just read and my mom had said, "It was so well written –
50 you just don't read things like that anymore," and my father had agreed, "No doubt, it's the only smart thing being written today." I'd loved it. Loved the snappy reviews and the witty cartoons and the feeling of being admitted to a special, members-only club for readers. I'd read every issue for the past seven years and knew every section, every editor, and every writer by heart.

55 Alex and I talked about how we were both embarking on a new stage in our lives, how we were lucky to be doing it together. We weren't in any rush to get back, though, somehow sensing that this would be the last period of calm before the craziness.

(808 words)

Excerpt(s) from THE DEVIL WEARS PRADA: A NOVEL by Lauren Weisberger, copyright © 2003 by Lauren Weisberger. Used by permission of Doubleday, an imprint of the Knopf Doubleday Publishing Group, a division of Penguin Random House LLC. All rights reserved.

Annotation
1 Brown University is an elite American university in Providence, Rhode Island.

Task I: Mediation Englisch–Deutsch *(The Devil Wears Prada)* 8 credits

Beantworten Sie die folgenden Fragen auf Deutsch.

1. Nennen Sie die Leute, deren Gedanken sich ständig um die „tollen" Menschen drehen, die man in den Elias-Clark Aufzügen trifft. 1.5 credits
   - _____
   - _____
   - _____

2. Die Erzählerin sieht die sündhaft teuren Frisuren der Frauen in den Elias-Clark Aufzügen. Was, neben dem Preis, wusste sie zu diesem Zeitpunkt auch noch nicht? 1 credit

   Dass es Leute gibt ...

   _____

3. Erklären Sie aus dem Kontext: "this widely bragged-about fact" (Z. 26) 1.5 credits

   _____
   _____

4. Was erfahren wir konkret über die berufliche Zukunft der Erzählerin und ihres Freundes Alex zum Zeitpunkt der gemeinsamen Reise? 4 credits

Erzählerin	**Alex**
langfristiges berufliches Ziel: • _____	berufliche Perspektive: • _____
zeitlicher Rahmen: • _____	Zeitpunkt: • ab _____
persönliche Gründe für den Berufswunsch: • _____	persönliche Gründe für den Berufswunsch: • _____
• _____	• _____

Text II: Forget the 'war on smuggling', we need to be helping refugees in need
by Alexander Betts

The refugee crisis in the Mediterranean, which has aroused worldwide attention, is a manifestation of a global displacement crisis. Around the world there are currently more displaced people than at any time since the Second World War. More than 50 million people are refugees or internally displaced and the current international refugee regime is being stretched to its absolute limits. For example, there are nine million displaced Syrians, of whom three million are refugees. The overwhelming majority are in neighbouring countries. A quarter of Lebanon's entire population is now made up of Syrian refugees. Yet the capacity of these states is limited. Faced with this influx, Jordan and Lebanon have closed their borders to new arrivals. But these people have to go somewhere to seek protection and, with few alternatives, increasing numbers are making the perilous journey to Europe.

The problem is that there is a fundamental inequality in the existing global refugee regime. It creates an obligation on states to protect those refugees who arrive on the territory of a state ("asylum"), but it provides few clear obligations to support refugees who are on the territory of other states ("burden-sharing"). This means that inevitably states closest to refugee-producing countries take on a disproportionate responsibility for refugees. This inequality is a problem within Europe, but it also exists on a global scale. It is the reason why more than 80 % of the world's refugees are hosted by developing countries.

In order to enable this system to function properly a serious commitment to refugee protection needs to be maintained by countries outside regions of origin. This is even more important when "we" arguably have a moral responsibility – through our foreign policies – for the destabilization of countries such as Syria and Libya.

Yet European politicians are taking the easy option of failing to understand the wider world of which Europe is a part. What is missing is meaningful international cooperation to address the real causes of the problem. Instead, Europe has focused on higher levels of rapid deportation, presumably to unstable and unsafe transit countries such as Libya. The humanitarian provisions of the plan have been vague and problematic. The EU has also committed to triple funding for Operation Triton. Yet unlike the abolished Mare Nostrum program, that border security operation has never had a search-and-rescue focus. And Europe has proclaimed a "war on trafficking". However, this fails to recognize that human trafficking does not cause migration; it responds to an underlying demand. Criminalizing the smugglers serves as a convenient scapegoat, but it cannot solve the problem. Rather like a "war on drugs", it will simply displace the problem, increase prices, introduce ever less scrupulous market entrants and make the journey more perilous.

The refugee problem is far broader than a border control issue; it goes to the heart of the way in which we deal with refugees and displaced populations. In the aftermath of the Second World War we collectively created the global refugee regime, based on the 1951 Convention on the Status of Refugees. The aim was to ensure that people facing persecution would have access to effective protection and assistance by another state. Around the world, the core principles of this regime are under threat. Yet the rights of refugees to seek asylum have to be sacrosanct. As in the early 1950s, courageous European leadership is again needed to repair that international system and reinforce human rights standards, within and beyond the EU.

There are instructive lessons from history on the kinds of international cooperation that could make a difference in the Mediterranean. After the end of the Vietnam War in 1975, hundreds of thousands of Indochinese "boat people" crossed waters from Vietnam, Laos and Cambodia towards south-east Asian states such as Malaysia, Singapore and Hong Kong. Throughout the 1970s and 1980s, the host states, facing an influx, pushed many of the boats back into the water and people drowned. Like today, addressing the issue took political leadership and large-scale international cooperation.

In 1989, a Comprehensive Plan of Action (CPA) was agreed for Indochinese refugees. It was based on an international agreement for sharing the burden. The receiving countries in south-east Asia agreed to keep their borders open, engage in search-and-rescue operations and provide reception to the boat people. However, they did so based on two sets of commitments from other states. First, a coalition of governments promised to resettle all those who were judged to be refugees. Second, humane solutions, including legal immigration channels, were found for those who were not considered refugees in need of international protection. The plan led to millions being resettled and the most immediate humanitarian challenge was addressed.

The Indochinese response was not perfect and it is not a perfect analogy to the contemporary Mediterranean, but it highlights the need for international cooperation and responsibility-sharing. It's high time for political leaders to come up with creative solutions for refugees on a global scale. But that will take political courage and leadership.

(828 words)

© *The Guardian (25. 04. 2015); http://www.theguardian.com/commentisfree/2015/apr/25/war-on-trafficking-wrong-way-to-tackle-crisis-of-migrant-deaths (abridged and adapted)*

Task II: Gapped Summary *(Forget the 'war on smuggling')*   9 credits

Fill the gaps in the summary with appropriate words or expressions (one word per line) from the corresponding sections of the text. Do not make any changes or adjustments. Please also provide the number of the line in which you have found the word/expression.

According to the author, the fact that so many refugees set out for Europe is part of a _____ _____ (l.   ) spanning the whole world. Since most refugees flee to poorer countries nearby, some of these countries feel overwhelmed by the task posed to them. But a lot of richer countries further away don't do enough to help refugees that have not reached the countries' _____ (l.   ). This has to change. After World War II, states _____ (l.   ) accepted their obligation to help asylum-seekers. But obviously this refugee regime does not work properly any more. So countries further away from the crisis areas, especially those that have contributed to the situation that makes people flee in the first place, have to accept their _____ (l.   ) and thus have the obligation to share the burden.

However, the EU seems far from doing so. It has chosen the _____ _____ (2 words, l.   ): it has not done anything about the fundamental problem but has only addressed the symptoms. For example, fighting the smugglers does not improve the situation at all. As long as there is _____ (l.   ) for such people, the ones caught will be replaced by others.

Decision-makers will finally have to pluck up the _____ (l.   ) to tackle the problem. Perhaps a look at history can help them find solutions. When many of the so-called "boat people" were in a situation comparable to that of today's refugees in the Mediterranean, the UN brokered a Plan of Action that solved the problem.

Countries in the region _____ (l.   ) to take care of the refugees on condition that other countries gave those who got refugee status a home and also helped those who were not accepted as refugees. A similar _____ (l.   ) to the crisis in the Mediterranean is necessary today.

Text III: A Master's Degree in … Masculinity? by Jessica Bennett

Michael Kimmel stood in front of a classroom in blue jeans and a blazer with a pen to a white-board. "What does it mean," the 64-year-old sociology professor asked the group, "to be a good man?" The students looked puzzled. "Caring," a male student in the front said. "Putting other's needs before yours," another young man said. "Honest," a third said. Dr Kimmel listed each term under the heading Good Man, then turned back to the group.

"Now," he said, "tell me what it means to be a *real man*." This time, the students reacted more quickly. "Take charge; be authoritative," said James, a sophomore. "Take risks," said Amanda, a sociology graduate student. "It means suppressing any kind of weakness," another offered. "I think for me being a real man meant talk like a man," said a young man who'd grown up in Turkey. "Walk like a man. Never cry." Dr Kimmel had been taking notes. He pointed to the Good Man list on the left side of the board, then to the Real Man list he'd added to the right. "Look at the disparity. I think American men are confused about what it means to be a man."

You've heard of women's studies, right? Well, this is men's studies: the academic pursuit of what it means to be male in today's world. Dr Kimmel is the founder and director of the Center for the Study of Men and Masculinities at Stony Brook University, part of the State University of New York system, which will soon start the first master's degree program in "masculinities studies." It's called "masculinities" (plural!) to acknowledge that there is more than one way to be a man. The case for women's studies has long been clear. The first programs were founded in the 1970s during the height of the women's movement, and served as a kind of academic arm to the era's political struggle. It's safe to say that without women's studies, we would not have many of the gains that women have made over the last 45 years. Women's studies proved the pay gap between men and women, and showed the disparity in money spent on men's and women's health. The mere fact that we count the number of women in state legislatures is because of women's studies. All in all, women's studies produced research, theory and activists who worked to write women into the history books from which they'd been largely absent. Men's studies on the other hand never really seemed necessary until recently. Literature was essentially a study of the things men wrote, art history an exercise in what men painted, etc.

That viewpoint has been changing, albeit slowly. The American Men's Studies Association was formed in 1991 from a series of men's consciousness-raising groups called NOM, for the National Organization for Men, later renamed the National Organization for Changing Men. Over the years, a number of universities have begun offering courses in men's studies.

A full-fledged program for the study of masculinity, Dr Kimmel said, would incorporate scholarship across disciplines – from social work to literature to health. It would ask questions like: What makes men men, and how are we teaching boys to fill those roles? It would look at the effects of race and sexuality on masculine identity and the influence of the media and pop culture. It would also allow scholars to take seemingly unrelated phenomena – male suicide and the fact that men are less likely to talk about their feelings, say, or the financial collapse and the male tendency for risk-taking – and try to connect the dots.

The new academic discipline is not without controversy, of course. Like many new fields, masculinities studies brings with it varying degrees of scepticism. Some academics have suggested that it's too trendy to be of real academic merit. Others fear that it siphons money away from women's studies. And a small but vocal group of champions of male studies (not to be confused with "masculinities studies") views Dr Kimmel's work as insufficiently pro-men. "He is waging war against what I say is real men," said Dr Edward M. Stephens, a New York City psychiatrist and the chairman of the non-profit Foundation for Male Studies.

But Dr Kimmel's audience is growing [...] which is the product of a few things. For starters, the discussion of women's equality seems to be everywhere (including the familiar debate about whether women can "have it all"), with new attention being paid to the role men play in helping women achieve equality, and why it's good for them, too. Over the last 40 years, there's been a huge shift in gender roles for men and women, and yet most of the academic study has focused only on its impact on women. A recent survey by the Shriver report shows how necessary it is to focus on men, too: Four in nine men said it was harder to be a man today than it was in their fathers' generation, with most citing women's economic rise as the reason.

And then, there's the sad reality that everywhere we turn, it seems, there is another news story about men in crisis: mental illness, suicide, terrorism, rape, mass shootings, jetliner crashes or young black men being killed by the police. "This stuff is all around us," said Dr Kimmel. "We have a mass shooter in the U.S. every few weeks. And every time it happens, we talk about guns. We talk about mental health. But we don't talk about how all of these mass shooters are male." He paused, then said, "We need to understand how masculinity affected their experience."

Masculinity touches so many aspects of our lives that you almost don't notice it: As partners and husbands, whether we do our fair share of housework and child care, whether we opt to take paternity leave (even when companies offer paternity leave, research has shown that many men are reluctant to take it); our relationships with other men; how fast you drive; whether you choose to serve a ball underhand or overhand – literally anything. "Take the Disney movie," Dr Kimmel said. "For a long time, we've been having the conversation about how princess movies are bad for girls. But what are they telling men? The men swoop in and interrupt the woman's story. And then we're surprised when men interrupt women in boardrooms."

(1.062 words)

Jessica Bennett: A Master's Degree in ... Masculinity?
From The New York Times, August 8th, 2015 © 2015 The New York Times. All rights reserved.
Used by permission and protected by the Copyright Laws of the United States. The printing, copying, redistribution, or retransmission of this Content without express written permission is prohibited.

Task III: Multiple Choice *(A Master's Degree in … Masculinity?)*   7 credits

Mark the most suitable option by crossing the appropriate letter.

1. Dr Kimmel's classroom activity is described to illustrate the …
   A suitability of the title of his new degree program.
   B interdisciplinary nature of the new degree program.
   C fact that women are interested in men's studies.
   D prevalence of male stereotypes in men's studies.

2. The first university courses in women's studies …
   A helped launch the women's movement.
   B supported the struggle for female emancipation.
   C produced major female political leaders.
   D celebrated the new employment opportunities for women.

3. "That viewpoint" (see l. 32) refers to the opinion that …
   A there is a strong case for women's studies.
   B women's studies and emancipation belong together.
   C men clearly play the key roles in history.
   D a number of academic fields already cover the achievements of men.

4. By trying to "connect the dots" (l. 44) Dr Kimmel and his researchers try to match …
   A causes and effects.
   B problems and solutions.
   C problems and examples.
   D similarities and differences.

5. Which of the following criticisms is **not** thrown at the new field of studies?
   A It is an unwelcome competitor for funding.
   B It will lead to more conflict between the genders.
   C It won't exist long enough to be taken seriously.
   D It doesn't value the idea of manliness.

6. There is an increasing interest in masculinities studies.
   One of the reasons is …
   A male arrogance about
   B female ignorance of
   C the academic neglect of
   D the public's obsession with

   … the effects of female emancipation on men.

7. According to Dr Kimmel, concepts of masculinity …
   A are attacked by media productions for females.
   B don't affect everyday family life.
   C may be responsible for a lot of the world's misery.
   D have almost disappeared in post-feminist society.

Aufgabenteil: *Writing*

Task IV: Mediation Deutsch – Englisch 12 credits

Fassen Sie den folgenden Artikel zusammen, indem Sie die unterstrichenen Textstellen sinngemäß ins Englische übertragen. Erstellen Sie hierfür einen zusammenhängenden Text im Umfang von etwa 150 Wörtern.

Beginnen Sie mit: "The world may just be falling apart …"

Urlaubssaison – Sonne, Strand, Stress

Die Welt mag gerade aus den Fugen geraten, die Deutschen aber reisen. Die Flüchtlinge an den Grenzen und im Mittelmeer mögen sie betreten machen, die Reisewarnungen und Terroranschläge manchen bewegen, doch noch umzuplanen. Zu Hause bleibt deswegen aber kaum einer. Der Deutsche Reiseverband nennt die Lage „erfreulich", bei den Buchungen wie auch beim Umsatz liege man über dem Vorjahr. Zwei von drei Deutschen verreisen in diesen Wochen. Sie stehen im Stau kurz vor der Nordsee und treffen in Myanmar ausgerechnet den Arbeitskollegen, baden nackt auf Ibiza oder reisen verhüllt durch den Iran, drängen sich mit tausend Campern unter Pinien oder teilen die Einsamkeit Kareliens mit tausend Mücken. Der Urlaub dient, wie es so schön heißt, der Erhaltung und Wiederherstellung der Arbeitskraft. Wäre dies tatsächlich Sinn und Ziel des Sommerurlaubs, würden wohl viele Menschen einfach zu Hause bleiben, die Rollläden herunterlassen und mal ordentlich ausschlafen. Aber der Urlaub samt der mit ihm verbundenen Reise hat ja längst diesen profanen Zweck hinter sich gelassen. Er ist heutzutage Teil des Lebensstils und der Lebensdeutung. Er stiftet soziale Orientierung und Sinn. Der Urlaub ist einer der selten gewordenen Orte gemeinsamer freier Zeit. Er unterbricht den Alltag, er schafft Riten, er lässt ahnen, dass es andere Welten und Wirklichkeiten gibt. Der Theologe Johann Baptist Metz sagte einmal, Religion bedeute die Unterbrechung des gewöhnlichen Lebens. Wenn das so ist, dann hat die Urlaubsreise fast religiöse Züge angenommen.

Die Überhöhung des Urlaubs hat ihn aber auch anstrengend und angestrengt gemacht. Man fährt ja nicht mehr einfach weg. Man setzt ein Statement, Ziel und Art der Reise sind begründungspflichtig. Es geht in den Londoner Regen, damit die Kinder Englisch lernen, nach Kuba, bevor dort alle sind, nach Lesbos, um zu zeigen, dass nicht jeder Deutsche Schäuble heißt. Wer all inclusive am Sonnenstrand gebucht hat, muss sich schon was einfallen lassen, vielleicht: „Wir waren beruflich so eingespannt (ah!), dass wir das jetzt brauchen." Und, wo fahrt ihr hin? Kaum eine Frage bringt sicherer soziale Unterschiede an den Tag und die feinen Abstufungen einer Wohlstandsgesellschaft. Wer auf die Malediven fährt, gilt als neureich unter Verdacht, der Pilger als Selbstverwirklicher. Und wer gar nicht fahren kann, gehört oft zu den Ausgeschlossenen im Land.

(362 Wörter)

© *Matthias Drobinski, Süddeutsche Zeitung (01. 08. 2015);*
http://www.sueddeutsche.de/reise/urlaubssaison-sonne-strand-stress-1.2590150

Task V: Argumentative Writing 24 credits

Choose **one** of the following topics. Write **at least 220 words**.

1. **Composition**

   Some people believe that vegetarians and vegans are better people. What is your opinion?

2. **Composition**

   Rich people should be made to pay higher taxes. Discuss.

Lösungsvorschläge

Aufgabenteil: *Reading*

Task I: Mediation Englisch – Deutsch *(The Devil Wears Prada)*

1. Klatschkolumnisten / Promis / Medienmanager

   Hinweise:
   Die Elias-Clark-Aufzüge werden in Zeile 2 genannt und diejenigen, die sie benutzen („riders of those sleek and quiet lifts"), in den Zeilen 4/5. Dazwischen finden sich die Menschen, deren Gedanken sich um die Liftbenutzer drehen („obsessed over the flawlessly made-up [...] riders", Z. 3/4): die „gossip columnists", „socialites" und „media executives" (Z. 3).

2. ... die mit einem Blick in der Lage sind, zu erkennen, wer die Haare gefärbt hat.

   Hinweise:
   Die relevante Textpassage zu den sündhaft teuren Frisuren lautet: "I [...] didn't know [...] that others in the know could identify the colourists after a quick glance at the finished product." (Z. 5–7)
   Beachten Sie in der Aufgabenstellung die Formulierung „neben dem Preis", d. h. dass die Information „cost six grand a year to maintain" (Z. 6) hier nicht zur Antwort gehört. Eine vollständige Antwort muss dafür den Aspekt „after a quick glance" einschließen.

3. Die Brown University bildet sich etwas darauf ein (ist stolz darauf), dass sie ein so breites Spektrum an Aktivitäten und Optionen anbietet.

   Hinweise:
   Eine vollständige Erklärung im Kontext muss folgende Aspekte abdecken:
   – Was verbirgt sich hinter „this [...] fact"? – Ein breites Angebot an Aktivitäten für jeden Geschmack („endless activities and classes", Z. 22/23; „[w]hatever intellectual or creative interest I wanted to pursue", Z. 24).
   – Was bedeutet „widely bragged-about"? – Jemand prahlt mit etwas, bildet sich etwas ein, ist stolz auf etwas.
   – Wer ist stolz? – Die Brown University (vgl. Z. 22).

Erzählerin	Alex
langfristiges berufliches Ziel: • **Autorin/Journalistin beim Magazin *The New Yorker*** *"I was intent on finding a job in magazine publishing. [...] I was determined to be writing for them [= The New Yorker]"* (Z. 44–46); *"It was [...] the only place I'd ever really wanted to work"* (Z. 47/48)	berufliche Perspektive: • **Englischlehrer** *"He was so excited to start teaching English"* (Z. 41/42)
zeitlicher Rahmen: • **innerhab von 5 Jahren** *„before my fifth reunion"* (Z. 46/47), d. h. vor dem fünften Klassentreffen nach dem Abschluss	Zeitpunkt: • **ab September** *"he had the rest of the summer to kill before starting in September"* (Z. 35/36)
persönliche Gründe für den Berufswunsch: *Für 1 BE müssen zwei der folgenden vier Gründe genannt werden:* • **Eltern schwärmen für den *New Yorker*** *"my mom had said, 'It was so well written [...],' and my father had agreed"* (Z. 49/50) • **die besondere Qualität des *New Yorker*** *"Loved the snappy reviews and the witty cartoons"* (Z. 51/52) • **das Gefühl, einer exklusiven Leserschaft anzugehören** *"the feeling of being admitted to a special, members-only club for readers"* (Z. 52/53) • **sie hatte jahrelang jede Ausgabe des *New Yorker* verschlungen** *"I'd read every issue for the past seven years"* (Z. 53)	persönliche Gründe für den Berufswunsch: • **möchte junge Menschen prägen/formen** *"shaping young minds"* (Z. 43) • **möchte sich für die Ärmsten und am meisten Benachteiligten einsetzen** *"mentoring the poorest and the most neglected"* (Z. 43)

Task II: Gapped Summary *(Forget the 'war on smuggling')*
Hinweise:
- Achten Sie auf die Zusätze „one word per line" und „from the corresponding sections of the text"!
- displacement crisis (Z. 2): Bezugspunkte zwischen Gapped Summary *(GS)* und Originaltext *(OT)* sind: „spanning the whole world" *(GS)* vs. „global" *(OT Z. 2)*
- territory (Z. 15): Bezugspunkte zwischen GS und OT sind: „have not reached the countries' […]" *(GS)* vs. „of other states" *(OT Z. 15)*
- collectively (Z. 39): Bezugspunkte sind: „After World War II" *(GS)* vs. „In the aftermath of the Second World War" *(OT Z. 38/39)*; „states" *(GS)* vs. „we" *(OT Z. 39)*; „accepted their obligation to help" *(GS)* vs. „global refugee regime" *(OT Z. 39* – „regime" bedeutet hier so viel wie „Vorgehensweise, Management") und „The aim was to ensure […] access to effective protection and assistance" *(OT Z. 40/41)*
- responsibility (Z. 22): Bezugspunkte sind: „those that have contributed to the situation that makes people flee in the first place" *(GS)* vs. „through our foreign policies" *(OT Z. 22/23)*; „have the obligation to share the burden" *(GS)* vs. „moral" *(OT Z. 22)*
- easy option (Z. 24): Bezugspunkte sind: „the EU […] has chosen" *(GS)* vs. „European politicians are taking" *(OT Z. 24)*; „has only addressed the symptoms" *(GS)* vs. „What is missing is meaningful international cooperation to address the real causes" *(OT Z. 25/26)*
- demand (Z. 33): Bezugspunkte sind: „does not improve the situation" *(GS)* vs. „cannot solve the problem" *(OT Z. 34)*; „such people" *(GS)* vs. „human trafficking" *(OT Z. 32)*; „as long as there is […]" *(GS)* vs. „does not cause migration; it responds to an underlying demand" *(OT Z. 32/33)*
- courage (Z. 66): Bezugspunkte sind: „Decision-makers" *(GS)* vs. „political leaders" *(OT Z. 65)*; „to tackle the problem" *(GS)* vs. „to come up with creative solutions" *(OT Z. 65/66)*
- agreed (Z. 54): Bezugspunkte sind: „Countries in the region" *(GS)* vs. „receiving countries in south-east Asia" *(OT Z. 55/56)*; „to take care of the refugees" *(GS)* vs. „to keep borders open, engage in search-and-rescue operations and provide reception" *(OT Z. 56/57)*; „on condition that" *(GS)* vs. „they did so based on two sets of commitments" *(OT Z. 57/58)*
- response (Z. 63): Bezugspunkte sind: „similar" *(GS)* vs. „not a perfect analogy but […]" *(OT Z. 63)*; „is necessary" *(GS)* vs. „highlights the need for" *(OT Z. 64)*

According to the author, the fact that so many refugees set out for Europe is part of a **displacement crisis (l. 2)** spanning the whole world. Since most refugees flee to poorer countries nearby, some of these countries feel overwhelmed by the task posed to them. But a lot of richer countries further away don't do enough to help refugees that have not reached the countries' **territory (l. 15)**.
This has to change. After World War II, states **collectively (l. 39)** accepted their obligation to help asylum-seekers. But obviously this refugee regime does not work properly any more. So countries further away from the crisis areas, especially those

that have contributed to the situation that makes people flee in the first place, have to accept their **responsibility (l. 22)** and thus have the obligation to share the burden. However, the EU seems far from doing so. It has chosen the **easy option (l. 24)**: it has not done anything about the fundamental problem but has only addressed the symptoms. For example, fighting the smugglers does not improve the situation at all. As long as there is **demand (l. 33)** for such people, the ones caught will be replaced by others.

Decision-makers will finally have to pluck up the **courage (l. 66)** to tackle the problem. Perhaps a look at history can help them find solutions. When many of the so-called "boat people" were in a situation comparable to that of today's refugees in the Mediterranean, the UN brokered a Plan of Action that solved the problem. Countries in the region **agreed (l. 54)** to take care of the refugees on condition that other countries gave those who got refugee status a home and also helped those who were not accepted as refugees. A similar **response (l. 63)** to the crisis in the Mediterranean is necessary today.

Task III: Multiple Choice *(A Master's Degree in ... Masculinity?)*

Hinweise:

zu 1: Dr. Kimmels Master-Studiengang heißt „masculinities studies" (Z. 19), also soviel wie „Untersuchungen zu Formen der Männlichkeit". Die beschriebene Szene im Seminar (Z. 1–14) zeigt, dass es tatsächlich sehr verschiedene Vorstellungen und Rollenerwartungen zu angemessenem männlichen Verhalten gibt – der Titel des Studiengangs ist also passend gewählt (= „suitability of the title" in der Aufgabenstellung).

Zu 2: Die ersten Seminare zu Frauenstudien waren so etwas wie die universitäre Ebene des damaligen politischen Kampfes („academic arm to the era's political struggle", Z. 22/23) für mehr Gleichberechtigung von Frauen („gains that women have made", Z. 24).

Zu 3: Die Zeilen 27 bis 31 zeigen auf, dass die „Women's Studies" den Frauen einen Platz in der öffentlichen Wahrnehmung erarbeiteten („write women into the history books", Z. 28/29), während das für Männer nicht nötig erschien („never really seemed necessary", Z. 30), da ihre Leistungen (= „achievements") auf vielen Gebieten (= „academic fields"; „literature", „art" etc.) außer Frage standen.

Zu 4: Das Forscherteam um Dr. Kimmel befasst sich mit scheinbar voneinander unabhängigen Phänomenen („seemingly unrelated phenomena", Z. 41/42), wie z. B. der Finanzkrise und männlicher Risikobereitschaft, und versucht, Verbindungen herzustellen („connect the dots", Z. 44), also daraus Schlüsse zu Ursache und Wirkung (= „causes and effects") zu ziehen.

Zu 5: Option A bezieht sich auf „it siphons money away from women's studies" (Z. 48; „to siphon away" = Geld abziehen). Option C entspricht „it's too trendy to be of real academic merit" (Z. 47). Option D passt zu „a small but vocal group of champions of male studies [...] views Dr. Kimmel's work as insufficiently pro-men" (Z. 48–50). Die richtige Lösung ist also Option B.

Zu 6: Obwohl sich die Rollenerwartungen für beide Geschlechter enorm verändert haben („huge shift in gender roles for men and women", Z. 57/58), hat sich die Forschung fast nur auf die Auswirkungen dieses Wandels auf Frauen konzentriert („most of the academic study has focused only on its impact on women", Z. 58/59). Diese Vernachlässigung der Auswirkungen auf Männer (= „academic neglect of the effects [...] on men") ist einer der Gründe für das zunehmende Interesse an den „masculinities studies".

Zu 7: Im vorletzten Absatz zählt Dr. Kimmel eine Vielzahl von Taten auf („suicide, terrorism, rape, mass shootings" etc., Z. 63), die Leid verursachen (= „may be responsible for a lot of the world's misery") und überwiegend oder gar ausschließlich von Männern begangen werden. Daran anschließend regt er eine Auseinandersetzung mit der Frage an, inwieweit Vorstellungen von Männlichkeit (= „concepts of masculinity") damit zu tun haben könnten ("We need to understand how masculinity affected their experience", Z. 67/68).

Option A: Die erwähnten „princess movies" (Z. 75) erscheinen in einem ganz anderen Kontext.

Option B: Das Gegenteil ist richtig (vgl. Z. 70–74).

Option D: Auch hier ist das Gegenteil der Fall, wie das Beispiel aus den Tagungsräumen („boardrooms") zeigt, wo Männer oft immer noch sehr dominant auftreten (vgl. Z. 76/77).

1 A
2 B
3 D
4 A
5 B
6 C
7 C

Aufgabenteil: *Writing*

Task IV: Mediation Deutsch – Englisch *(Urlaubssaison – Sonne, Strand, Stress)*

The world may just be falling apart, the Germans, however, keep travelling.
The refugees, travel warnings and terrorist attacks may cause (prompt, move) some to change (reconsider) their plans.
But hardly anyone (almost no one) stays at home.
(Alternative: But for most people this is no reason to stay at home.)
People say that the idea behind a holiday is to maintain one's work productivity (to maintain the physical and mental skills needed at the workplace).
(Alternativen:
Holidays are said to be about remaining powerful and productive at work.
People say that going on holiday is about keeping fit for one's job.)
If this were actually (in fact) the purpose of a summer vacation, many would simply stay at home and have a good night's sleep (sleep like a baby, have a long sleep, sleep late).
(Alternative: If this were the real reason behind a summer holiday, many would rather stay at home and get some extra sleep.)
Yet, today (nowadays, these days), one's holiday has become part of one's lifestyle.
It gives life meaning, it provides social orientation and has almost become something like a religion (has almost assumed a religious touch).
All this has made going on holiday stressful, though.
(Alternative: However, these high expectations have made vacationing something of a strain.)
The vacationer makes a statement.
(Alternative: It's about making a statement.)
"So, where are you going?" – this question reveals (brings to light, makes evident) social differences.
Those going to the Maldives are considered nouveau riche, and the pilgrims are regarded as keen on self-fulfilment (and the pilgrims are said to be seeking self-fulfilment).
Those who cannot go on (afford) a vacation at all are often among those excluded from society (are social outcasts).

(about 150 words)

Task V: Argumentative Writing

1. Composition

Hinweise:
Die Aufgabenstellung könnte dazu verleiten, sich ausschließlich mit den Motiven auseinanderzusetzen, warum Menschen auf den Konsum tierischer Produkte verzichten. Im Zentrum der Themenstellung steht jedoch die Frage, ob Vegetarier und Veganer bessere Menschen sind.
Aufbau:
(1) Kurze Hinführung zum Thema
(2) Argumente, warum man Vegetarier/Veganer als bessere Menschen bezeichnen kann
  – consumption of animal products causes serious problems: methane emissions, waste of land resources, use of pesticides and herbicides, bad practices in animal rearing and slaughtering, etc.
(3) Argumente, warum Vegetarier/Veganer keine besseren Menschen sind
  – historically, man is an omnivore
  – affordable animal products bridge the gap between wealthy and poorer people
(4) Abrunden des Aufsatzes, z. B. mit einem Resümee oder einer persönlichen Einschätzung

It is a mild summer evening. After grabbing some best-price pork chops at their local supermarket, thousands flock to rivers, lakes or parks, where they set up their barbecue equipment and enjoy their low-priced meat products. Are these people simply careless? And are those who do care and deliberately go without meat better? As often in life, there are two sides to the coin.

It is true that the consumption of animal products is related to serious problems. In order to produce affordable food for the masses, agriculture has been industrialised. Pigs, dairy cows and hens are kept in barns and batteries unnaturally by the thousands. They are given antibiotics to prevent disease. And large herds of cattle emit huge amounts of methane, a greenhouse gas which has an effect on the climate worse than that of carbon dioxide.

In addition, the cultivation of animal fodder, especially soy and corn, requires the extensive use of pesticides, weed killers and fertilisers. In some parts of the world it also leads to deforestation and the waste of land resources.

Last but not least, neither the technique of fattening animals within a very short period of time nor the methods applied in slaughterhouses can be considered ethically acceptable.

As a result, it can be established that vegetarians and vegans have not only opted for a healthier lifestyle but help to largely avoid most of the downsides mentioned above.

However, man is an omnivore, at least historically. In many parts of the world, humans still depend on meat in order to survive. Moreover, the extension of production has made meat and other animal source foods affordable for the vast majority of people, at least in industrial societies, regardless of their social status or income. Finally, a diet including animal products is not necessarily unhealthy – as always, this is a question of moderation.

Nevertheless, bad practices in animal rearing and cultivation, and the risks of climate change pose a grave threat and a moral challenge to society. Cruelty to animals must be stopped, cattle and pigs must be kept in a more natural environment, and free-range eggs must replace eggs from battery farming. However, the advocates of fundamental change must be aware of the social divide that inevitably comes with more expensive animal products.

At the end of the day, vegetarians and vegans are not "better" people but they seem to live life more consciously and have the potential to drive change in people's attitudes by example. *(412 words)*

2. **Composition**

   Hinweise:
   *Der Aufgabentyp „Discuss" verlangt die Auseinandersetzung mit **Pro und Contra**.*
   Aufbau:
   (1) Kurze Hinführung zum Thema
   (2) Argumente gegen die These, dass Reiche mehr Steuern zahlen sollten
   *   – may annoy hard-working people*
   *   – could lead to a stronger tendency to avoid taxation*
   (3) Argumente für die These, dass Reiche mehr Steuern zahlen sollten
   *   – increasing social divide between the haves and have-nots*
   *   – income from capital gains, rents, inheritance etc. is distributed unevenly*
   *   – little respect for the performance of ordinary employees*
   (4) Abrunden des Aufsatzes, z. B. mit einem Fazit, Ausblick oder Appell

In the context of the diesel crisis, newspapers revealed that the manager of a German automobile company was given a contract guaranteeing him a monthly pension of € 60,000 after retiring at the age of 62. A few weeks earlier, the French football club Paris Saint-Germain cancelled its contract with coach Laurent Blanc, who then received compensation to the amount of € 22 million. These two examples highlight the tremendous amounts of money which are earned in some businesses and make many people shake their heads in disbelief. Would it not be only fair if people who were that well-off were made to pay higher taxes?

On the one hand, higher taxes for the rich may annoy hard-working people. Business leaders, freelancers and artists, to name just a few, do not have nine-to-five jobs, they are willing to take risks and they might feel their 60- to 80-hour working week should pay off. In an achievement-oriented society you should get what you deserve, which involves a payment based on performance.

In addition, with higher tax rates there might be a stronger tendency for top earners to avoid taxation, legally or illegally. In this way, the state might end up with less money – the opposite of the effect intended.

On the other hand, individual wealth is not necessarily the result of extraordinary individual effort.

Numerous international surveys suggest that the social divide between the haves and the have-nots is increasing. A major cause of this inequality, obviously, is that the well-off usually get additional income from rents, inheritances and capital profits. They can let their money work for them – a possibility which less wealthy people do not have (or to a far lesser degree).

Apart from that, there are plenty of ordinary jobs, for instance in health care, shift work or agriculture, which are highly demanding both physically and mentally, but are not as well-paid as certain leadership positions by far.

So, to my mind, higher taxes for the very wealthy would be justified. It would be appropriate to tax income from capital and property more highly than income from productive work. This would help to counteract an uneven distribution of income and to increase social justice; otherwise the social gap described above will continue to widen.

Furthermore, the Panama Papers scandal tells us that it is necessary to take steps against the widespread practice of tax evasion. *(397 words)*